Who Was Dustin Thomas?

By

Patrick M. Browning

ISBN: 0-7596-6751-9

This book is printed on acid free paper.

1stBooks – rev. 01/03/02

Chapter 1

The two men rode along in silence. The only audible sounds were the horses breathing and the ordinarily soothing creaking saddle leather, but this was not an ordinary ride. These life long friends were as different as beings from separate planets, yet in many ways were very similar. After last night, they have more in common than they ever thought possible. They were wanted and were on the run for their lives.

Their thoughts roamed back over the events of the past few days. Disbelief, apprehension and trepidation filled their minds. Even a little fear and nervousness, maybe, but absolutely no remorse or regret.

All things change. That's pretty much an accepted fact. Few change as rapidly as did the lives of these two men. Just days ago, Matt Morton was a quiet man who owned his own business. Matt had always minded his own business as well. His saloon was one of the most popular watering holes, for citizens and soldiers as well as desperadoes and dark characters, in this raw, new, western territory.

This territory all used to belong to Mexico and Matt purchased the place from the old Mexican Innkeeper who was about to be run out anyway. Things aren't always fair. These Mexicans held their land for four hundred years. Taking it away from them was given no more thought than it took to write the phrase, "Manifest Destiny". Most Mexicans took it hard and many fought for their homes. They were greatly out manned, out armed and out financed. America had claimed from the Atlantic to the Pacific and would not be stopped by a few stubborn foreigners, even if they had all been born there.

Matt was one of the few gringos the Mexicans looked on favorably. His treatment of the Cantina's former owner raised his standing in the community considerably. Even when he raised his prices to a point the common Mexican peon could not afford to frequent the place, the locals viewed it as just a business decision, not as discrimination. Matt's place, The Confederate Cantina, was a little pricey. The customers did get their money's worth in good liquor and entertainment unequaled for hundreds of miles in any direction.

The other silent rider never had settled down like his friend Matt. Dustin Thomas, Dusty to his few friends, had been an adventurer his whole life. He was raised by Matt's family and treated like one of their own. He never did, however, allow himself to become a full family member. His memories of his own parents and their savage deaths kept him a little aloof from the Mortons. He respected them as one would his own mother and father but from the night he arrived at the Morton's, he stayed down at the barn. Dustin would not crowd them more than necessary. Mr. Morton seemed to understand Dustin's feelings more than anyone else and made the rest of his family respect Dustin's need for space.

1

There was another reason Dustin did not want to be considered a full sibling to the Morton children. He had always been proud to call Matt brother, the problem was, Matt had a sister, Cindy, that Dustin always had feelings for. They had attended school together in the little one room shed that served as a church and school house. This was at the Carter ranch, located closer to the fort than either the Thomas or Morton places. Cindy was two years younger than the two boys and had caught a hold on Dustin's heart long before he moved into the Morton home. Dustin was always looking out for Cindy and she seemed to count on him to do so. He was as dedicated to her as any person can be to another. Even when Cindy, at age fourteen, ran off with the new school master, Tim Burns. Dusty held her blameless. Mr. and Mrs. Morton were worried sick about Cindy and had almost given up any hope of ever finding her. Just over a year later word came from her in St. Louis asking for someone to come get her and bring her home. Mr. Morton sold his team of good work mules and wagon in order to make the trip and return with his daughter. He'd figure out how to manage the place without his team later, right then he was going to get his little girl. Upon his arrival Mr. Morton was a little surprised to find his daughter with a child of her own, but not very. He'd feared this would be the case when he received her letter.

Dustin had moved out of the Mortons' just after Cindy ran away. The popular opinion was he'd spent the entire year looking for her, unsuccessfully. Matt and his sister had always been close. He felt bad that Dustin had gone after Cindy and he hadn't. He wanted to go but just didn't. He'd never quite forgiven himself.

Dustin was still away when Mr. Morton returned with his wayward daughter and new grandchild. Dustin could both read and write well and maintained contact with the Mortons. Mrs. Morton sent word to the Kansas City Stockyards, which was Dustin's last known whereabouts, that Cindy had been abused and abandoned by the school master. The letter wasn't received in time for him to meet Mr. Morton in St. Louis. Apparently Dustin did make the ride from Kansas City to St. Louis anyway, but was not heard from for several months.

A letter, with no return address, was received about a month after Cindy's return home. Inside was no note or name, simply a St. Louis newspaper clipping telling of the local constable finding a body identified as one Mr. Tim Burns. The article reported that the man had been brutally beaten and had died soon after. All indications were there had been no weapon used as there were no entry wounds in the body. No evidence or witnesses to the beating were found. No other information was in the envelope. The address was written as if intentionally altered so as not to be identifiable. Mr. and Mrs. Morton shared the clipping with Matt but chose to keep the information from Cindy, for now at least.

About six months later, Dustin came riding in on a different horse than he'd rode out on and looking much older than his seventeen years. The Mortons were happy to see him, Matt most of all. Cindy, however, was very distant toward her protector of years before. In fact, she'd been a little cold to her whole family since her return. Mr. Morton was afraid the troubles they were to have with his little girl weren't all over yet. He had no idea how right he was, especially where Dustin would be concerned.

Chapter 2

Years before Dustin's father, Franklin Thomas, had moved his young family west after his participation in the unpleasantness against the north. Franklin, as many other defenders of the Red and Gray, left his southern homeland for less ravaged landscape in the west, a new frontier free of the carpetbaggers of the reclamation. Franklin found there was no escaping the bitterness left in the hearts of all who were involved in this horrible event in our nation's past.

A large number of the Union soldiers, who remained in service after the conflict, were sent to the frontier to help with the great western migration and settlement of the plains. They rebuilt forts left abandoned during the war and built many new ones as well. Many of these Union men were absolutely intolerant of southern sympathizers and took every opportunity to inflict any anguish upon them possible.

With the renewed Indian activity, which had commenced in earnest during the time the soldiers from these western forts were pulled to support the troops against the Confederates, along with the Mexican dissidents who were defending their homeland, you would think the cavalry would have had little time for harassing the very western adventurers and settlers they were being paid to protect. This was not always the case. Many of the soldiers were fair and reasonable in their dealings with the new inhabitants of the lands under their jurisdiction, but a few of the recently relocated officers were so concerned with future political aspirations and the possibility of a reassignment back home in the east, that some of the decisions they made were ludicrous or cruel and often even fatal.

To make things even worse for Franklin Thomas, the commander of the local fort, Colonel L.J. Armstrong, had been severely wounded at Shilo. His injuries left him with the use of only one arm and a painful limp as well, and as fate would have it, Franklin's unit of Confederate raiders had been responsible for the commanders wounds. Franklin and a handful of his fellow Southerners escaped capture but most were killed or arrested soon after the raid. Colonel Armstrong knew of Franklin's involvement in the raid and went far out of his way to gain some small grain of retribution at every possible opportunity.

Franklin Thomas, trying to put the past where it belonged, worked hard to build his future in the west and raise his family as safely and healthy as possible. This was no easy task in this wild country full of hostels, both Indian and Mexican as well as the harshness of the land itself. This was brutal country at best. Franklin settled on a piece of wild land not far from the Rio Grande where it runs south toward the Mexican settlement of Socorro.

A life long friend and fellow Confederate, Jim Morton, moved west with the Thomas family and settled on the land next to Franklin's. Jim had been in the

Confederate navy and had distinguished himself as a bold and honorable man on several occasions. The two men were friends long before the war. They both had wives and young children hopefully waiting for their safe return during the war years. Both families were of the lucky few whose loved ones actually returned. Scarred and hardened as they were, they were alive and whole. Seeing the devastation of their once beautiful homeland, Jim and Franklin packed their very few belongings, which had neither been confiscated or destroyed, and their families in a rather high quality buckboard Franklin had acquired from a Union Army camp, along with the beautiful four mule hitch attached to it. The mule's freshly altered U.S. brand had become Franklin Thomas' 08 brand and would fool only the most gullible of investigators. These mules would in fact become a tremendous liability to their families before this was over. For now they were the only transportation these two families had and would be defended as such.

The Morton home had been burned in the conflict and these adventurers were leaving behind only a two room shed like building which was all that remained of the Thomas home. They left it in flames when they went. It would not have been much good to the Union as it was, but it would be of none at all now. It was odd but none of them even looked back at what had been their home. Each man had a saddle horse and the kids rode in the wagon with their sparse belongings. The women alternately walked or rode horseback while the men walked.

Chapter 3

The trip was no different than the trips made by several thousand other displaced Confederate families. It took many weeks and was hard as expected. Not really any harder than life was for poor folks at the time anyway, just mobile. The women became used to the routine quickly and the men soon felt some of the weight, the burden of war had placed on them, lifting. In this ever more opening country was a chance of a new life with no constant dread of death to deal with. Everyone dies and has to deal with death sometime. War, however, especially this heinous chapter in American history, dealt death in a frequency seldom ever seen before or since.

Jim Morton witnessed death and injury by the ship load, hauling injured and dead Confederates from the mouth of the Mississippi to the safe port of Galveston. Franklin saw death first hand as it was being dispensed, dishing out more than an ample share of it by his own hands. He was a wonderful horseman and stealthy raider. Franklin threw himself into the effort with all his heart and soul. He had been a peaceful man, almost gentle in nature. Large and strong but sensitive and caring at the same time. When the killing started, it was like someone pulled a veil over Franklin's very soul. He became a ruthless assassin and cold killer. When Richmond fell and all was lost, the veil was lifted and Franklin returned to his former quiet manner, at least it would seem so.

Both men knew when they reached the east bank of the Rio Grande that home lie on the other side. They found enough open land, not yet claimed, for two nice places. At first the two families lived together in a little, brush arbor shanty the men threw together. Later two separate dwellings a little over three miles apart were built. Humble as they were, they were very comfortable and served both families adequately. The families worked hard and made lives for themselves in this unsettled territory, facing hardships as they came and overcoming any obstacles thrown in their way by nature or man.

One stumbling block that was becoming more and more difficult to handle was Colonel L.J. Armstrong. This menace to humanity was more concerned with punishing ex-confederate soldiers and their families than tending to his duties as a United States Army officer. The country was all but overrun with renegade Indians and dissident, displaced Mexicans. Armstrong's lack of control in his territory was of great concern back in Washington. This added pressure from his superiors made Armstrong even more angry and intolerant. He had several citizens hanged publicly and had executed one of his own scouts by firing squad. The reasons were always a bit cloudy as to the why of these actions. "Order must be gained before it can be kept." He was oft times quoted. Armstrong had not nearly gotten a hold on the handle of control in his territory. He had requested help from forts to the north and south of his area as they seemed to be having less trouble than he, but Armstrong was never satisfied with the suggestions made by these assisting officers and was always offended at their questions as to the reason behind his failure to govern his sector of the new frontier. To most of his contemporaries, Armstrong was so far off the mark in his assessment of the local situation, several wrote Washington themselves suggesting a change of commanders at the fort. The change seemed very slow in transpiring, considering the importance of the territory that was being virtually overrun by the hostels and bandits.

While all this was going on, the newcomers had their hands full making a life in the wild, new land. Protecting their families and ranches was more than many could handle. Some left the territory, a few traveled further west. Others returned to their southern homeland where poverty and abusive northern reclamationists were their only adversaries. Many more lost their ranches to the bandits or their lives to the hostels.

The Mortons and Thomases were here to stay. They had chosen their new ranches well and had very defensible locations for their homes. They did however, often times wish the houses were closer together. Their idea of the location, one on each end of the little valley, was for protecting and holding their newly acquired livestock and using the natural lay of the land to do so. The two hard riding men took advantage of some of the thousands of cattle gone wild, roaming west from the Texas plains and north from Mexico, to stock their ranches. They had so effectively gathered these wild cattle as to necessitate looking for a larger range to handle their holdings. The 08 brand soon became one of the largest in the territory.

Col. Armstrong's refusal to use any beef raised by ex-confederates for either the fort or the reservation Indians caused multiple problems for both the Army and the 08 men. Even though Franklin and Jim had found a ready market for their beef at the forts both north and south of their own territory, this required long drives in very dangerous country. While the men were gone on one of these drives, the home ranch was raided, a great deal of stock driven off and one of the smaller Thomas children had been shot, injuring her severely. This raid changed things greatly. There had been some question as to who the raiders actually were. Both Mrs. Thomas and Mrs. Morton said the riders appeared to be Comancheros, Mexican Indian thieves who had been plaguing the country for some time. What troubled Franklin and Jim was that both women reported hearing no Spanish or Indian spoken but each were sure they heard orders being given in clear English. The raid was violent, rapid and well organized. Not at all like the normal savage attacks by the wild, unorganized Comancheros. The men would avenge this violation of the sanctity of their homes and families with all the ferociousness they possessed.

Franklin, having more hands on experience in combat than Jim, went into action immediately, gathering the two families together and leaving Jim in charge of their protection and that of the ranches. Sally, the injured Thomas girl, had taken a bullet in the spine at the base of her neck and was paralyzed. Mrs. Thomas was a dedicated nurse and mother. Mrs. Morton aided by caring for the other children as much as possible. Jim and the oldest boy of each family took on the ranch responsibilities in Franklin's absence. The boys, Dustin Thomas and Jim's boy Matt, were big enough to be some help but Jim had his hands full. Fences had been torn down, the main barn burned and numerous animals shot dead or wounded so seriously as to necessitate destroying them. Jim and the boys had to drag the carcasses into piles and burn them. They were able to jerk some of the beef but most was too far gone to save by the time it was discovered. This devastating blow was nearly fatal for the 08 ranch enterprise and would soon prove to be completely so for many of the perpetrators of the raid.

Franklin had many friends near the fort and knew an old Mexican Cantina owner who disliked the Union soldiers as much as he did. Juan Rodriguez was the saloon keeper's name and his was one of the many families, who like the rebels of the south, had been run off of their own land. He refused, however, to abandon his business and because of its public service fulfillment of providing liquor and ladies, both hauled up from Mexico, he was allowed to keep it operating. Juan knew he would eventually be forced out but for now he stood his ground. Franklin gained valuable information from Juan as to the identity of the participants of this cowardly act. Some talk had been overheard that Armstrong did not participate in but did organize the raid. It was, in fact, as Franklin suspected, soldiers dressed as Comancheros acting on the order of Armstrong.

A short list of names was gathered for Franklin and his work began in earnest. Reverting back to his gorilla war state of mind, this righter of wrongs waited patiently and ambushed participants of the raid as they left the fort or wandered from camp. He then snuck into the fort itself and went inside the barracks where forty men lie sleeping. Not a sound was heard. When the bugle sounded revelry in the morning, four more men lie still in their bunks, throats cut all. The other bodies were soon discovered outside the fort and a panic ensued in the ranks. It became apparent that only the participating members, knew anything about the raid. There was an immediate call to arms and a patrol sent to the Thomas Morton ranches with vengeance in mind.

Franklin had arrived home ahead of the soldiers, under cover of darkness and returned to the Morton house where his family was waiting. He moved them back to their own home, still before light. He and Jim, with Dustin and Matt, were trying to salvage some of the contents of the barn when the patrol approached, headed by Armstrong himself. Franklin, with Jim at his side, both carrying rifles at the ready, stepped directly into the path of the soldiers.

"Hold it right there and identify yourselves," Franklin said menacingly.

"You know damn well who I am, Reb!" was Armstrong's reply.

"Well, you do look like a blue belly officer I once shot at Shilo, but it seems around here lately looks can be deceiving," Franklin responded without taking his rifle barrel off of Armstrong even for a second.

"I'll not stand for that insubordination from any gray dog like you. I'll have you shot!" Armstrong shouted back.

"That'll be right hard to pull off, Yank, considering you'll be dead if you open your mouth again," Franklin said so coolly that several officers very quietly backed their horses away from the Colonel's.

"Easy Franklin. Let's see what they know or think they know," Jim whispered.

"I've changed my mind and decided to let you talk some more, blue belly. What are you doing on my property again so soon? I ain't even cleaned up the mess from your last visit."

"I don't know what you're talking about, Thomas. I've not set foot on this place before now!" Armstrong stated.

"No, I didn't actually figure you'd have the nerve for a raid. You received all your war wounds in the back running for cover, didn't you?" Franklin said.

The Colonel's face looked as if it were going to burst and he was about to loose all control. A captain stepped his horse forward afraid Armstrong would say something life ending to this cool and obviously dangerous southerner.

"Mr. Thomas, I'm Captain Perron. We had a dozen men killed last night. Four of them found dead in their bunks. The Colonel thought you might have some information about what happened to them."

"Your Colonel has all the important information, Captain. You get him to tell you what happened out here and I'll tell you what I know about what happened in there. You seem to be an intelligent man. I can tell by your eyes you had no part in this or even any knowledge of it. Some of the men in this patrol do know what happened here, I can see that as well. If they come clean and testify against Armstrong for giving the orders for the raid, their lives will be spared. If not, no one will be getting much sleep at the fort until they do," Franklin said to the Captain as if they were all alone.

"Dad, that man's riding one of the horses from the raid. I recognized the white spot on his hip," Dustin said.

"Shoot him, Jim!" Franklin said without removing his aim from Armstrong.

"No! Please, I didn't mean for no kid to get shot! The Colonel told us to just do some damage and scare you all off!" shouted the Sergeant riding the horse with the tell tale spot.

"Shut up, you fool! I'll shoot you myself," Armstrong screamed while reaching for his pistol.

Before he could pull it, the Captain stuck his own weapon in the Colonel's chest.

"Just sit easy, Sir. I'll be relieving you of your weapon and your command until we get this cleared up. Lieutenant, place the Sergeant Major and Colonel under arrest. Any of you men involved in this will be given partial immunity for your testimony. Don't anyone do anything stupid. Mr. Thomas, don't leave the territory. I'll need to talk to you about the murders at the fort. I have nothing except the suspicion that you were involved. If I find any evidence pointing to you, I'll have to bring you in as well."

"Captain, I'll not stand a military trial. If you think you can prove I did anything, I'll turn myself in to the civil authorities for a public hearing. That's the best deal I can make you but I give you my word on that," Franklin said.

"That's good enough for me, Mr. Thomas," said the Captain.

"I'll see you hanged for this, Captain Perron. This is treason. You men better listen to me or you'll be just as guilty as he is," Armstrong pleaded.

"We've already listened to you too much, Colonel. This got way out of hand. Mr. Thomas, I'm sorry I had anything to do with this. I sure didn't want anyone to get hurt. When this is all over, I'll come back and help make things right," Sergeant Major Michaels said.

"If you pull this off, I'll be back too! I'll make things right, you low life rebel trash. I'll kill you all this time," Armstrong said.

"You might want to be careful what you say, Sir," reminded the Captain. "We'll be forced to testify as to your statements."

"That went easier than I ever dreamed, Franklin," Jim said as the troop rode off.

"This ain't over by a long shot yet, Jim," Franklin said watching the soldiers riding away toward their fort several miles distant.

"What do you mean, Franklin? There's nothing tying you to the killings at the fort, no witness, no evidence and we'll all testify you were here the whole time. Besides, what judge would believe one man could slip into a heavily armed military post and assassinate a dozen soldiers and get out again without ever being noticed," Jim assured his compadre.

"We'll see. Armstrong won't lie down easy. He's still got some loyal followers too. We'd best keep our eyes open for a while," Franklin said matter of factly.

Things went along as quietly as could be expected for the next few months. The men couldn't spend much time trying to rebuild the herd by gathering more wild cattle. They were too worried about a retaliatory strike against the ranch at the hands of Armstrong's supporters who had become vocal of late, threatening to clean the territory of all confederates should the Colonel be convicted. This appeared about to be happening as the remaining six raiders had all testified against Armstrong.

Little Sally Thomas died of her injuries about a week after the visit from the troops. None of the men knew who's bullet had struck the little girl and all shared the burden of guilt. The court martial and dishonorable discharge of Armstrong was a very hotly discussed subject in the territory. Because of their testimonies against Armstrong, the soldiers participating in the raid were dealt with somewhat lightly considering the gravity of their actions at the 08 ranch. All were reduced in rank but none imprisoned after the military trial. Two of the men chose the discharge offered them by the tribunal in lieu of remaining as privates. Both of these men returned to their former homes in the east. Hopes were that Armstrong would do so likewise. This would not be the case. His disgraceful discharge from service was more than Armstrong could bare. The war had left much more than his body crippled. His mind and very soul had sustained much damage. This new blow from the Rebels was not going to be tolerated.

He was blameless in his own mind and felt he had been dealt with unjustly. Somehow being held responsible for what was, obviously to him, Franklin Thomas' own deserved punishment for being an impudent Confederate marauder. Franklin's days of causing pain and disgrace to Armstrong were about over. Armstrong was quickly able to assemble a gang of undesirables who were sympathetic with him and his mission of revenge against the Rebels, Franklin Thomas particularly.

Left all but penniless and afoot after the trial, Armstrong's first work for his new band of discontents was mounting and arming themselves properly for battle. The forth coming raids and robberies were held in the name of justice. The Colonel's new army of thieves rode with confidence known only by men who believed in what they were doing and had faith in the cause they were about. They boldly rode into Mexican ranches and took what horses and food they required, many times leaving several bodies of harmless victims behind. Always in the name of cleansing the territory of unwanted "foreigners" like the Confederates who came here the same time many of the Union soldiers had, the Mexicans who had been here four hundred years now, and the Indians who had been here long before that.

The territory plagued already with the menace of bandits and renegade Indians, now had a real threat to its peace and even its very life. Now there was Armstrong without even the small amount of restraint his position in the military had formerly held on him. He was now absolutely out of control.

The men of the 08 ranch were struggling, trying to put things back together, still waiting for an attack from Armstrong who had not been seen lately but was being held responsible for several more raids on Mexican ranches. He'd amassed quite an army and they needed to be supplied.

They also were worrying about charges being brought against Franklin for the deaths of the soldiers that had participated in the raid at the 08 ranch, all while rebuilding the herd and trying to reestablish some normalcy in their lives. Franklin and Jim had decided to build two separate sets of corrals and smaller barns nearer their houses instead of the one larger centrally located one that had been all but completely destroyed in the raid. The men figured, in case of raiders, they might save part of the livestock this way.

Franklin's oldest son, Dustin, used to attend school with his little sister Sally. They would take the old Union wagon and the mules by the Morton's and pick up the three youngsters of that family who attended school also. Matt, Cindy and the youngest Morton, little Kathy would climb into the wagon with the Thomas kids and ride to the neighboring Carter ranch where the school house was located. This little one room shed was also used as a church house on Sundays and several ranch families attended regularly.

One morning while Dustin drove over to pick up the Morton children for school, he thought how much he missed little Sally and how he wished his father would work with Jim so the two men would be together in case of trouble. Franklin had told his young son that he and Jim were working their own places so they could watch their families better. Franklin also told Dustin not to worry, everything would be all right, that the trouble here was over. This reassuring lie was the last thing Dustin ever heard his father say. That day while he was at school, another life changing event took place at the Thomas ranch.

At first sight of the massacre, the carnage would indicate the most savage of Indian attacks. Upon closer look at the bodies of several of the attackers, one saw that these were, in fact, known members of Armstrong's army. Franklin, who had obviously fought ferociously by the number of bodies belonging to the raiders, was killed and mutilated as were all the remaining members of his family. All but young Dustin, that is, he was at school of all places. He should have been at home to help his family. He too would have been killed, and that is how he wished it was. Every animal not stolen was killed and the house and new barn burned to the ground. Dustin was spared the horrifying sight by Mrs. Morton who rode to the school to bring the children to her house after Jim had seen the smoke from his partner's and had run to give aide. All was lost before he arrived. He did see a large band of riders crossing a ridge far to the west as he was nearing the scene of the murders. Jim rode to the fort to report the attack.

The new commanding officer, Brigadier General Stewart, had been sent to the west to take charge of all operations west of Fort Dodge, Kansas, north to Canada and south to Mexico. He had distinguished himself and risen to his position of power and trust through intelligence and cool headedness under fire in his handling of the repulsion of Lee's troops on their move north. General Jim Stewart had a great deal of family and property in the south. Most noted was a cousin, Jeb Stewart, who fought heroically for the southern cause. Still the Union never once questioned Jim's loyalty. His actions were always toward a quick end of this terrible ordeal and a just peace was his foremost concern. His compassion in his dealings with the Confederate officers held capture and his administration of the prison camps in general, led to his selection of ranking officer of the new frontier and Indian reservations.

Armstrong's actions had, here to for, been an objectionable affront to this new governing officer of the settlements and had certainly kept the Indians and Mexicans stirred up. Now this murderous attack on white settlers was so vile as to demand more direct and immediate action. An aggressive man hunt for Armstrong's army was ordered. Stewart felt partly to blame for this devilish deed because he'd not pursued Armstrong before and hanged him as he felt he should have. That could not be changed now. It could, however, be rectified. He would put together a special force to aid in the pursuit and capture or annihilation of Armstong and his army.

This would be led by Captain Perron, his personal testimony and handling of the court-martial was so professional and impartial, Stewart had counted on him as his aide de camp since the trials. Perron took this important and prestigious command very seriously. His easy manner and firm control of his new troops, even the officers, developed a loyalty necessary but seldom ever totally gained in a military outfit. Perron was assuming that Armstong was fleeing to old Mexico between raids and sent several scouts south to try to locate the fugitive band of murderers and thieves. Not to be foiled, Perron also sent scouts to the Indian Nations to the east and north and more to the west as well. He had word sent to the nearest telegraph in Kansas to fill the wires with notice that Armstrong's army was wanted for the murders of the Thomas family and all members bore the weight of large rewards for their capture, dead or alive!

The reward for Armstrong himself was much more alive than dead. Stewart wanted to hang the ex-Colonel publicly as a declaration that the war was over. The activities of the Union marauder would not be tolerated in the west anymore than those of the rebs in the south would be. This was the United States of America once again and Stewart intended to govern it as such. Armstrong's raid and murder of the Thomases had made the papers of the east and south. The few newspapers still having Confederate ties were having a field day with the Union Colonel gone bad. Stewart knew he must stop this quickly and cleanly.

Perron was also aware of the pressure being placed on General Stewart to quail this situation expeditiously as possible. All haste was made. Every lead was followed but still no Armstrong. It was as if he'd fallen off the planet. Captain Perron soon sent some highly trusted, expertly trained men under cover to infiltrate the dark world of the Comanchero butchers from which Armstrong had recruited his most villainous soldiers. These spies selected by Perron had to be carefully chosen. None could have ever been seen before by Armstrong or any of his men. Because of this Captain Perron had to refuse to accept ex-Sergeant Major Michaels, who's insistence that he be allowed to go caused no little suspicion among those who were being selected for this mission as to his true loyalties. Michaels went A.W.O.L. when Perron insisted the Sgt. not participate in the covert part of this action, causing Captain Perron even more anguish.

No one knew exactly just who all was riding with the ex-Colonel and this made things even more difficult for Perron. This became a purely volunteer mission after a few select candidates were chosen. All volunteered without hesitation. Captain Perron explained how because of the fragile nature of the public opinion of the military at the moment, all knowledge of their actions would be disavowed should they be caught before Armstrong was taken. They would be held responsible for any crimes committed by themselves and dealt with as deserters. Captain Perron turned his back and continued talking to these select men, explaining that if any should decide to recant his decision to volunteer, he could simply return to his barracks now and it would never be mentioned again. This was, after all, probably a suicide mission at best. No one would ever think less of any man not participating. Perron stood quietly for a moment and then turned back around. Every man remained. Pride filled Perron as he looked into the faces of these six brave men.

He then continued, "Upon the return of Armstrong to General Stewart, you will receive full amnesty for any necessary actions taken by you to illicit his capture. Am I understood, gentlemen?" Perron asked.

He received the affirmative from all.

"Good luck then, men. You'll not report to anyone until you have Armstrong or bring information of his exact location. You are undertaking an assignment few could accomplish. I have all faith in your ability to do so. God speed."

Chapter 4

Jim Morton was staying close to home now and all lived in fear. This was a very troubled time and everyone felt there would be no relief until Armstrong was captured and hung. When his murderous gang was perpetrating their heinous crimes, all the settlers were scared and huddled in their homes. It was even worse when Armstrong would vanish and no word of him came for weeks at a time. Men could not work their ranches or their fields. Livestock had wandered off to a point that many places failed. More and more families moved to the forts for help from the military to keep from starving to death. Some did starve, others tried to return east or south only to find their demise on the same plains they had not long before successfully crossed heading west. Such was the life on the frontier for the next several months.

Dustin became even more quiet in nature than before. He spoke seldom and never smiled. Never, that is, except when he was watching little Cindy Morton at play or when she brought him his meals. The loss of his entire family was such a devastating blow to Dustin, some feared he might lose his senses all together. He was a Thomas and was too strong for anything like that to happen. He would survive and grow even stronger and would someday be a man his father would have been proud of.

His affection for Cindy was what kept him centered for now. Many school boys felt the wrath of Dustin's protective nature when play turned too rough or hurtful toward his little Cindy. Size, age or number did not enter into his mind when in her defense. One time some boys were teasing Cindy about a dress her mother had made her. Dustin and Matt were sitting under a big tree talking about what they were going to do with their lives when they saw Cindy run into the schoolhouse crying. Dustin never hesitated to find out what had happened. He flew into the largest of the boys with a savageness that comes from within so deeply most men are never able to call it up, regardless of cause or situation. Dustin knocked the larger boy down and was pummeling his head against the ground while his two friends stood speechlessly watching. They soon gained their wits and kicked Dustin off of their overwhelmed leader. They continued to stomp the avenger until the cries of the crowd of fellow schoolmates drew the attentions of the schoolmaster, who was able to stop the beating just short of it becoming a murder. Matt ran over to his fallen friend and knelt beside him. Matt felt badly because he hadn't gone to Cindy's defense and worse because he hadn't tried to stop Dustin's beating. He wanted to, but he just didn't.

The school master allowed the Morton children to drive Dustin home in the wagon. On the drive home, Dustin knew that he had some cracked ribs and more sore places than he could count. He felt as if he were drowning and was concerned he'd punctured a lung. He'd seen a horse fall on a cowboy once and the man died in his bunk that evening. Dustin's father had said that a broken rib had pierced the fellow's lung causing his death from drowning in his own blood.

Matt drove the wagon with his little sister Kathy seated beside him. Dustin lay in the back with his head in Cindy's lap. She had just turned fourteen and he coming on sixteen now. Looking into her eyes made him feel more like a man than he ever had. Suddenly Matt shouted that there were riders coming. Dustin could barely sit up to see who it was.

"Armstrong's men. Run for it Matt. We'll try and beat them home!" Dustin moaned.

Matt just stopped the wagon and stared at the rapidly approaching men.

"Run, damn it! They'll kill us for sure," Dustin repeated.

Still Matt sat frozen. The men rode up and a particularly scrubby man dressed like a Comanchero rode up along side the wagon.

"Well, look what we've got here, boys! U.S. Army mules with the 08 brand on 'em. You kids are mule thieves for sure. I'm confiscating these mules and wagon before you get into trouble," the ragged man snarled sinisterly.

Matt never spoke but Dustin pulled himself to his feet in the wagon bed.

"You ain't taking nothing, you sorry trash," he managed to say though it was hard for him to even breath from the pain of his broken ribs.

The Comanchero pulled his pistol and pointed it directly into Dustin's face.

"I'll kill you first then I'll take whatever I want."

"He's just a boy, Sanderson. The Colonel's got enough heat on him without us killing more children." This voice came from a large man across the wagon from the first.

"Boy or not, I'll kill him for talking to me like that!" Sanderson said.

"Let's take the wagon and go. This kid's already been in some kind of wreck. Look at him. He's beat all to hell," the second man said.

This time Dustin got a good look at this interloper and saw something very different in his eyes than the other Comanchero's had. On closer look, Dustin thought he recognized this man as a soldier he saw at the fort talking to Captain Perron the last time they'd gone in for supplies.

"By God, I'll do as I please, Ned. You ain't been with this outfit long enough to give me orders," the first one said.

"Look Sanderson, you go ahead and get in the wagon. Let's get the hell out of here," Ned said sternly.

"Hell, he ain't worth shooting anyway but I'm taking the girl with me," Sanderson said menacingly.

"You touch her and I'll kill you!" Dustin said in a manner which left no doubt he meant it.

Sanderson struck Dustin across his face with his pistol and Dustin fell. Dustin went down but not out. Sanderson stepped off his horse directly into the wagon and grabbed Cindy's arm. Ned drew his own pistol and pointed it at Sanderson, ignoring the cheers of the rest of the gang.

"Let the girl be, Sanderson. We'll throw them kids into the road and take the wagon and mules. We'll get us some grown women when we get back to Mexico! We don't need no damn little girl slowing us down."

"By God, I'll take her if I decide to! You or nobody else will stop me either. Damn you Ned, you're acting awful prissy. What the hell's the matter with you? This girl ain't nothin to you," Sanderson asked, wanting an explanation.

Ned looked cold and deliberate and spoke slowly, "I had a daughter about her age, Sanderson. The Indians got her. Now throw them kids out and let's get. We've taken too long already. They'll be after us and the Colonel will raise hell if we don't get back with this loot. The wagon will slow us down enough."

This all seemed reasonable enough to Sanderson. He turned Cindy's arm loose and slapped her out of the wagon and picked up Dustin, still about half stunned from the pistol blow, and threw him down beside her. Matt grabbed little Kathy and jumped off the wagon seat and ran back to the other two children.

"This damn wagon ain't worth getting caught for," Sanderson said. "Cut the mules loose and we'll at least take them along."

Two of the bandits stepped off their horses and unhooked the mules then handed their lines to Sanderson.

"You stole them, you lead them," one of the Comanchero's said.

"What a bunch of sissies I'm riding with. Wait until I tell Colonel Armstrong the way you all are acting when he's not around. You'd think we were a bunch of Sunday school teachers. Come on you damn mules, let's go," Sanderson finished and rode off south, the rest of the men following him.

Ned looked back directly at Dustin making eye contact, then he dropped something and rode to catch up with the others. Dustin struggled to get up and with Matt's help stood. Dustin walked over to see what Ned had dropped. There was an empty crumpled envelope with the letterhead of the Mission Inn from Magdalena, Mexico stamped in the upper left hand corner where the return address goes.

"What is it, Dusty?" Matt asked.

"Just trash, Matt. Let's get started for home. It's closer than back to the Carter's place. We've got to bring back some horses and get the wagon. You all right, Cindy?" Dustin asked.

She nodded yes. Her face reddening from the slap. Dustin and Matt walked the two girls back to the Morton home and Matt returned with his father to get the wagon immediately, as it was the only one they had left after the recent raids.

Dustin excused himself to tend his many cuts and abrasions from his earlier thrashing and found he needed Mrs. Morton to sew up a gash above and behind his right ear, left by Sanderson's pistol. Dustin made his way out to his room and asked not to be brought supper. He'd rather get some rest. This proved to be a near fatal request. Sometime in the early evening Dustin succumbed to his injuries and blacked out. His fever raced higher and higher to a more than dangerous point. If not for Matt coming out to apologize for not trying to make a run for it with the wagon, Dustin would have surely died.

It was several days before Dustin was out of danger. Jim Morton had carried Dustin into the house and made a pallet for him off to one side in the main room. Mrs. Morton and Cindy watched over Dustin night and day. On the evening of the third day, his fever broke and Dustin came out of what was almost his final sleep. A few more days saw Dustin up and around. Except for the occasional deep cough and the spitting up of some blood, he was near well. His anger was not channeled solely at the older boys who nearly kicked him to death, but rather at the man, Sanderson, who had slapped Cindy and stolen his father's mules.

Dustin could not get the man, Ned, out of his mind. He wasn't sure why, but he somehow knew that this man had saved him from being killed and Cindy a fate even worse.

Dustin never officially returned to school but did follow the road leading away from the Carter ranch, the road taken by one of the older boys involved in the beating. Much in the manner his father waylaid the soldiers outside the fort, Dustin waited for this large lad to head home. Not fully understanding gorilla warfare as his father had, Dustin ignored the size difference of the enemy and rather than hide and ambush, he sat his horse dead center of the road. This big fellow rode his own mount up to Dustin's and was about to say something to him. Dustin did not pause to hear this young man's speech. He leaped headlong into the big fellows chest knocking him off his horse and all the wind from him as well. Dustin rose first and though coughing still, proceeded to stomp as much life out of ol' biggen' as possible without committing a homicide. He explained to this pitiful, whipped fellow that the thumping he'd just received was not for beating him but for the remarks he'd made to little Cindy hurting her feelings.

That night at the Morton's home, Dustin became ill again from his activity of the afternoon. In spite of Jim Morton's urgings, Dustin had returned to the barn. Jim went down after supper to check on Dustin to find him doing rather poorly. Dustin explained the events of his day, after much insistence from Jim. A tear came to Jim's eye when he realized Dustin had been beaten so terribly for defending little Cindy's hurt feelings. Jim started talking to Dustin about the days when he and Franklin were young men. About the terrible war and Franklin's valiant service to the Confederate cause. He told Dustin of the many raids his father had led and the gorilla tactics he'd employed. He filled the evening with the tales he'd never told Dustin before about the heroic deeds his father had performed against overwhelming odds. He told a boy who was becoming a man, of a father who had truly been one. One he could always be proud to be the son of. The last thing Jim Morton told young Dustin was that he was a son any man would be proud to have, as well.

A good nights rest helped Dustin to gain his strength back enough to get around some the next day. One week later Dustin was again on the Carter road the other side of the schoolhouse. The other two boys lived near enough so they walked to and from school. This time Dustin was waiting in a thicket of young mesquites, bordering their road home. As they strolled homeward, unsuspecting due to the lapse of time and the adage of safety in numbers, they were suddenly jerked off their feet. Dustin simply rode out behind the brothers and roped them around their waists. He then took a wrap around his saddle horn and drug them back towards the school. He drug them over the road a ways and then off the road through cactus and rocks, through brush and thistle. When he stopped and stepped down to release them, there was no fight left in them. He repeated his declaration as to the cause of their punishment and left them crying and picking thorns out of each other.

Dustin did not return home that night. He'd told Jim Morton he would be gone for a while and not to worry about him. Jim said he'd not try to stop him but he would still be worried about him until his return.

Dustin rode toward the fort and stopped at the cantina of Juan Rodriguez. No reliable information about his mules or the whereabouts of Sanderson could be attained. Juan let Dustin stay the next few nights in his back room. The first night the story of a fight and desertion came from the fort to the cantina. Dustin could hear most everything that was said. What he heard confused and upset him greatly. The man who had deserted was none other than the ex-Sergeant Major Michaels. No real reason was given, just that Michaels had gotten into an argument with an officer and had been placed under arrest. On the way to the guard house, Michaels knocked out the soldier escorting him, stole a horse and escaped under a barrage of rather heavy pistol fire. A detachment had been sent after him to no avail. Dustin had hoped he would find an ally in Michaels because of his heart felt, emotional apology to his father the day of Armstrong's arrest. Now with him gone, Dustin would be absolutely alone in his search for the mules and Sanderson. Alone that is, except for the man called Ned who had already saved both his and Cindy's lives.

Dustin stayed two more days and then his break came. Ned came into the cantina with several other Comancheros but the man, Sanderson, was not with them. Dustin laid quietly in his spot in the storehouse listening as carefully as possible. He wasn't able to hear as much as he wanted to but he'd already decided to follow Ned and the others when they left.

He slipped out back and got his horse and gear ready. He made sure his father's pistol, which he now wore proudly, was properly loaded then slipped back into his little nook in the storeroom to wait.

He was surprised to find that another group of rough looking men had entered the cantina while he was out back. Ned was sitting with two of the new comers. Their new location was the closest table to Dustin's hiding place. Their conversation, although near whispers, was easily heard by the nearby eavesdropper. The content seemed very strange but not too big of a surprise to Dustin. It seems Ned is not really a Comanchero butcher, nor were the two other men at the table with him. They were apparently after Armstrong themselves. The one they called Black Jack was scolding both Ned and the other man for going off alone. The only chance they had was to stay together. He continued that no word had been heard from their three companions in several days and if anyone of them is found out, all the new men in Armstrong's army would become suspect.

"What's this crap I hear about you standing down Sanderson in front of his men, Ned, over some damn mules?" asked Black Jack.

"It wasn't over them mules! Hell, they was already stole once, from the army. It was those kids. That son-of-a-dog was going to take that little girl. I'll be damned if I'll sit still while some scum pile like Sanderson has his way with a child," Ned said in his own defense.

"I hadn't heard about the kids, Ned. You done the right thing," Black Jack said in as close to an apology as he'd ever given.

"It was all for nothing anyway. We was being chased and them mules wouldn't keep up so that idiot Sanderson, shot them dead in their tacks to keep anyone else from getting them. He seemed real proud of himself when he done it too," Ned finished.

Dustin's heart sank and he paid less attention to the rest of the conversation. It seemed to be mainly about the deserter Michaels, anyway. They all seemed worried about what trouble he might cause.

"Hell," the third man said, "Ol' Mike might slip in and kill or capture Armstrong all by himself and save us all the trouble."

"If anyone could, I guess it would be him. I didn't know him but have sure heard some hair raising stories about his escapades," Black Jack stated.

The three agreed not to get separated again regardless of circumstances and rose to walk out.

"Where to now?" asked Black Jack.

"Magdalena, Mexico, boys! Armstrong's main force holds up there. These little bands like Sanderson's just raid around here to keep the heat off the main camp," Ned said almost too loudly for the comfort of his companions.

Dustin rode back to the Morton's and as it was very late, he rode up behind the barn and made as little noise as possible. When he stepped into his little room, he was grabbed from behind and his mouth covered by a huge hand.

"I'm gonna turn ya loose Laddie, don't yell out. I'll not hurt you. You just snuck up on me. Sorta spooked me, I guess. You're the boy recognized my horse, ain't you?" said Michaels.

"Yes, Sir," Dustin replied still a little rattled.

"Sorry I scared you, son," Michaels apologized.

"I ain't scared and I ain't your son," Dustin said very matter of factly.

"No, no of course you ain't. What's your name then?" Michaels asked.

"Dustin Thomas," Dustin stated proudly.

"Me friends, when I had friends, calls me Big Mike," he said and reached out a big paw in form of an introduction. Then continued, "You're just the man I'm looking for."

"What you looking for me for?" Dustin asked.

"Well to help ya lad, to help ya," Big Mike said.

"Help me do what?" Dustin asked actually confused.

"You're not a bright lad, are ya? I came to help ya kill the man what took yer family from ya, laddie," Big Mike said.

"How you going to do that. Nobody knows where he is, for sure," Dustin said.

"I do, Laddie. I do! I can ride right to him. Remember I rode with the Colonel for years before he lost his mind. Can ya use that gun you're a packin'?" Big Mike asked.

"Yes, Sir. My father taught me to shoot," Dustin replied.

"Well then, are ya willin to use it, then?"

"Yes!"

"Ta kill a man?"

"That man and his bunch, yes sir!" Dustin said coolly.

"Fine then, fine! Are you willin to go with me laddie?" Big Mike inquired looking straight into the eyes of the young man.

"Yes, sir. We can leave when you're ready," Dustin answered.

"Good then laddie. We'll head to Magdalena as soon as I get my stuff gathered up. You seem to be packed already."

"Yes, Sir. I've been gone to the cantina trying to get my mules back that a man named Sanderson stole, but he shot them later, so I came back. Some soldiers at the cantina said you'd run off and they wasn't sure what you were up to," Dustin said.

"Keepin my promise to your pa, Laddie. I always keep me promises. Tis a good habit to get in to," Big Mike said then, "Soldiers? What else did they say?"

"They were dressed up like Comancheros and the one called Black Jack said they were headed to Magdalena to get Armstrong."

"How many were there?"

"Three and they said there were three more somewhere but they hadn't been seen for awhile," Dustin responded.

21

"Good, they've found the old man's hiding place. We'll have us some help when we get there. Now all we have to do is cross a couple hundred miles of mean desert full of hostile Indians, Mexicans and Armstrong's own men; charge into the middle of several dozen armed killers and shoot the old gentleman. Nothing to it, hey, laddie?" Big Mike actually seemed to like the sound of his plan.

"No sir, nothing to it," Dustin said as convincingly as he could.

"Fine, laddie, fine," the big man repeated as they got their horses ready and then rode south toward Mexico.

Chapter 5

Big Mike thought it would be easier to do all their westward traveling deeper south in Mexico, then the only adversary would just be the native Mexicans and the land itself. Dustin made no suggestions and learned to accept Big Mike as a man who could survive and more importantly, help him survive almost any situation. As they traveled, the two talked about their lives and Big Mike told stories about fighting in the war and the terrible shame of how much family he'd lost during its course. Dustin had never talked about the war with a Yank before and would never have guessed one could feel as his father had about it. Dustin soon found he genuinely liked this man and felt there was much to learn from this warrior and he would make it his business to learn it all.

The trip itself was more exciting and adventure filled than Dustin could have ever imagined. Traveling cross country with a wanted man did have many disadvantages. In addition to the obvious necessity in traveling every back trail, they had to travel a great deal at night. Dustin soon adjusted to the rigorous trip and even started enjoying the demands it placed on him, body and soul.

Big Mike proved to be absolutely proficient at this life of forced marches and food and sleep depravation. He shared his experiences with Dustin and taught him how to ignore hunger, fatigue and even to a great extent, nature. Survival was the ultimate concern to a man in the wilderness, all else was meaningless unless you lived. Dustin realized soon that he was with the right man from which to learn the art of survival. Big Mike noticed everything. Nothing passed by without meeting his scrutiny. Anything out of place or unusual would bring Big Mike to a halt at the ready. Dustin quickly picked up the habit of looking before leaping, also. Big Mike would test his young companion as they traveled along.

"How many horses crossed that wash before us, Dustin?" he would ask.

At first Dustin might not have even realized they had crossed a wash. Pretty soon he learned to try and figure out things that might be important. He would often venture a guess if he didn't feel confident in an answer. He liked the way Big Mike explained why his answer was either right or wrong. Either way, Dustin always learned something from his giant companion. Two ambushes, three long chases by unknown parties and one unsuccessful hold up attempt, which ended fatally for three Mexican banditos, got the two travelers across most of Mexico and within striking distance of Armstrong's hold up in Magdalena.

"Little man, you've done real good so far but I'm afraid I'll have to go in alone from here," Big Mike said.

"Like hell you will! I've come this far and I'm going on in. You'll be no more welcome there than I will be, besides I got a plan," Dustin demanded.

"You've got a plan do ya? Well boy, let's hear it then," Big Mike was actually interested in what Dustin had to say.

"OK, first thing is, you got to knock me over the head," Dustin started.

"Whoa, there little fella! I ain't about to be hitting you over your empty little head. Let's get that straight. I might kill you," Big Mike said puzzled.

"Just listen, Mike. Please! You won't hit me hard enough to kill me, just hard enough to make it look like you tried to and I at least put up a fight. Then you tie my hands in front of me and you ride in behind me, holding your gun on me. This will do two things, first, it will get you all the way in to see Armstrong and second, you will already have your gun out. I'll have mine under my jacket and will be able to get to it quick when the fun starts. Any other way and they will either shoot you on sight or take you prisoner and take away your guns and I'm pretty sure we're going to need them to get out of there," Dustin said very calculated.

"Goodness! You thought that all up yourself? I can't believe it. I've rode into enemy fire many times on orders from generals who hadn't thought things through that well. Have you given any thought as to how you and me is going to get out after we kill old Armstrong? There will be fifty of them damn Comancheros around him, you know and just two of us," Mike said.

"There are at least six soldiers undercover headed to Armstrong ahead of us and maybe some scouts as well. I'm counting on them helping when this dance starts, but even if they are all there, we won't have enough men to shoot our way out. We'll have to take Armstrong out alive and use him as our right of passage. We might pull it off even if the soldiers haven't arrived yet," Dustin explained. Then continued, "Just remember Mike, if things go bad, be sure you kill that sorry bastard, Armstrong. It makes no difference what happens to me. I'd rather see him hanged at the fort but letting him get away is not an option. Agreed?"

"Agreed! When do you want to go in?" Big Mike asked.

"Let's get as close as we can and then lay low until they're mostly asleep or drunk, whichever comes first. If we can slip in unnoticed that's much better but I ain't counting on it," Dustin said.

"It all sounds good to me but I ain't going to whack you over your head and that's that! Can't you just wrap a rag around it and pretend?" Big Mike almost pleaded.

"No, they might look and if they get suspicious, we're both done. I'll take care of the bump on the head, you big sissy," Dustin teased.

"I will spank your damn behind for you, you little smart aleck," scolded Mike.

"That would be the wrong end, big fella. Just calm down and I'll get this done," Dustin said, soothing the big man's hurt feelings.

Dustin got a piggen string off his saddle and walked over to a big Mesquite tree. He tied one end of the rope around a limb about the size of your arm, then the other he wrapped around the trunk and pulled the limb back until it was curved like a bow and tied it off.

"This would sure be easier on me if you'd just whack me over the head," Dustin taunted.

"I ain't agonna do it, I told you!" Mike insisted again.

"All right then, here goes," Dustin said as he reached up and cut the rope close to the limb while standing directly in its path.

Wham! The lights went out. The first thing Dustin remembered was Big Mike holding him and washing blood off of his face with cool water. All the time he was muttering something about a damn fool thing to do. Dustin had underestimated the power of that green limb, not to mention the thorns. It had knocked him plumb out and nearly ripped half his face off to boot. Big Mike said that stitches would be nice but not necessary. Mike also said that if the rest of Dustin's plan went as well as this part had, they would both be way past needing or caring about stitches by morning. Dustin reminded him that he'd wanted his large companion to simply whack him over the head but he'd refused. The tree had at least given the effect Dustin wanted. They would damn sure believe he'd been forced to come along.

"Hell boy, Armstrong won't even recognize you with your face tore up like this!" Mike said worried like.

"Damn is it that bad, Mike? It hurts some but it don't feel terrible," Dustin asked.

"It's that bad kid. We'll just have to wait till the swelling goes down or take our chances he remembers you good," Mike assured him.

"I'd rather not wait, Mike. The soldiers might make their move first and I want to be a part of this. Let's go on in and take our chances," Dustin encouraged.

"I'm with ya, general. It's been nice knowing you Laddie," Mike said grimly.

He tied Dustin's hands so they would stand an inspection if necessary yet with a little effort, Dustin could get them undone quickly. They stashed two pistols under Dustin's shirt for easy access. Big Mike loaded his own rifle and the shot gun he'd brought along for crowd control and loaded Dustin's rifle also.

The two rode into the camp about three a.m. and things seemed pretty quiet. They rode past several guards, all drunk or asleep and were nearing the center of the compound completely unnoticed. At that instant, shots were fired. Dustin looked at Mike and untied his own hands.

He grabbed a pistol and Mike said, "Hell they're not shooting at us. Let's go get involved. I'll bet our soldier boys are in a fix."

They rode steadily toward the gun fire. It had picked up some and now there were men running, from all directions, some still half drunk. Mike never looked back as he hollered over his shoulder, "You can still get out if you go now, Laddie."

"I want a closer look. Lead the way, I'm in this to the end," Dustin responded and cocked his daddy's pistol.

When they arrived at the spot the shooting was coming from, Dustin could see men penned down across a court yard. Apparently these were the soldiers and their secret had been discovered. What else Dustin saw was nearly unbelievable. There directly in front of them was Armstrong and several of his men shooting from behind some boxes and barrels. They were completely exposed from this side and as he and Big Mike approached, Armstrong shouted at them without even looking.

"You drunken bastards, get up here and help. These damn spies are shooting us to pieces."

Without answering, Big Mike shot two of Armstrong's men. As they fell dead by his side, the Colonel turned and looked at the assailant. First terror then anger came over Armstrong's face. Dustin ran his horse directly into the Colonel, jumping off on him as he fell. Startled, the rest of the Colonel's men watched as this kid pummeled him with his pistol.

In a moments time, the little group that had been with Armstrong were either all dead, captured or fleeing for their lives. The four remaining undercover soldiers that were still able, had rushed to Big Mike's side to help take control of the situation.

"We've got two men down over there by the wall. Are you two all right?" Ned asked after he'd pulled Dustin off of the unconscious body of Colonel Armstrong.

"Yea, we're fine. How many more of these Comancheros are there?" Big Mike asked.

"They're like ants, they are everywhere. I'd guess at least sixty-five or seventy more all together. I even saw some women take off when the shooting started but I don't know how many," Ned answered. "You're Sergeant Major Michaels, aren't you? I saw you at the fort."

"I was," is all the response Mike gave and continued, "Let's hole up here. I assume you have help coming."

"I hope so, Sergeant. I don't know if our man got through or not. Help could be here any time now or not at all," Ned said a little uncertainly.

"Listen! That's gun fire," Mike said suddenly.

No one knew if this was a good thing or bad. They did know it was getting closer, in fact there was now firing inside the compound. The four soldiers, Big Mike and Dustin knelt facing the oncoming onslaught of gun fire. Armstrong started coming around and Dustin grabbed him by his shirt front and pulled him into a sitting position and spoke directly into his face.

"I'm Dustin Thomas. I'm the son of the brave man you murdered along with the rest of my family. I am going to kill you myself as slowly and cruelly as I possibly can or see you hanged at General Stewart's convenience. It makes no difference to me. Either way will do. You just behave yourself and you'll get out of here to hang real civil like," he said coldly.

Ned who was apparently in charge since Black Jack was one of the downed soldiers shouted, "Steady men. Here they come."

After a pause of several heart pounding seconds, the first approaching man appeared stealthily easing along the east wall of the court yard.

"Hold your fire. It's Captain Perron's men," Big Mike hollered.

He addressed the soldier by name and the greeting was returned. The rest of the soldiers came forward and sent the medic and stretcher bearers from the cavalry ambulance to assist the two fallen soldiers behind Ned and the others. The first of the soldiers was reticent about Big Mike still being well armed. He was, after all, a deserter and was wanted.

Captain Perron rode in with his aides and looked around at the men standing in front of him.

"Good job Lieutenant," he said to Ned then he looked at Dustin and Big Mike. "Is this what you ran off to do, Sergeant Major?" Perron asked.

"It is Captain, but he done that to himself," pointing to Dustin's face. "I swear it!" Big Mike answered.

"Yes, Sir. It was part of my plan, Sir," Dustin said.

"Part of your plan? Son, what<*#!> are you doing with a >%#**&!!>plan?" Perron queried, using language quiet out of character of an officer and a gentleman.

"I'm not sure what you mean, Sir," Dustin said.

Big Mike grimaced and started to speak. Before he could, Dustin spoke up with, "I'd found out about this place here in Magdalena back at the cantina near home. I'd started here to kill Armnstrong. Big Mike apparently tracked me here and arrived just in the nick of time to save my life and Armstrong's as well."

"The hell you say! Sergeant Major, is that what happened here?" Perron demanded.

"Close to it, Sir. I'd rather not correct the young gentleman, Sir. He's been through quite a lot you know," was Big Mike's answer.

"Lieutenant, will you tell the truth about what happened here?" Perron asked Ned.

"Yes, Sir. We were found out, trapped and about to be overrun when I saw this young man ride straight into Armstrong and take him down. Then I saw Sergeant Major Michaels standing behind him firing at the Comancheros, killing several and saving our lives. That's what I saw, Sir," was Ned's response.

"Wonderful, that's the way all reports will read then. Am I understood men?" Perron said to all officers in his command.

Simultaneously, "Yes Sir," came from all addressed.

"Tell me about your face, son. What in the hell happened to you?" Perron inquired.

27

"Sir, would you believe I fell off my horse and hit my head?" Dustin asked almost comically.

"Son, tonight I'd believe anything. Let's get you doctored up some and get you back to the Morton's. They've been worried about you since they saw you and Sergeant Major Michaels ride off together. It's a good thing Jim Morton found this crumpled envelope by your bunk or we'd never have found this place."

Then Perron turning to Ned as the Lieutenant spoke, "My man didn't make it back to the fort, Sir?"

"No, Lieutenant. We found his body as we came into Magdalena. We came looking for young Thomas here with the crumpled Mission Inn envelope as our only clue," Perron said.

"Let's get this mess cleaned up men and get moving. We're wasting time standing around talking," Big Mike ordered then looked a little sheepishly at Captain Perron. "Have I been reinstated, Sir?"

"Yes, Sergeant Major. I'll decide later if any action needs to be taken. The guard you knocked out looks like he'll live. Take charge of this detail and secure the prisoner. I don't want anything to happen to him until we hang him," Captain Perron explained.

As the troop rode out, Dustin rode beside the Captain. They rode in columns, military style and Dustin enjoyed the camaraderie among the troops. He especially liked the scouts who seemed to have a free run of the frontier ahead of the troop. Dustin asked Captain Perron what it took to be a scout. Perron said you needed a good knowledge of the country and its inhabitants. Strong nerves and a cool head made for a good scout.

"How would a man get hired on as a scout? Who would I talk to?" Dustin asked.

"Well, if an eighteen year old man with the qualifications I just mentioned came to me at the post, I might be able to find a position for him," answered Perron.

"Do they have to enlist or how do they work?" Dustin inquired.

"They subcontract out to the government. They work for us but they operate under a different set of rules than the soldiers do," the Captain explained.

"Fine, Captain. I'll look you up as soon as I can pass for eighteen. In the mean time, I'll learn the country. I speak some Mexican now. I'll learn as many dialects of Indian as I can, as well," Dustin said as matter of factly as he could.

"Excellent, Dustin. We pay our interpreters a lot more than we do even the best scouts."

They were back home only a few days until the hanging of Colonel Armstrong was scheduled. The force at the fort was increased considerably to prevent any attempt at a rescue. It was unnecessary, for it seemed the arrest of Armstrong and the attack on the Magdalena hide-out broke the back of the

Comanchero's organization. There were still small groups of raiders seen around the country but the real threat of large scale assaults were to be buried along with Armstrong himself.

The hanging went off with no complications. Dustin and Matt went in with Jim to see the execution. Dustin was surprised that he didn't feel better about Armstrong's death than he did. The beating he was able to hand the Colonel actually was more satisfying to him. Dustin realized that justice by one's own hands was the most gratifying kind. This is a lesson he would remember and implement often in the years to come.

Chapter 6

Life back at the ranch just wasn't exciting enough for Dustin anymore and he was gone often. When his little Cindy ran off with the school master, Dustin went looking for her as soon as he found out she'd gone. He never once referred to her absence as running off, he preferred to say she'd been taken away. This laid the blame directly on the shoulders of the teacher and that's exactly where Dustin placed it. He spent nearly a year looking for her and when he received word from Mrs. Morton she'd been in St. Louis and was being retrieved by her father, Dustin went on to find Tim Burns, the schoolmaster.

He found, followed and killed Mr. Burns bare handed. Burns had taken and soiled the one pristine person in Dustin's life. He paid with his life for his moment of passion and foolishness. Once again, self dispersed punishment was in fact the surest and most vindicating kind.

Dustin stayed out several months after the demise of Mr. Burns in case he had over looked any tell tale clues or failed to see any witness to the execution of Tim Burns' death sentence. When he returned to the Morton place, Cindy never asked where he'd been. She seemed somehow quiet and a little far away. This made no difference to Dustin. He held his high opinion of Cindy as he always had. He would always be there for her. Someday she would need him and come to him for help and he'd be ready. She'd realize he was the one man for her and she had always been the only girl for him.

Matt and Kathy went back to school but Cindy stayed at the ranch and mainly day-dreamed. Mrs. Morton took care of the baby and continued her household chores. A woman's work on a frontier homestead involved much more work than one can possibly imagine. Cindy could have been a lot of help, but wasn't. Her mind was far away, thinking about the big city and the other places she'd seen. She knew there was more out there than this ranch and hard work.

She'd loved the time with Tim Burns until her pregnancy advanced to the point of keeping her from hiding the fact she was indeed with child. Even when Burns had started leaving her in the seedy hotel room on a St. Louis back street, she had still at least been in St. Louis. She loved the lights and laughter of the crowds in the cities. People there talked of the wild Indians and banditos of the western frontier and of its many other hardships. However, they didn't have to live in fear of loosing their very lives or living without so many things that they took for granted.

She missed the gayety of the high society which for a while she and Tim had enjoyed. Soon he gambled his little savings away and the company they kept changed considerably. Burns had fallen so far in debt, before long he used little Cindy to pay some of his gambling notes. This lasted until long after her pregnancy became so obvious that very few of even these low life gamblers would take her as payment. Burns seemed always to find some who would!

Burns began begging drinks and in his drunkenness beat Cindy terribly. He hoped she'd loose the child or leave, either one would be fine with him. Pregnant she'd become a burden instead of the asset she had been with her beautiful young body still fresh and undistorted. When it first started, the naive, young Cindy felt beautiful and wanted. The men, in the beginning anyway, were kind and gentle with little Cindy. As the money ran out and the crowds got rougher, things were becoming harder and harder on Cindy. Her pregnancy rending her worthless to Burns made things more difficult for her. She still felt less afraid here in the city than out on the ranch. No one ever really knew how the deaths of the Thompson family had affected Cindy. Her fear of being savagely killed by raiders weighed so heavily on her mind that nothing else seemed to worry her at all. She felt less in danger in the back room of a sleazy gambling hall filled with filthy buffalo hunters and assorted other low life ne'erdo wells. Even when the beatings began, she was seldom in fear for her life. There was at least law in the towns. Not like out on the frontier where the only law was at the fort many miles away and the man in charge had been a man so vile and prejudice as to instill a fear in a young girl not to be forgotten soon, maybe never. Cindy was back home now and Armstrong was dead and buried. Still there was little out here to keep her interested in life or the living of it.

Matt was doing well in school and working hard on the ranch as well. Jim wanted Dustin to keep control of his father's half of the ranch but Dustin insisted he'd rather not be tied down to the ranch and wanted Jim to use it as part of his own. Dustin spent most of his time working with the different traders traveling to the Indian reservations. He was surprised to learn that many of the Indian leaders spoke good Spanish. In a very short time, he was speaking several Indian dialects quite fluently.

Cindy's behavior and indifferent attitude toward her baby bothered Dustin considerably. He blamed himself for not being able to find her sooner. He thought his inability to pursue the seemingly obvious trail the two runaways had left was unforgivable. Dustin felt sure his failure to rescue Cindy in time was the reason behind her somewhat cool treatment of him since his return. Surely she had learned of his righting the wrong she'd been forced to endure at the hand of Burns. That didn't matter now, he'd been too late finding this lewd and vulgar abductor of helpless children to prevent his ravaging of little Cindy. Dustin made himself a promise that never again would he lack the skills necessary to come to her aid in a more timely manner. He set out to become the best, most knowledgeable tracker and scout in the territory.

That was to be quite an undertaking seeing the territory was well saturated with the best known scouts in the world at this time. Dustin was determined and worked methodically toward his goal. He hired out to shotgun on a load of

31

supplies a trader was taking north to the eastern slopes of the Great Rocky Mountains. They traveled through the terrifying Raton Pass, through the little town of Trinidad, then west to Alamosa and on again north to the little settlement of Salida. Here an explorer had located a pass over the Rockys to the western slopes. Many settlers were trying the Monarch Pass which was shorter than the more traveled northern passes albeit more difficult and dangerous.

Once in Salida, Dustin was surprised to find the trader had decided to take his profits from this very successful trip and proceed over the pass, moving his operations to Grand Junction and Montrose on the western side of the mountains. Dustin was entertaining the idea of traveling back to the New Mexico territory alone when he was approached by a Mexican gun runner who had been supplying weapons to the renegade parcels of different Indian tribes still fighting the inevitable invasion of their homeland by the whites. Dustin felt this supplying guns to the warring Indians to be wrong and passed on the offer to go along. He wasn't rude or aggressive in his handling of his rejection of the job offer and even let the old Mexican explain his feelings about his occupation.

The Mexican told Dustin how he hoped the Indians could stop the white soldiers from taking over the whole country. The Indians and Mexicans had been sharing it for many years and only a small amount of fighting had occurred. Not much more than between the Mexicans themselves. Now that the white soldiers have come, everyone was fighting everyone all the time. He'd like to see all the whites run back where they came from. Dustin took no offense to this opinion, it was after all an honest one. He still declined and wished the Mexican good luck on his journey.

Dustin rode back down to Trinidad and was hired by a wagon master to help his train over the Raton Pass. Each wagon had to be hoisted up each steep grade by several teams and the use of an intricate series of blocks and tackle tied to the largest of trees at the top of each section of incline. Once on top, the process was reversed letting each wagon down the other side with just as much effort and difficulty. Dustin's experience with mules made him very good help and earned him a pocket full of gold coin for his weeks work.

After watching the struggle of the other wagons in his train, Mr. Coldwell decided not to attempt the crossing and to stay in Raton to open shop there. He could see that the future would bring a great number of pioneers across this pass and most would rest up and resupply before attempting to cross this major obstacle on their route. Mr. Coldwell was a dry goods man and business was his strong suit. He had a large sum of money and had earned every dime of it. He took advantage of a situation most were suffering from and let it make him quite rich. He purchased items from the travelers that proved to be too heavy or to cumbersome to make it over the pass. Many a valued heirloom was simply picked up out of the road that had been discarded by a weeping, frontier wife. Mr. Coldwell sold much of this plunder to the settlers heading south and east that had left their similar articles on the other side of the pass. The rest of their journey being relatively flat, these items could be replaced with the price being the only burden.

Mr. Coldwell had an assistant, Dan James by name. Coldwell told James to take an extra horse and some money, return to Santa Fe and bring a wagon load of items they would need to supply the adventurers with on his return. Dan was nervous about the journey alone and asked if Caldwell would hire someone to travel with him. If not, possibly he could wait until a train headed east that could be joined. Coldwell insisted he go immediately and return as quickly as possible.

Dustin had helped Coldwell into the little pueblo of Raton and to set up his wares. He offered to accompany Dan to Santa Fe for a small fee. He would not be able to return with him and the supplies but would make sure he joined a train for the journey back. Coldwell wouldn't hear of paying anyone to ride along with Dan. He would, however, waive any charge to someone for going along under Dan's protection. Dustin could not believe this man Coldwell even considering trying to charge him like a passenger to travel through the hostile country between Raton and Santa Fe. He would not only have to show Dan the way but baby-sit him along the trail. Dan was a good enough fella but he'd just barely made the trip west riding in a wagon. Dustin was sure Dan was a real hand in a mercantile, but this trip would be a little different. Dustin stuck to his position that he had a service to offer Coldwell and would be paid for rendering it or not go along. Coldwell got his temper up and would not compromise.

"I'll not pay you a cent for using my man for protection on your way home. You have to go that way anyhow. You should be glad to have the company," Coldwell insisted.

Dustin declined this offer as he had the first, respectfully but adamantly. He bid Dan farewell and nodded good day to Coldwell and rode off to the outskirts of town where there was considerable activity and a tent city being erected.

As Dustin approached, he could see this was a U.S. Cavalry outpost. Dustin rode right into the hustling mob and inquired as to the whereabouts of the officer in charge. He was shown to a large tent already set up on the canvas town's eastern most side. Standing in front of this tent was a man in a Lieutenant's uniform talking to several other soldiers, each of lesser rank.

Dustin waited until the officer finished speaking to his subordinates then inquired, "Sir, are you in charge here?"

The Lieutenant turned around and just stood there smiling.

"Hello, Ned! What the hell you doin' here?" Dustin said a little amazed to see his friend so far from home.

"I'll tell you Dusty. We should be looking for you! Seems like anywhere there is action you soon show up," Ned said walking over to Dustin to shake his hand.

"What's happening here, Ned?" Dustin asked.

"You mean you don't know? That damn fool Indian, Nacatan, stabbed the Indian agent to death and got a hold of some guns somewhere," Ned continued.

Dustin interrupted, "Rifles?"

"Yea, how'd you know?" Ned asked.

"I think I met the old Mexican who's been supplying them," Dustin said.

"Damn, if you ain't always where the action is, just like I said," Ned went on.

"Hell, he offered me a job. If I'd a took it, you'd be hunting me right now!" Dustin said not really joking.

"We weren't looking for no gun runner, Dusty, until now that is. We're just hunting Nacatan and those sorry tramps that run with the old scoundrel. They're mean as devils sober and even worse drunk. They stole three cases of whiskey that was in route to the fort along with the entire Quartermaster's supply order for the month. It'll be short rations until the next shipment," Ned ended.

"Why do you figure Nacatan will cross here, Ned? Seems to me Indians would use the higher mountain pass just north of that highest peak over there," Dustin shared.

"What pass, Dusty? Our scouts said this is the only way over. Are you sure?" Ned inquired.

"Yes, I've been over it. I found it by accident chasing a run away mule. It's well traveled too. Whoever has been using it keeps both ends covered with brush and sweeps their tracks where they enter the main route," Dustin assured him.

"Could you show us this hidden trail?" Ned asked real official like.

"You have scouts with you, Lieutenant. Can't they show you?" Dustin asked.

"I told you, Mr. Thomas, our scouts say this is the only pass. I have the authorization to contract more help if I need it. Again, can you show us the way to the pass?" Ned inquired.

"Yes, Lieutenant!" Dustin answered.

"Good, you're hired. Go over to the Quartermaster's wagon and get anything you need for the trip," Ned instructed.

"Sir, my outfit's fine. We can go when you are ready," Dustin answered in a very military manner.

"How long will it take to get there, Dusty?" Ned queried.

"Three days each way with a big troop. A little faster with just a few mounted men," Dustin reported.

Ned turning to another soldier, "Sergeant, get seven days rations and give each man a hundred rounds," Ned ordered.

"A hundred rounds, Sir? You going to a war?" the Sergeant asked.

"We might have just been given the way to stop one, Sergeant. Get the men ready. We leave within the hour," Ned repeated.

"Yes, Sir," was the only reply.

"Dusty, tell me about this mule that finds secret passages," Ned inquired.

34

"I was helping a wagon train over Raton. About fifty wagons, most over weight and under harnessed. We were on top resting the teams we'd taken up to work the block and tackles when one idiot, younger mule broke loose and run off. I jumped on my saddle horse and went to retrieve him. Just over the next rise there is a cut in the mountainside that apparently goes nowhere. People been passing it for years without giving it a second glance. I'm right behind this damn fool and he just plumb disappears. I rode ahead a little ways looking for the runaway but saw nothing. I started back over the trail looking for his tracks. When I get back to where I saw him last and picked up his trail, it led into what seems to be a blind wall. On closer inspection I see where there's a huge bush uprooted and placed in the narrow entrance to a rather large opening. Just beyond this was a large, well traveled pass, recently used. I followed the mules tracks all the way across the mountain. A much faster, shorter crossing than Raton. There are a few narrow places that would keep wagons from going through without some trouble but it's still better than the other trail. Horses and men pass easily. I believe even small artillery could make it, Ned. Anyway, I got my mule caught at the brush plugging the other end. They had already started down with the wagons when I returned. I never mentioned my find to anyone. I guess its importance didn't really hit me until I saw you all encamped here and heard your story," Dustin explained.

"You know, Dusty, it is not all that unusual that this idiot mule led you to the pass. It seems to me, runaway jackasses have been leading the military for hundreds of years already. No reason this should be any different," Ned joked.

Dustin led the Lieutenant and his company to the mouth of the pass. Ned set up sentries high above the canyon on each side at strategic locations and where the canyon narrowed forming a funnel. Ned placed two groups of snipers on each side of the pass.

"This should be a good place to capture Nacatan," Dustin said.

"My orders are not to capture him, Dusty," Ned said firmly.

"Damn, Ned. This will be a slaughter!" Dustin said solemnly.

"Dusty you've filled your contracted obligation by leading us here. If you want to leave now, you may," Ned assured his young friend.

"No, Ned, I'll stay. Life ain't always pleasant. When this is over I'll help you find the gun runner also. Maybe I can help put an end to all of this," Dustin said solemnly.

Without much delay, only a few hours in fact, a band of Indians was reported to have entered the canyon They were traveling down it instead of up as had been presumed. Ned gave a few quick orders and made the necessary changes. This put Ned and his entourage on the lower end of the trap instead of his preferred first sight vantage, he'd counted on. Dustin was with Ned's group and was the first of them to see the approaching Indians, already completely inside the trap of the narrowing canyon.

"Ned, hold it! I saw those Indians in Salida last week. They couldn't have been with Nacatan when he killed those settlers."

Dustin had not quite finished his proclamation when some nervous soldier at the upper end of the trap opened fire. His shot was followed by a panicky screaming from the canyon and reports from the other rifles trained on the helpless Indians trapped below. It was over in just seconds. Seconds that seemed like an eternity to Dustin. He stood looking down into the canyon where moments before had existed life in several forms. Now horses, dogs and humans were lying grotesquely everywhere below. There were the bodies of women and small children lying crippled among their dead or dying pets and mounts. Dustin could only see a handful of boys or braves of fighting age.

"Ned, what have we done!" Dustin nearly wept.

Ned stood speechless, helpless to call back even one of the hundreds of rounds mistakenly fired into the innocent, slaughtered victims below. Ned didn't speak to Dustin for a while but busied himself giving some quick, rash orders to several men standing near him. These men went to work, sharing Ned's apprehension and grief over what had just happened. Dustin realized things were happening to conceal this terrible mistake. Several soldiers carried heavy boxes and barrels from the support wagons which had just moments before arrived. Finally, Dustin realized Ned was going to attempt to conceal the bodies by blowing the canyon shut at the narrow passage.

"Ned, even if this works someone's going to find out. Hell, there's over a hundred men involved in this. One of them will let his conscience run off with his good judgment and bring us all down with him," Dustin tried to reason.

"I can't worry about that now, Dusty. I can't undo what's happened here. All I can do is postpone the inevitable for a little while. At least until I get a chance to explain this mess to Captain Perron," Ned said almost despondently.

"Ned, are you open for suggestions?" Dustin asked.

"I'm blowing the canyon shut Dusty and that's the end of it," Ned replied.

"It don't have to be Ned. Let's dress up about twenty men to look like Comancheros or Armstrong stragglers and place them under arrest for the slaughter of these innocent Indians. We'll parade them through town some and make a big show of it. Then we'll make out like we shot all of the murdering bastards. We'll then dress them back up like soldiers and go back into town and let everyone see there ain't no Comancheros left. Hell, nobody's going to count all your soldiers to miss twenty the first time through town and after who'll even notice? It'll scare the real Armstrong men left, that you mean business and show everyone you'll not tolerate anyone treating Indians roughly. It'll also throw the Indians and Comancheros to fighting and there'll be no rest for the last few Armstrong men," Dustin finished.

"Damn Dusty! Did you figure all that out just now? That sounds crazy enough to work," Ned reasoned.

"Sure it'll work. Don't blow the canyon until we parade the men through Raton. We'll bring them up here to execute them. We'll pretend to bury them with the Indians in the canyon. We'll have to post a good guard around the perimeter. We want town folks to watch but not really see anything. Then later even if some damn fool weakens and spills his guts, no one will believe him," Dustin proclaimed.

"OK Dusty, but you're out of this. I'll tell my men it's my idea and if hell busts loose, you got no part of this. You'd better scatter on out of here now and I'll put this thing together," Ned more ordered than requested. "Take this letter by any fort paymaster and draw your money whenever you want," Ned finished and turned to make the necessary preparations.

Without turning around again, Ned spoke one last time rather harshly," Good-by, Dustin. Go now and good luck. I don't expect to see you again until I see you back at the fort."

Ned had seldom, if ever, called him Dustin, so he knew he was serious. Dustin rode out south and had not ridden too far until darkness settled in. He stopped, made camp and questioned how he felt about what he had seen at the canyon.

Death was something he'd had to deal with too often already for a man his age. It worried him more than a little that he was able to become numb to any remorse or passion about the lost lives of today. He'd been able to cope with his losses to this point, by dismissing the life gone as being something that happens to everyone and everything sometime. Some just sooner than others. As Dustin tried to fall asleep the term "cold blooded" was ringing in his head. He tried to raise a little compassion for the dead or their families left behind but could not. This line of thought was making him restless. He dealt with this as he always had, he mainly thought of Cindy. With a smile on his lips and contentment in his heart, he went to sleep.

Dustin decided to go over to the fort near home and see Cindy and the Mortons for a few days. Then he thought he might ride over to south Texas and have a little look around. On the trail ahead still some miles away, Dustin saw a column of smoke. He didn't remember seeing any homesteads this far out before, so he thought he'd better hurry in case someone needed a little assistance.

As he approached, he saw that the fire was north of the trail a ways. Dustin soon found where a wagon had left the main tracks and headed cross country. The tracks showed that the horses were traveling at break neck speed when they left the road. As he drew closer, Dustin saw an overturned wagon burning, a severly wounded horse struggling with his death dance and an even less fortunate man stretched out naked on the bare earth. This poor fellow had been gutted, scalped and other wise mutilated beyond all recognition. The three surviving horses from his four horse team had been led away. They had been the only enticement for the attack as the tracks were shallow showing the wagon had been empty.

Dustin walked over to the still smoldering wagon and put the horse out of its misery. He turned toward the dead man, contemplating a fitting burial for a waylaid traveler. His eye caught sight of a small leather valise partially sticking out from under a chaparral bush. The Indians had gone through it and found it of no interest. Dustin looked at the contents and his heart sank. Inside were a letter of introduction, list of goods to be obtained and instruction to open an account. The funds to be deposited in the name of, no other than, Mr. Coldwell. That was Dan James laying over there!

Dustin prepared a shallow grave and looked for something to wrap Dan's ravaged body in but only found his trousers with a belt still in them. The Indians had either torn up or taken his other articles of clothing with them. Dustin felt he should at least put the poor man's pants on him for burial. As Dustin was preparing to buckle Dan's belt, he realized it was tremendously thick and the light came on in Dustin's mind.

"Hell, this here's a money belt!" he said out loud. "Them Indians hadn't gotten the money after all. Ol' Dan out smarted 'em!"

Dustin pulled off the belt and without even looking into it, buried the loyal employee. After making the best job of covering the body one could do without the aid of tools, Dustin got the belt and rode away toward the valley. He'd already spent too much time here. He rode carefully, always looking for the perpetrators of this horrible murder.

He arrived at a secluded campsite he'd used before, near the river and settled in for the night. Isolated as he was, Dustin still built a very small fire, after taking care of his horse which was his custom. He knew all too well a man on foot in this country was doomed to a near certain, terrible end. As he settled in, Dustin retrieved Dan's belt from the saddle bags where he'd stashed it. All the time from the moment he found the belt, Dustin had been thinking how he would handle any funds it contained, if in fact there was money in it at all. It might just contain Dan's personal papers. Either way, Dustin was about to find out. This was a fine belt and its contents had actually been sewn into it, making detection and access difficult.

When Dustin cut the thread and laid the leather open, momentarily he couldn't catch his breath. There was more cash, U.S. currency, here than Dustin had ever heard of, let alone seen. He counted the large bills time and time again.

"Twelve hundred dollars! That can't be right, let's see, nine, ten, eleven, twelve. Damn, twelve hundred dollars!"

It took quite awhile for Dustin to have a bout with his conscience. This money really belonged to Mr. Coldwell. If the Indians would have found it, they'd have taken it. If he hadn't accidentally felt the belt, it would have been buried with Dan. If he hadn't come along, it might have never been found that far off the trail. All this and more was rushing through Dustin's head. He felt he had to ride to the fort and report Dan's murder to Captain Perron. He'd better get his scout's pay even if he kept the money, to throw off any suspicion that he'd found it. No one with twelve hundred dollars in his pocket would ride all the way into the fort to collect the eight dollars wages he had coming. Twelve hundred dollars would buy and stock a nice size ranch and leave enough operating capital for a man to get a good start.

He'd ride into the fort and tell Perron about Dan then he'd go talk to Cindy. He would ask her to marry him and he'd build them a good life ranching and he'd raise her child, little Wesley as his own son. They would have children of their own as well. He could buy Cindy all the things she craved. With this new found fortune, he could build her a big house and she would have the best of all things.

Dustin made the fort in three more days and went directly to Captain Perron's office. The Captain was out on patrol as the Indians were raising hell again. Apparently some Comancheros had massacred an entire village of migrating Indians above Raton and had then been captured and summarily executed for the heinousness of their crimes. Things were a mess in Raton as well. Nacatan had slipped by the soldiers and sacked the town, killing many of its inhabitants. Dustin waited to hear if maybe Coldwell was among the dead but no names were given and he didn't ask.

Dustin made an official report to the officer of the day about poor Dan's violent demise.

There was no mention of recovered funds in the report. He went to the pay master's and called to the soldier behind the desk. When he looked up it was Sergeant Major Michaels.

"Laddie, how ya been?"

"OK, Mike. I've sure seen some of life I might have been better off not seeing here lately," Dustin replied honestly.

"I'll get someone to relieve me and we'll get something to eat over at the mess hall," Mike said.

"I need to head home, Mike. I'm just here on business."

"What business you got here, Laddie?" Mike asked.

"Pay role business. I did a little scouting for Ned," Dustin answered and handed the letter to Big Mike.

"Scouting? I'll be damn! You're a mover ain't ya Laddie?" Mike smiled then continued reading.

"Says here you're hired full time as a free lance scout! I don't think I know what that is exactly. Let's see what else ol' Ned says here. I see, you're on a special assignment going to report to the Lieutenant directly. All right then, Laddie. Says here I'm to assign you a payroll number and give you a months wages," Mike finished.

Dustin knew there was some mistake but he just wanted gone so said nothing.

"Here is thirty dollars, Laddie. Sign here," Big Mike said very officially.

"What the hell you going to do with all that money?" Mike kidded.

Dustin keeping as straight a face as possible said, "I think I'll get married and by a ranch, Mike. How does that sound?"

"I've known lesser men start with worse stakes than that Laddie. I'll bet you make it. Remember the twenty fifth of each month," Mike said.

"What about it, Mike?" Dustin asked puzzled.

"Pay day, Laddie, Pay day! Every month you go by the nearest fort and give 'em this number and they'll have you thirty dollars. That's how it works," Mike explained.

The two friends talked about things that had happened to each of them since they last saw one another. Most interesting of all was Big Mike told Dustin about the Army's big plan to secure more beef for the reservation Indians and even buy cattle for building herds for the different tribes, even the ones way up north. Mike told Dustin about the need for horses up north too and said he had a friend in Wyoming that would sure buy all someone could deliver.

The two talked until Dustin just had to go see Cindy. He had his own plans to talk about, with the girl he loved.

Before he left he turned, "How long is it good for Mike, I mean the job?" Dustin asked.

"Until the Lieutenant fills out all the necessary paper work, notifies you officially and files the termination papers. If not, I guess it just goes on forever or until you get yourself killed. If you don't get by a fort each month, it accumulates too. So if you get way out somewhere, you'll have a pile waiting for you when you return. Good luck Laddie," Mike said and shook Dustin's hand.

Chapter 7

Dustin bid his friend farewell and headed home to Cindy. He arrived home to find things much as he'd left them. Cindy was as removed from her surroundings as she could possibly be and still be physically present. Jim was working at making a go of the ranch with a little help from Matt. Mrs. Morton was busy raising little Wesley and still running her household with little or no help. Kathy tried her best to be of some assistance but Cindy might as well be on Mars. Dustin thought he saw some small amount of excitement in Cindy's eye as he rode by the house toward the barn. Jim and Matt were working on some harness out in the shop.

"Hello, Dusty! Where ya been this time?" Jim asked friendly as always.

He'd learned to stop worrying about Dustin, that boy could take care of himself.

"Been thinking I might ride down the Rio Grande to Texas and look around. I'm working for the Army as a free lance scout. I got paid once already!" Dustin said real proud.

"What's a free lance scout?" Matt asked.

"Me!" Dusty replied.

"I think Matt meant what the hell does a free lance scout do, Dustin?" Jim asked chuckling.

"Well, damned if I know, Jim. But I sure enough am one anyway. It says so right here."

He showed the Morton boys his official papers.

"I'll be damn. A free lance scout, look here, Matt!" Jim said.

"I still ain't got no idea what you do, Dusty," Matt repeated.

"Soon as I find out, I'll write you and let you know, Matt. You got my word on it."

They all laughed and then Dustin continued, "I think I'm going to do my scouting and free lancing toward Texas, sure thing Jim. I'd like to see more of the country down south near Mexico. I didn't get to look around much when Big Mike and I went through, I'll bet it would be a good place for ranching."

"Hell, Dusty, this is a good place for ranching and you already own a ranch here," Jim reminded him.

"I know, Jim. I don't reckon I could ever live over there no more. It's your place now, yours and Matt's. I want you two to have it. If I ever need a place to stay, maybe you'll let me put up there awhile," Dustin explained.

"It'll always be your place, Dusty. We'll take care of it for you and use the feed but it'll be waiting for you when you decide to run it yourself."

Dustin waited until Cindy's usual after supper walk to speak with her about a future. He was not nervous as much as excited. No one thought anything of it when he accompanied her as he had done so many times over the years. He knew this evening was different, special and very important. They walked along quietly for a distance.

Dustin started with, "Cindy, you know how I have always felt about you."

"Yes, I suppose so," she answered softly.

"Good, I have something to tell you and then something to ask you," Dustin stumbled on without a response from Cindy. "I came across some money, a lot of it. I want to get a place in south Texas and I'd like you to come join me when I get it set up. Cindy, will you marry me and let me take you away from here?" he queried very emotionally.

"Away from here!" with no pause at all, "Yes!"

Dustin wasn't absolutely sure what she'd said yes to but he wasn't going to take any chances so he just continued, "Wonderful. I'm the happiest man in the world. I'm going to leave the money with you for safe keeping while I run down to look for a place to build our ranch."

"How much money do you have?" Cindy inquired innocently enough.

"Enough to start us a good life. With hard work and some luck, it's enough to do it all first class," Dustin answered with pride.

"Enough to travel?" Cindy inquired.

"All the way to south Texas. We have just over twelve hundred dollars, Cindy," again very proudly.

Her eyes lit up for the first time since her return from St. Louis with little Wesley, "South Texas! That's enough to see the world," Cindy said actually excited about Dustin's news.

He felt like he was floating on air.

"I'll not tell your parents until I've got everything setup," he explained to her.

He was so happy he talked on and on about the plans he'd made for the two of them and little Wesley. Cindy sat quietly by his side. She was smiling a big smile that made Dustin warm inside.

The very next day he prepared for his expedition to the south. When all was near ready he said his good-bye's to the Morton's and then went to find Cindy to finish making their plans. She was back at the spot they'd sat the evening before waiting his arrival.

"Cindy, I'm being paid as a scout by the Army. I'm not really sure why but I am. I'll have all the money I'll need so I'll leave all of this with you to take care of for us," he explained as she sat silently, still smiling that wonderful smile.

"I'll not try to buy a place now. I'll select a few that will work and we'll pick out ours together after we get there. I'll come back up and get you and little Wesley once I've looked around some," he said.

"Little Wesley? Oh, of course," Cindy said almost to herself.

Dustin knew she was excited but he was thrilled now to see she was so much so as to almost forget about her child. He handed her a tin box some canned meat had come in and said, "Here's our future Cindy. You hang on to it so I don't get robbed or loose it. It's too important to us to take needless chances carrying it around with me." Then, "Cindy, we'll make us a good life. You can have some of the nice things you've been wanting. We'll be able to give little Wesley a fine start in life. Cindy, you've made me very happy."

Dustin leaned over and gave her a kiss on the forehead and said good-by. He explained that he would write her before he returned for them and for her to start thinking about how she wanted her house to look. She sat looking at the big tin in her lap and didn't rise as Dustin left. He headed south with a happier feeling deep inside than he'd known before. He was going to Texas to find a home for Cindy, Little Wesley and himself.

He rode the river to make it an easier trip. Dustin had to keep an eye open to avoid having problems with the border gangs or Mexican bandits. He rode down to Presidio then back up toward Ft. Davis following a tributary of a small river Dustin did not know the name of. The country he passed through on his trip north from the Mexican border up to Ft. Davis suited Dustin well. The grass was lush and deep even in this year of uncommonly harsh drought. The elevation was climbing as he neared the fort.

He could see Fort Davis in the distance from a ridge of pine covered mountains. Dustin decided this was the place for Cindy and himself to build their lives. He would ride into the fort and ask around about the whereabouts of the land's owner or if the land was even available.

First, Dustin would ride every inch of this area and decide on the very best possible location for their new home. Dustin spent the next two days looking around and thinking about where he'd build the corrals and horse trap, barn and sheds but most importantly locating the perfect home site. Finally satisfied with a little valley isolated yet accessible, Dustin headed into the fort to see about obtaining his new ranch land.

There was only a small part of Dustin's land privately owned. That by a land speculator out of Laredo. The rest could be purchased from the state land office in Austin. Dustin headed east to the capital to secure the title on his future. Late on the second day of travel, Dustin came to a little community in the middle of nowhere. He rode up to an old adobe building no larger than a carriage house. It had a sign nailed to the front which simply said, "Drinks". Dustin turned his horse, General Lee, into the rail next to the two horses already standing there then dismounted and walked into the little dirt floored room.

The place was crowded with just three other patrons and a barkeeper. Dustin asked if he could get something to eat and was told he could.

"Just have a seat over there in the corner on that nail keg and I'll send little Manuel to bring you some food. What ya drinking?" the barman asked.

"What you got?" asked Dustin in return.

"Bad beer, worse whiskey!" came the reply.

"I'll have some of the bad beer then," stated Dustin. "Should I ask what I'll be eating?"

"You won't be able to tell and don't really want to know. What's the matter are you fussy?" the barkeep asked.

"No, I guess I ain't. I was just a little curious," Dustin replied.

In a very short time a little Mexican boy came in and asked the barman which fellow got the food and when told Dustin was to receive it, he brought it over to him. It turned out to be a delicious meal of red chili con carne with tortillas, rice and beans.

"The cook should shoot you, barkeep! This is plumb fine. How far is it to Austin?" Dustin asked not really knowing why.

He hardly ever talked and never just to be talking.

"Ain't never been that far. Several days I'd expect. You going all the way to Austin?" the barkeep asked kind of impressed. "That's a fer piece. Got family there?"

"No I'm just going looking for a job in a new county," Dustin answered figuring it better not to let on he was a land buyer and might be carrying money with him.

He could get way laid like ol' Dan before anyone found out he didn't have no real amount of money with him. Leaving it with Cindy was the smartest thing he could have done. He ate his meal and drank the justifiably labeled bad beer then rose to leave.

"Want some more?" came from the bartender.

"No thanks, just need a place to put my horse and get some sleep," Dustin replied.

"I got a little shed with a stall in it out back you can use for a dime," the barman stated.

"That'll do," Dustin said putting the extra dime on the counter along with the price of the meal.

As Dustin stepped outside, there were two men riding through town. One was leading the two horses that had been standing out front of the cantina when Dustin came in and the other one was leading Dustin's horse, General Lee. They apparently hadn't heard him come out as they appeared to be in no particular hurry. Dustin pulled his father's pistol from its holster and leveled it on the man leading his horse.

"Excuse me fellas, my horse ain't allowed to go nowheres without me," Dustin said real friendly like.

The men turned around excitedly. Their surprise was just slightly greater than was Dustin's. The man holding General Lee was Sanderson, the Comanchero who'd left that bad scar on Dustin's head and had been going to take little Cindy.

"What did you say boy?" came the gruff reply.

"I said I am going to shoot you dead, Sanderson!" was Dustin's reply.

Sanderson sat up startled by this announcement and made the mistake of reaching for his own gun. He never heard the report of the pistol. He saw the flash, felt the impact and then just fell dead. The second man fired two shots at Dustin and spurred his horse away in the opposite direction from the one they had been heading.

The occupants of the little cantina had started out to see what the first shot was about. They stopped and then came again more cautiously when the next two shots rang out. One of these shots splintered one of the old boards of the cantina door directly behind and ever so slightly to Dustin's right, just missing him.

"What in the world's going on out here," asked one of the men from the cantina.

"That fella lying over there was stealing my horse! When I caught him at it, he went for his gun and I shot him. The second man shot this direction and ran. The dead guy's name is Sanderson. He's wanted. I'm a scout for the U.S. Cavalry. I've run into him before. I'll tie him to his horse and take him to the nearest fort in the morning. They'll be glad to get him," Dustin explained.

"That would be back to the west at Fort Stockton or on east to Fort Lancaster. It's a little further but it's the way you're headed," the barman told Dustin.

The men were buzzing with speculation about how this kid could have out drawn Sanderson. He'd been one of the fastest, meanest outlaws in this area for some time. Dustin didn't know what they were whispering about or didn't care much. He also didn't realize that by not telling them he already had his gun out when he called to Sanderson, he was causing himself more trouble, not less.

Early the next morning Dustin headed toward Ft. Lancaster riding General Lee and leading the body of Sanderson thrown across the bad man's own horse that Dustin called Sled. This was the no leadingest horse he'd ever come in contact with. After several long hours, Dustin decided to ride Sled and lead General Lee. The change was made and only required moving Sanderson's body and not changing saddles. It seems being a bandit must pay well, for Sanderson had a much better saddle than Dustin's. This new arrangement worked well. Sled rode wonderfully and General Lee led just as good as he rode.

Dustin stopped for the night in a clump of cottonwoods sheltering a little spring which lie in a bend of a rather deep canyon. This made a very safe place to camp and Dustin relaxed some considering what all had transpired. He felt he'd better look over Sanderson's outfit for identification. He'd already decided to keep the saddle if it didn't have Sanderson's name on it anywhere. He unloaded Sanderson's body from General Lee then unsaddled him and turned him loose, hobbled to graze.

Next, he unsaddled Sled and hobbled his front feet like General Lee but also scotch hobbled a front foot to a hind one. He didn't want to wake up and have to hunt a horse. Now Dustin started through Sanderson's things. He had not even gone through his pockets before, he'd just removed his gun from the holster so it wouldn't fall out. He had had every man present sign a letter he'd written describing the events of the shooting and verifying it was Sanderson that had been shot. Dustin did this in case he needed witness or backing of his story at the fort. In this wild country, one never knew who'd be friend and who'd be foe.

Dustin opened Sanderson's saddle bags first. On the left side was the usual supplies carried by most distance riders. Things like an ample supply of tobacco, a few store bought matches in an air tight bottle, some extra cartridges, a large skinning knife, two small tins of potted meat and a sack of coffee beans you'd have to first grind or smash before boiling into a drinkable liquid. There was also an extra cinch ring and fencing pliers. Thieves used this as a running iron and the more proficient ones could copy even the most intricate or complex brands with an ease which was impressive to say the least.

The other bag contained a large wallet buckled tightly shut. It had the initials H.H. beautifully engraved into it. Inside there were many business papers, several deeds for land adding up to almost forty thousand acres. This land was further south and a little more southeast than where Dustin's dream ranch was located. There was also two beautiful watches, one of which had those initials H.H. on it, over a hundred dollars cash and coin and a bag the size of a tobacco pouch full of what Dustin assumed to be gold dust weighing well over a pound, as close as Dustin could guess. At over thirty dollars an ounce a pound of gold would be worth almost five hundred dollars. Dustin knew that Sanderson had held up a stage or rolled someone in town or something. There was no telling just how much these deeds were worth. It was confusing to him that all the deeds were signed. Sanderson must have forged the owner's signature to make them valid and marketable.

There was also a hand held telescope in the saddle bag. Dustin had seen many cavalrymen use these looking for hostels and even a few cowmen looking for wild cows. He'd better hang on to this for his scout work. Sanderson's pistol was more modern and a better model than his dad's but he couldn't take Sanderson in without a gun with him and Dustin didn't want to give his father's gun away so he'd have to leave Sanderson's gun with his body at the fort. Maybe he could put in a claim for it or buy it from the officer in charge at the fort.

He'd already looked Sled over, no brands or marks of any kind. That was good. Dustin would try to buy him as well. A rancher would need many good horses and Sled would sure enough do.

After his investigation of Sanderson's personal effects, Dustin cooked some supper and lie back thinking how it hadn't bothered him any to kill Sanderson. It didn't unnerve him when Sanderson's partner shot at him either. He hadn't returned the fire on the second man because it would have been an unlikely shot with him riding away as fast as he was. Dustin had been watching his back trail all day expecting to see a lone rider following. Tomorrow he'd be expecting a large group of riders coming. He figured it all depended on how far away Sanderson's hide out was.

"Hell! You spooky little sissy. Maybe he don't have no gang or no hide out. Maybe it's just him and ol' chicken liver back there. He ran once, he'll run again. He might not even know about all this loot Sanderson got here. Or maybe he does and is waiting up front of me for an ambush somewhere. He probably knows this county some and I sure don't. Now that's plumb silly. The folks back at the cantina recognized Sanderson right quick but none of them had no idea who the other guy was. He sure as hell

ain't no crack shot. He was sittin' dead still and missed me twice standing not twenty five feet in front of him just big as day. Damn, I'm getting goofy sitting here talking to me in my own coffee cup," Dustin said and stood up to go check on the horses and put out the fire before turning in.

The next day found Dustin riding parallel to the main road to the fort, keeping a constant vigil for other riders. He'd seen no one all day when suddenly, as he came up out of a canyon, he found himself face to face with a buckboard traveling the main road. They were over a mile apart but Dustin knew he'd been seen and couldn't ride away leading a horse carrying a dead man. He rode straight toward the wagon.

"Hello, gentlemen! How much farther to the fort?" Dustin asked.

"Don't look like it'll matter much to your companion but it's just less than a days ride from here, almost due north," the driver said.

"Thanks. He ain't my companion. This here's the Comanchero butcher, Sanderson!" Dustin said a little hesitantly.

"Sanderson! I'll be damn. I guess his luck finally run out. Hell, just a couple of weeks ago down south, where we're from in Del Rio, he won Hugh Hendricks entire land holdings and almost a thousand dollars in gold dust. Damn fool won it fair and square. Drew to an inside straight and busted two pair to do it. That hard headed Hendricks put up all that land to cover less than a five hundred dollar bet he was so sure he had Sanderson beat. Then the poor fool stepped into the ally and blew his own brains out. What did Sanderson do to get himself finally killed? Beat someone else out of his life's savings?" the driver asked.

"No, he was caught stealing horses and got hisself shot for his effort," Dustin explained.

"Damn man, who in the world was fast enough or bold enough to gun down Sanderson?" asked the driver.

"I did. Fast didn't even enter into it. He didn't get his gun out of his holster."

The two men were silent for a moment then the passenger asked, "What's your name young man, if you don't mind me asking?"

"Dustin Thomas, Sir. Why do you ask?" Dustin asked.

"Well Mr. Thomas, I have a feeling I'll be telling people I actually met you once. That I saw you leading the dead body of Sanderson to collect the reward!" the passenger responded.

"Reward? What reward?" Dustin inquired.

"Damn it, he didn't even know about the five hundred dollar reward," the driver said to his passenger.

"Good luck, Mr. Thomas. I hope to see you again someday," the driver said as he and his passenger drove away. Then continuing, "Can you imagine, he's so fast Sanderson didn't even clear leather."

Dustin thought he should explain what he'd meant by fast not being important but the men were already driving away and he didn't really want to stop them for even more conversation.

He reached the fort by dark and went to the officer of the day, with his ripening charge in tow. A crowd had gathered around as this young man rode into the fort leading this once notorious bad man's remains behind him. Dustin reported to the officer in charge and turned over the body to the Army. He filled out the proper papers to collect the reward and also filled out the forms necessary to claim the personal effects of the recently deceased Sanderson. The cash and gold were omitted from the report. There was some controversy as to Dustin's claim to the effects of Sanderson. Hendricks was dead and the Colonel and the local civil magistrate ruled in common it was no longer Hendrick's land. It was, in fact, Sanderson's property. If none of Sanderson's family, if he had one, came to claim them, the deeds would be treated as any other found property and after a sixty day waiting period from the public notice, the deeds would become the property of the finder. For now, Dustin would just have to wait.

He would write Cindy and tell her all he had done and found here in the beautiful country of south Texas. He found he liked this part of Texas even better than that he'd already chosen. He'd look around more before settling on a spot. He sent his letter via military escort which was in the form of a supply train taking necessary provisions to their New Mexico sister garrison.

Dustin rode south to see this Del Rio. When he arrived, he made a deposit in the local bank. Upon receipt of his reward and at the advice of the banker, Mr. Rogers, he put the funds from cashing in the gold dust, which in fact amounted to just under 1,000 dollars, in an investment deposit with the newly developed Chicago Stock Yards. The banker had helped develop this fledgling company after the war and knew its workings inside and out. The company was long visioned and was about to develop into one of the largest beef processing plants in the world.

Mr. Rogers told Dustin of the recent attempts, both successful and failed, to drive cattle to the railroad, either the new spur in Kansas City or St. Louis. Soon there'd be new track laid further west to Wichita and Dodge. No matter where the herds were driven they would end up in Chicago and that was where the real money was going to be made in cattle.

Dustin told of his desire to start ranching on his own and would need all of his money but not for awhile.

"Good then, let's let it work for you in the interim period," the banker said, giving Dustin some more papers to sign.

With all his business taken care of, Dustin had in his possession over one hundred dollars cash, five hundred in an interest bearing savings account and one thousand dollars stock in the fast growing Chicago, Illinois Stock Yards Inc. This did not include counting the twelve hundred dollars Cindy had or the long shot possibility of his acquiring through the courts forty thousand acres of good Texas grasslands, buildings included. His entire family had never earned, all told in their lives, as much money as Dustin had at this very minute.

Dustin was sure walking in tall cotton now. He got a room at the Grand Saloon and Entertainment Emporium. This place was the office for many of the larger cattlemen in the country, often being used for the Cattlemen's Association meetings which were being held more often lately. Dustin attended every one and listened intently. Their frequency was not increasing solely because of the liquor or fine company to be had in the Grand Saloon, rather because the Texas cowmen were in trouble. They had gathered many of the cattle that roamed the land wild during the war and had built great herds. Now the problem was getting them to market. Here in Texas they were only worth what their hides would bring and that wasn't enough to pay for skinning them. They were cattle poor and things weren't getting any better. Dustin listened to their problems and as always, he had a plan. The cattlemen were open to at least listen to any suggestions. This one, presented by a young Army scout who had just bested the desperado Sanderson in a gun fight, was heard with enthusiasm.

"Gentlemen, I know that the army needs more beef for the ever growing reservation population. I have heard the officers at several Forts discussing the problem facing them now that Congress has raised the quotas for beef to be allotted each family of peaceful Indians staying on their assigned reservations. The government wants to establish cowherds on the reservations as well. This will be a one time opportunity to save your fortunes and provide these cattle. The Army wants fifty-thousand three and four year old steers and ten-thousand cows from two to five year olds with an appropriate percentage of bulls to cover the cowherd. I can bid the contract for this beef from Fort Lancaster. You have something no other area of the country has, that's numbers, Gentlemen, numbers! The government wants twenty-five thousand head delivered to Montana. No one rancher could possibly handle the order. You as an association could supply this amount readily."

While Dustin spoke, no one interrupted, until now.

"It's a long damn way, from here to Montana," one skeptical rancher said.

"Yes, and good water and feed every step of the trip. Your cattle would actually gain weight on the way. There's been a few short drives to the rail yards in St. Louis and even to the new spur in Kansas City. They've had trouble with weather, robbers and water due mostly to poor planning. These cattlemen were victims of panic. They left at a bad time of the year and caught bad weather. They didn't know the country they were traveling through or took unintelligent gambles and made no preparations to protect or defend their herds. A well planned trip over known country with a well armed, well mounted crew of top quality cowhands led by someone with a vested interest in the cattle, could be very successful. It is not necessary for these trips to be the hazardous risks the few who have tried and failed make them out to be. They will be hard and dangerous. They can also be profitably undertaken if properly planned and financed in the beginning. I'll talk to the Colonel and request he contact General Stewart, his headquarters are at the fort near my home, to obtain the contract for the new, northern Montana reservations.

We'll need to leave early as possible in the year in order to arrive before the fall storms hit Montana. We'll travel the Pecos all the way to where it ties back into the Rio Grande at Santa Fe. Stay with it to Alamosa, cut over to the Arkansas then over to the South Platte all the way north through Cheyenne, then cross country to the Platte up to the Seminole reservation. Then we'll jump over to the Bighorn all the way north to the Musselshell, over to the Missouri and then the Cow River. That will take us to Fort Assinniboine and Fort Belknap and their associated reservations where the cattle are to be delivered.

This route will give us the opportunity to sell some of the extra cattle we've swept up on our way north. The miners along the eastern slope will pay top dollar for fresh meat as will the little towns along the way. The forts and Indians we pass will be more helpful if we grease the wheel of commerce as we go. Your cattle are worth twenty-five cents a head here, if you're willing to spend twenty cents a head to have them skinned. I can get you fifteen dollars a head delivered, at a cost of about a dollar a head total."

Dustin remained standing while the entire room of cattlemen, most two and three times his age, sat silently absorbing all they just heard.

"What guarantee do we have you can pull this off? Hell, you're just a kid!" one reluctant rancher said.

"He's the kid that killed Sanderson and lived to collect the reward!" shouted another.

The room came alive with debate, some for and some against the proposal.

"I could give you all the five cents a head you would clear on your cattle here and cut you out all together. That wouldn't help you all much and I don't really need the money enough to cover the whole deal myself. You cattlemen have always been gamblers, you've had to be. This is the best deal you're going to get.

"I'll put the whole thing together and lead the drive myself for 10% of the deal, plus anything over $15.00 a head I can get. You come up with half the expenses up front, the other half on delivery and payoff with a bonus of twenty-five percent of everything sold along the way and also of any bonus the military pays for either early delivery or extra good condition of the cattle.

"That's my offer, Gentlemen. Think it over, you have sixty days to put your road herds together and get your cowboys and remudas ready. The cowboys wages will be your regular wages plus a bonus on delivery. I'll only take good men you all know well. I want at least one hundred-fifty men and will take up to one hundred seventy-five. I'll not start short handed. Every man must be willing and know how to fight if necessary. I also intend to have extra help from soldiers along the way.

"I'm going to give away a lot of your cattle to encourage a military escort as much of the way as possible. I'm going to give some more to the Indian beggars who's land we'll cross also. Several of these smaller drives refused to give two or three head to these roadside indigents and have had whole herds stampeded during the nights, loosing over half of their cattle or even more.

"I speak Spanish and several dialects of these southern Indian languages and will employ the services of other military scouts further north who will interpret for me the tribes above Cheyenne."

Dustin finished this dissertation with a confidence and air of conviction that elicited a unanimous vote of approval by the near desperate cattlemen. They now had a plan. Somehow this confident youth had made this never before attempted adventure seem very plausible. He hadn't hidden any of the likely dangers of the trip, he had simply explained how they needed to handle each problem as it arose.

"Most difficulties are only mere inconveniences if one is prepared before they happen."

Dustin then explained that they should start gathering every available qualified man and start throwing their cattle together.

"We will brand all the cattle with the road brand '08'. Every rancher should have an accurate count of his starting cattle numbers. All should be aware that every cattle owner will share equally by percentage of cattle they started with in all profits and any loss as well. Any stampedes or losses of any kind will be shared by all. This becomes one herd with each of you owning whatever percentage you start out with."

"Also Gentlemen, any of you physically able to endure this trip are more than welcome to come along. I'll need five captains, for I intend to move this herd as one unit with five divisions within it. I would encourage and welcome your company. You will have the opportunity to watch first hand history being made. All authority will be signed over to me before we leave. There will be no pulling off on your own after we start. You all are honest men here at home joining this drive with all the best intentions. Still I must prepare for any obstacle that might jeopardize the success of our drive. Anyone of you could be as major a deterrent to arriving intact at our destination as Indians, bandits or the land itself. My first instincts tell me not to even allow any of you owners to come along, let alone encourage your participation. I know that you gentlemen have your very survival riding on this trip of ours, and in spite of my gut feelings against doing so, I again extend a sincere welcome.

"Colonel Gibson, sir, you seem to be the head of this association and I would like to leave you in that well deserved position in the organizing of this undertaking here at home. You'll need to put together five separate companies of men each with its own support system of chuck wagon, bed wagons and cowboys all under a captain. Please Sir, remember I desire an excess of all possible needs, especially men.

"I'm paying the men out of my percentage and I'll not have this mission fail for the lack of a few extra hands. A few of the smaller, shorter drives have failed because of tired, over worked, under fed men. Usually the result of poor planning, cheap or greedy trail bosses have cost many cattlemen everything they owned by cutting corners of just a few dollars.

"Are you willing to take on this responsibility, Sir?" Dustin asked the stout old gentleman.

"Young man, the 'Colonel' in front of my name was not placed there as an honorary title. I proudly earned it on the field of battle in the recent unpleasantness. I lost my home and fortune in our defeat. I moved to Texas and built another life and again amassed a nice fortune here. Now circumstances have placed me in the position of facing a total loss again. I am, however, this time too damn old to build yet another life. This one must be saved at all cost. I gladly give any and all aid I may be able to on this venture. If these men, my neighbors and fellow cattlemen, each as near financial ruin as myself, will indeed follow my lead, I'll put this thing together and have all ready in sixty days," Colonel Gibson said to a round of applause in a show of total acceptance and approval of his selection as head of this endeavor.

"Good, Colonel. I'll rely heavily on your good judgment and knowledge of these men. I'll require ten head of horses for every man. I believe I can sell the whole horse herd to a buyer in Wyoming I know. We'll trail them back down after we deliver the cattle in Montana. There is also a good chance we can sell the top end of our saddle stock to the Army. They're in constant, desperate need of good mounts. I'll take the same percentage and bonus on the sale of the horses.

"The wagons can also be sold or driven back at your choosing. There will be a market for them that far north. That decision can be made in Montana.

"I'd prefer not to have any mules in the wagon teams if at all possible. They are usually more problem than good horses and nearly impossible to catch out of the remudas.

"I'll want the cattle to be open (not bred) if possible and we'll keep the bull herd separate until the last three months of the drive. The calves are worthless to us and heavy cows will slow us down. If one calves along the way and we knock the calf in the head, the cow will worry us needlessly trying to return to the spot she had it. Open cows and cows that have recently calved that can be relieved of their burden are what we need for an easier drive. This will not be easy to accomplish but remember the calves we sacrifice now will increase our chances of completing this drive successfully.

"I'll want two herds of five thousand cows with one thousand steers mixed in with them. Also, two herds of five thousand steers following the lead herd of one thousand bulls and the remaining three thousand contracted steers. Add to these fifteen hundred older steers to be used for trade or gifts to prevent any surprise. I'll go to the fort and secure the necessary papers from General Stewart while you organize everything here," Dustin finished.

"Well boys, you heard the man! We've got work to do. Let's get an inventory ready. All the wagons, horses, men, weapons, supplies and of course cattle. I know most of you are like me and most of your cattle are running over thousands of acres. The only place large enough to hold all these cattle for the time it takes to get them all gathered is Millers place on the river. We'll all work together and start throwing all the cattle in the country down to his big river pastures to hold. Let's get busy." Colonel Gibson took charge like Dustin hoped he would.

Colonel Gibson was once again in charge and fighting for his way of life. He was alive with enthusiasm and it was contagious. The rest of the cattlemen sat at their places, some with help of a friend or neighbor who could read and write, making lists of what they had to contribute to the drive. Dustin left things in competent hands and headed to the fort.

Dustin had some luck on his side as Captain Perron was visiting all the forts under General Steward's regime collecting bids for the Montana reservations cattle, as well as tending to other, more routine military business. He would be at Fort Lancaster within a few days.

Dustin checked the post mailroom as was his custom when near a fort as it had been long enough now to have received a return letter from Cindy. Nothing today again. The mail was slow, he'd hear from his future bride before long he was sure. For now he had a lot to do.

He wanted to arm a guard with the most modern weapons available. Possibly he could borrow these from the armory. He'd wait until he talked with Captain Perron before securing the necessary armament. Dustin returned to Del Rio. Again it was wait as patiently as possible. Dustin spent a great deal of time with Colonel Gibson never telling the old gentleman he hadn't yet secured the military contracts for the Montana reservations. Dustin wasn't worried. If the military didn't buy these steers, the markets in the mid west could. He'd just change the destination of the drive. He'd have to hold the herd on the plains and deliver the cattle in small parcels as the stockyards could handle them. He'd make something work. The benefits to the spirit of the community and especially Colonel Gibson was worth any uneasiness on Dustin's part.

If, in fact, the cattle could be gathered, there should be adequate numbers of each class to fill Dustin's order. Saddlestock was being brought in from near and far and more than enough had been secured or soon would be. Two of the larger ranches had a special blacksmith wagon built and supplied. Many of the previous short drives failed or were miserable adventures due to bent or broken wagon wheels or lame or barefoot horses. This would not happen on this drive. Harness were being repaired and extra trace chains, collars and leather for future repairs were stored in wagons to be used as bed wagons. Dustin kept reminding the Colonel that having several extra of anything is better than having just one too few of that same thing. Plenty is good, extra is better. This was Dustin's credo.

Several more days passed. Finally Dustin received word of Perron's arrival and to Dustin's continued good fortune, Captain Perron had not received any acceptable bids for the beef and cows for Montana.

After listening to Dustin's plans, somewhat in amazement, Perron said, "If you think you can put this together Dustin, you can have the contract!"

"It's already in motion, Sir! Has been for over a couple of weeks now. I was counting on no one else being able to raise a herd so large as the one you require. I'll want to sell the extra horses also. Captain, could you see about helping me find a buyer? Most will be good Texas cowponies. I know the military likes taller mounts but these will sure be fit when we arrive. Might work good for the Army," Dustin said.

"You've thought of everything again, haven't you Dustin? I tell you what, I'll purchase every sound horse you wish to sell at Fort Belknap along with the cattle. You've not mentioned price, Dustin. I'm sure you haven't over looked that part. Are you waiting for me to make an offer?" Captain Perron said wearily.

"Yes, Sir, I am. I know you'll be fair especially when I tell you that I'm bringing along many head to give the Army along the way just to ride with us for a while between forts especially through hostile country. I'm bringing extras for the Indians too. I'd rather give the beggars a few than have them steal a lot," Dustin explained.

"Very well done, young man. You are on top of things for sure. I'll give you twenty-five dollars per horse, eighteen dollars for each steer, fourteen dollars per cow and twenty dollars a head for each herd bull up to the contract number," Captain said, but not with absolute or final conviction.

"Sir, that sounds reasonable. I was hoping to receive a little more for the cows. I'm going to deliver them ready to calve in the spring so the Indians won't loose them all in the cold of winter," Dustin said.

"Fifteen per cow then!" Perron retorted.

"Done!" said Dustin, way more than satisfied.

"About the overage, Sir. I know I could be obliged to take less for anything above the contract numbers because I am anticipating having a sizable number of all three classes of cattle above the contract. I would like to present all the excess to you personally as a gift for your help in my successfully completing this endeavor. Please, before you try to explain that this would be any kind of conflict of interest, let me assure you that no improprieties are implied here. Your help in your official capacity as officer in charge of this acquisition is worth many times what little retribution I am able to offer. To show my sincerity and heart felt gratitude for all you are able to do to insure my success, I'll be honored to go halves with you on the overage. We can leave them in my name until your retirement from the service. At that time, whenever it might be, half of all the profits from the cattle you and I own will be in an account in your name in Miles City, Montana drawing interest. Please accept this offer in the spirit in which it is offered and remember we are both rendering a great service to the government of the United States by allowing them to keep their word to those poor Indians held captive on land we chose for them. Also remember, these Indians as well as the soldiers at both northern forts will surely starve without this beef. Only you have the power and authority to guarantee a successful trip," Dustin finished as humbly as an ignorant serf who had just explained the obvious truth to his lord.

"You're good young man! Really good. You have all the help at my command. The Army will buy the overage at the same prices up to an additional ten percent. Anything above that, we'll negotiate on delivery. Is there anything else, Dustin?" Captain Perron asked just a little indignantly but not too much so.

"Yes sir, as a matter of fact there is just one more thing. For the times we don't have a military escort, I'd like to arm a guard of men to prevent any unusual and unnecessary stress on the future wards of the government I'll be watching over. Captain, I would like to requisition enough rifles and ammunition for fifty men. The arsenal will be returned to the fort of your choosing upon completion of our journey," Dustin said.

"Consider it done, Dustin. Please give me an approximate itinerary for your trip. In the best interest of the government, I'll see you have the full cooperation and support of the military most every step of the way," Captain Perron said and stuck out his hand. "You didn't really think I'd accept the overage of cattle, did you, Dustin?"

"To be honest, I was hoping you wouldn't. You see they're only twenty-five percent mine. I'd of had to buy the rest out of my part. It would still be a bargain for me anyway. Thanks for the help, Captain. I'm sure I've bitten off more than I could chew alone," Dustin said shaking hands with Perron.

"Dustin, I think you can chew about as much as anyone I've ever seen all by yourself. It's a pleasure to be a part of this trip. Good luck, Dustin. I'll see you along the way some and I'll sure be in Fort Belknap to take the herd and pay off for the grateful government whom you are doing such a bold and noble service," Captain Perron said without a trace of sarcasm in his voice. He then added, "By the way, I was sure sorry to hear about Cindy's grandmother being ill. That's a tremendous trip for a young girl alone. All the way to England."

"Yes sir, it is a shame. Thank you again. Excuse me, I've got to go," Dustin said barely able to keep his knees from buckling under him.

Once outside Dustin ran to check the mail. There was a letter from Mrs. Morton. It was tear stained and short. It simply stated Cindy had run off the day Dustin rode south. They didn't know where she'd gone until Jim asked around the fort if anyone had seen Cindy. It seems she went to St. Louis with a patrol escorting an officer who'd been injured and was being sent back east. They've had no word from her but she couldn't have gotten far as she had no money they were aware off. They were all happy to receive his letter and are all glad to hear he's doing well. They were confused about his telling Cindy he'd come get her when he had everything ready. She asked him to please write and let them know if he had any idea where Cindy might be headed back east. They were quite confused by all of this. Why would she run away to the east, especially if she had secret plans to meet him in the south? She closed, "Love as always, Mom Morton," and added a postscript. "If Cindy is with you, please take care of her and tell her we love her." Cindy had apparently told the soldiers of her European destination, and Mrs. Morton had not heard about it at this letter's writing. He knew she had made it to Europe by now and there was little he could presently do to retrieve her.

Dustin sat down immediately and wrote out his story of finding a home, having Cindy join him there and making a life together. He told his foster mother about the money he'd had Cindy hold for him. He briefly told of his undertaking of the trail drive from the southern most part of Texas to the northern forts of Montana. He told her that he could be reached by mail sent to the forts along the way. When they received word from Cindy he would retrieve her or aid her to the best of his ability. Dustin didn't feel right about handling this through the mail but he really couldn't leave long enough to make the round trip. Dustin spent the rest of the night staring out the window of his hotel room.

The next morning he was out at the Gibson ranch with the Colonel going over the preparations for the up coming trip. This cattle drive had become Dustin's sole purpose in life the moment Caption Perron told him of Cindy's unexpected departure. He worked and behaved accordingly. He threw all his efforts into making sure every detail was gone over dozens of times. The less left to chance the better things would go.

The Colonel was as actively participating with the same enthusiasm as Dustin. The activity was medicine to the old Gentleman. He'd been a busy man his entire life until just recently when the pressure of the waning cattle business had driven him indoors to attend meetings too numerous to count. Bankers and Attorneys filled the hours of Colonel Gibson's days with a redundant rhetoric they offered up as an explanation of the financial problems at hand. Like too many others, Colonel Gibson was in a bad way

momentarily and felt compelled to at least attend these gatherings if not actually listen during them. Now things were different! He had purpose, his life had meaning. A true warrior needed a battle, a fight he understands, to participate in, in order to continue to exist. Colonel Gibson was a warrior in the first case definition of the word. This new battle was the most important he'd ever take part in. This one was for self first. To preserve this life he'd worked so hard to build. If he helped his fellow cattlemen as well, so much the better. He knew their help would be of great value to him and his new young associate but with or without them he'd find a way to carry this drive through.

A month into the preparations things were nearly ready. Colonel Gibson and Dustin spent countless hours in the saddle every day checking each detail personally. Anyone found to be cutting corners was instantly reminded that the success of this trip depended on every nut and bolt, cinch and latigo, rope and chain and every man and animal. All must perform their absolute best.

One late afternoon the two men were returning from rechecking the count on the cow herd. The steer herd had already come together as it was the least selective class of cattle to be gathered. There were many steers a year or two older than the contract called for but these would be used, if necessary, as toll payments in crossing Indian lands. The bull herd was also less selective and ranged from long yearlings to several over ten years old. These were sufficient in number to fulfill the requirements of the Army within the perameters of a reasonable age range and the younger and older bulls could be added to the average.

"We are having trouble filling the order for cows, Dustin," Colonel Gibson said needlessly, Dustin having been with him when making the count.

"Don't worry Colonel, we've got time yet and we're close now. I know it's going to be tough on the ranchers to knock all the calves in the head that are coming along every day now, so I've got a plan. If you'd like to hear it, Sir?" Dustin said knowing he had the Colonel's full attention.

"Dustin, everything I own is riding on one of your plans now. I believe I can stand listening to one more," Colonel Gibson said laughing out loud at himself.

"I kinda hate to see all these good young calves just killed and wasted. Let's let them nurse the cows for a few days to get that good first milk then we'll let all the kids around here raise them on goat's milk. It won't cost us anything much and when we get back we'll have a big crop of near yearlings," Dustin explained with heart felt conviction.

"Goat's milk? Where in hell are them kids going to get goat's milk?" Colonel Gibson asked incredulously.

"From goats, Colonel, from goats. I've seen more than enough goat herds just south of here to fill the need. It won't take as much as you think. We have around eleven hundred cows that will drop calves before we leave. We can kill them all or try to raise some of them. Remember it makes no real difference to me. They are your calves," Dustin finished a little put out at Colonel Gibson's skepticism.

"You're right Dustin, again. You are absolutely right. I hate to see the little fellows knocked in the head. I'll see what I can put together. There are enough children and women in the village on my ranch to handle five times that number. Hell, if we save just one, that's something," Colonel Gibson laughed again. "By God, goat herders! What next, Dustin? Should we maybe build a luxury wagon with a big six horse hitch and put my feather bed in it so's I can go along?" Colonel Gibson still laughing.

"As a matter of fact that is exactly what I wanted to suggest Colonel! That you yourself make this trip. I've been watching you for the last month. You can make it, Sir. Your leadership will carry you and this herd all the way to Montana and you back. These men, the ranchers that is, are following me now here at home mainly because you are really heading this up. Now before you answer listen carefully to me. I have everything ready for the safest smoothest trip possible. I am prepared for any event, even unforeseen acts of God. This will be the most successful cattle drive ever made and the easiest. It is still the longest drive that ever will be attempted unless some damn fool just circles around the country for nine months. It's over twenty-five hundred miles, if all goes well we'll make ten miles a day average. That's two hundred fifty days. Colonel, even if everything goes as planned that's a long time gone from home. There are going to be arguments about camp rules and town visitations. I made a mistake letting a few of the ranchers come along. Once the invitation was made I couldn't very well omit any of the association ranchers. I'm concerned I'll have to shoot several of these old war-horses when we get on the trail. Most of them aren't going to take orders from a kid, especially orders they don't like. We'll build you that luxury coach and I'll put a fine feather bed in it myself and a desk.

You can keep a log and take charge of all accounts for the trip. You are an invaluable part of my plan. You Sir, have something I can only hope to someday earn, the respect of those around you. Think about it, Sir. You'll be plumb pitiful around here watching over our goat herd!" Dustin stopped for a moment and smiled big at the Colonel who sat up clearly offended by the thought of watching a bunch of children feed baby calves goat's milk.

Then Dustin went on, "On second thought Colonel, you are getting pretty long in the tooth. Maybe sitting around the hearth side with a shawl over your shoulders with the added excitement of daily tending your herd of goats would suit you better. Yes, I'm afraid your old heart might plumb give out at the excitement to be had on this trip, especially when we arrive farther north than any cow herd ever has, and the site of all that money when the Army pays off...," Dustin was nearly knocked off his horse by the slap on the back of his head from the feisty old Colonel.

"Get off that horse you smart aleck. I'll kick your ass for you, that's what I'll do! By God, I ain't never heard no such thing as me staying home in a rocking chair while history's being made by no damn snotty nosed kid." There was a little pause while the color came back to the Colonel's face then, "Goat herder, my ass! I was thinking about coming along all the time anyway. Smart assed, damn kid. Long in the tooth? That's a hell of a thing to say!" the Colonel mumbled for the next several miles then added, "You be sure to make the coach plenty long and wide. I like a big bed!" Then both men laughed long and loud.

"Glad to have you along, Colonel," Dustin said earnestly.

Then in response, trying as hard as possible to still sound indignant while laughing, "It's a wonder you've lived as long as you have. Imagine me sitting home watching a bunch of damn goats. What would you have done if along the way some fancy newspaper man comes riding out to interview this soon to be famous trail herd. You'd say something and embarrass yourself for all of history. No, no indeed. It's mandatory I accompany this expedition to lend to it the cultural and intellectual fabric, that properly woven, holds civilized man above the beast of the field."

The Colonel spoke as if to all mankind in a very grandiose manner and tone while looking far off to a not seen horizon.

"That was beautiful, Colonel. Really it was! Spoken like a true goat herder if I ever heard one!" Dustin joked and ducked just in time to miss being slapped in the face with the Colonel's large hat he'd held in his hand to accentuate his regal bow at the end of his discourse.

"Smart assed kid!" the Colonel said as he rode off toward home a big smile on his face.

Dustin spent the next several days at the fort filling out requisitions already approved by Captain Perron for weapons and ammunition. Dustin also put in a requisition for an army ambulance and to his pleasant surprise received one. This

59

was an almost new rig which was fully stocked. This would be perfect for Colonel Gibson. It even had a special double spring seat which Dustin had the fort carpenter pad heavily and cover with high quality canvas ducting for the most comfortable ride available anywhere. He also had a fold down desk built with a metal lock box hidden in the floor.

"Perfect! I'll put the rifles and ammunition in the back for now and move them to the appropriate wagons later," he told himself.

He decided to test the limits of the fort's hospitality a little further and was a little embarrassed when caught. He was back at the Quartermasters office requisitioning enough kegs of ready made horse shoes and nails to last the entire trip. While the Quartermaster was looking through his books to see if in fact he even had enough horse shoes on hand to meet the order, a voice from behind Dustin called out, "Relax Sergeant, he'll not need the whole order now. I'm giving him an open requisition for any further supplies he may need along his way. No need in you carrying all that extra weight the entire trip. You can acquire what you need as you go." Then without pause Captain Perron continued, "I knew you would be concerned about the well being of the horses soon to become the property of the United States government. You are such a thoughtful young man!" Perron said with just the slightest smile but shaking his head. Then he continued, "Are you still on schedule, Dustin? Everyone along the route is ready and excited about your journey. General Stewart and an entire company of his special forces will accompany you on the last leg of the drive."

"Yes sir, Captain! Right on schedule. We'll leave right on time with all preparations complete. Thank you, Captain. I didn't mean to be too pushy," Dustin apologized.

"No problem, Dustin. These cattle delivered to Fort Belknap is a pet project of General Stewart's. The full cooperation of the entire western force of the United States Cavalry is at your disposal. I'm going ahead with my men to clear the way. I'll lie back now and then to let you catch up so we can visit. Good luck again, Dustin. I'm not too concerned about you needing any luck. You haven't left much to chance and with General Stewart backing your project this should be a stroll in the park. I'll see you up the line, Dustin."

Captain Perron left and Dustin waited for the part of his supplies he'd need for the first leg of the trip.

As time drew near, Colonel Gibson growing healthier and more spry all the time had everything ready, including a goat heard gathered that would have been the envy of the Pharaohs. Everything that is except the cow herd and this fact was weighing heavily on his mind. They were still short just over one thousand cows of proper age and hadn't gathered any that would fit their contractual requirements in several days.

"Dustin, I'm concerned greatly about this shortage. Do you have any ideas now? I'm worried we might not be able to fill this part of our contract. We've gathered lots of cattle most too old for the Army to use. I'm not sure what we're going to do," Colonel Gibson confided in his young consultant.

"Mexicans," Dustin said simply.

"Mexican what?" Colonel Gibson asked.

"Mexican cattle, Colonel. We can cross over whatever amount of cows the right age with just a few days notice. I met a charro that works for a Ranchero Grande, Don Diego Augustina. His hacienda is just across the river. We'll need to buy them from him before we leave. He'll take five dollars a head but he wants it when we leave," Dustin explained.

"Damn, that's five thousand dollars more than we have. Truthfully we are pretty short on your part of up front money. We were hoping you might take a bigger slice on the other end."

"Colonel, this has gotten bigger than just a cattle drive. Hell, we've got the whole cavalry going with us. We're not going to let a little money stop us now! I've got some in the bank and can borrow more if necessary against some stock I have. How much do you have?" Dustin asked.

"We have just under the twelve five you asked for up front," Colonel Gibson said apologetically.

"Hell, Colonel that's great! I'll tell you what. You pay the men on the other end out of your part instead of my paying them as we go and we'll split the extra profit on the Mexican cattle fifty-fifty and I'll take nothing up front for my part. You keep what's left from your combined bank rolls to purchase our needs on our trip. That'll give us the five thousand for the Mexicans and leave you over seven thousand dollars for road expenses and allow you to stake the men a little from time to time when we're near a town. They'll need a little blow out or two because I intend to run a dry camp. No liquor at all, not even for medicinal purposes. We have real medicine. How fair does that sound?" Dustin asked.

"Dustin, how can you go with nothing up front? I don't understand why you'd want to under take this for nothing," the Colonel questioned.

"Colonel, I'm going to make a large fortune on this trip. You are now paying all the expenses and I am just going along for the ride. I've got this set up pretty well and have all but guaranteed its success with the help of the military involvement. I'll take my part at the other end and will take it with a clear conscience and don't feel like I'm risking anything. Have we got a deal?" Dustin asked very business like.

"Yes, I've been given authority from the association to make any deal you want to make. We all know we'd have no military support without your involvement. We also realize you are the only one who's been over any of the country," Colonel Gibson explained.

"Okay, Colonel, we are still on. I'll go buy the Mexican cattle tomorrow. They'll have them ready within the week," Dustin explained.

"Wonderful, I'll have the money in the morning. Will you want an escort?" Colonel Gibson asked.

"No thanks, Colonel. I'll have Don Diego come to my hotel for the deal. I don't fancy going into Mexico with five thousand dollars," Dustin assured him.

That evening Dustin sent a peasant boy across the river to Don Diego's estate and arrangements were made for a meeting. Don Diego spoke beautiful English but was pleased with Dustin's show of respect in conversing with him in his native tongue.

Dustin explained to the powerful Don Diego that the Texans were having some problems raising the cow numbers necessary to fulfill their contract and the government needed them in the far north. Don Diego knew of the great need for beef by the military. His own ranch had been supported by his government's need during their seemingly constant state of revolution. Mexico was a poor country yet the cattle market was still strong. Dustin realized the negotiations had begun.

The two men had talked before of the large numbers of cattle Don Diego could supply and of his need for money on delivery. Dustin explained that the Texas cattle were all but worthless here but would bring a fair price in the north. He needed a thousand young, preferably open cows to satisfy his contract. Don Diego acknowledged Dustin's problem and assured him he could raise the necessary cattle. Don Diego's concern was that his cows were very valuable to him and the Mexican government. By not letting any outside cattle into the country and with the herds being reduced in size by American bandits along with the many wandering across the river to end up being claimed by the Americans, cattle in great demand and must bring a fair price. Dustin had never really talked about price with Don Diego before. He'd picked the five dollars a head out of the air and now was worried.

Some of the cattlemen had a fit at this apparent extortion on the part of Don Diego as there was already much bad blood between the Texans and Mexicans. The Texans realized that a shortage of cows would spoil the whole contract and the American ranchers they knew farther north and east would want part of the steer contract as well. They would triple their money on the Mexican cattle on delivery and now that Dustin wanted no money up front, they agreed to five dollars a head. It was, after all, money Dustin would have received anyway. Most of the cattlemen were glad he hadn't insisted on his money up front and purchased these cattle himself, with their money, and cut them out all together.

As Dustin and Don Diego set the stage for the transaction, each played his position with great skill. Don Diego from a position of power. He had the cows necessary to fill the needs of these poor Texans and the market in Mexico was not as desperate as it was just north of the border. Dustin's edge was he had much needed American gold coin he well knew Don Diego and his government could use to support their revolution. Dustin told Don Diego how the steers in

Texas were worth just twenty-five cents a head for the hides and the cows even less, times were very hard indeed.

Don Diego spoke without any sign of emotion, "That is very sad my young friend. My cattle are worth ten times that amount."

He did not move except for his eyes that had been looking at his empty glass and now pierced into Dustin's searching to see if his arrow had indeed struck its target. Dustin returned Don Diego's stare also emotionless.

"Senior Don Diego Augustina, you are a very powerful and wise man whom I respect greatly. Your word is your bond as is mine. I accept your words as fact. You say your cows are worth this amount then I know this must be so. Sir, here is the money for one thousand head of young cows to be delivered across the river within the week. There is twenty-five hundred dollars here my good friend, ten times their value on this side of the river. Thank you, Senior for your help in our time of need. I count on your good judgment on the selection of the cattle as to their quality," Dustin finished and pushed the money across the table toward Don Diego.

He simply motioned to one of his men to pick up the money as he said, "My wise and trusting young friend, it is not necessary to pay until you receive and count the cattle. It is customary and would be no insult to me."

"I am young and inexperienced in such matters, Senior. Please take the money now. I have the word of Don Diego Augustina. I see no need to wait payment or count cattle. I shall sleep comfortably with our arrangement, Senior," Dustin said eloquently.

Don Diego smiled and arose extending his hand to young Dustin. "My friend when you become king of the great country of America, you will not forget your good friend Don Diego?"

"Senior, we don't have a king," Dustin said a little confused.

"Not yet my friend but you are still young and have not fully applied yourself," Don Diego said sincerely with a great smile on his face. Then turning to his escort of men said, "Let's go. We have many cattle to gather for my dear friend, young Dustin Thomas."

Dustin rode back to Colonel Gibson's ranch via the bank. He left instructions with his new financial advisor, the banker Rogers, to hold this twenty-five hundred until the trip began. If Dustin did not come for it before he left, add it to the stockyard investment. At Gibson's ranch, Dustin was met by the Colonel with several other worried cattlemen.

"Did he go for the deal? Did you have enough money? Can he get the cows in time?"

All these questions and many more came in a barrage.

"Yes, everything is fine. He'll deliver the cattle this week. How's everything here?" Dustin asked turning the tide of questions back toward the cowmen.

"Everything is wonderful now that you pulled this cow deal off, Dustin. We'll never be able to repay you for all you've done for us," the Colonel said and all present agreed.

"Gentlemen, I'm going to get rich on this drive. You understand that, don't you?" Dustin asked feeling just the slightest bit guilty.

"Deservedly so, Dustin. Deservedly so!" again as a chorus.

"All right, I just don't want no hard feelings when this is over," Dustin added.

"Nonsense Dustin, we can all do the math and know full well you're going to make more than any of us. Hell, more than all of us. That's not important. The deal is we were going to lose everything until you put this together for us. Remember Dustin, we're all going to get rich as well. This is a big contract and there's plenty for all of us," the Colonel said.

"Good," Dustin said. "How about the wagons?"

"Hell Dustin, it looks like a wagon train instead of a cattle drive. We're taking along everything we could possibly want or need except whisky and women and I for one wish you'd reconsider both!" the Colonel said with an evil little smile on his face.

"Damn, you are feeling good! Just a little while ago I was going to leave you with the women and the goat herds. Hell, I'd be afraid to now!" Dustin joked and everyone laughed at the Colonel's expense but none harder than the Colonel himself.

"By God, I do feel great! I'm having the time of my life. I've acquired some ledgers to keep a log of our trip, Dustin. We'll show the world how these trips should be made. I've got the ambulance you brought me fixed up more comfortably than my office at the ranch. I'm bringing along six good gentle horses so I can ride some too. I don't want to spend the whole trip riding in the wagon," Colonel Gibson said.

"Of course you will ride, Colonel! I'm gonna ride in the wagon. You can wake me up when we get to Montana," Dustin said still laughing along with all the others.

Dustin spent almost no time in his Del Rio hotel room but kept it rented in case. In case of what he wasn't sure. He knew it was ridiculous but some hidden part of him thought maybe Cindy hadn't really gone to Europe after all. Maybe she had just gone east to get the things she'd need to make a good life for the two of them. He'd written letters to the Mortons regularly but had received few in return and no news of Cindy at all. He longed to see her again. To even just watch her from afar and imagine what it would be like to have her love him as he loved her.

Dustin was spending almost all of his time helping brand the trail herd and waiting the arrival of Don Diego's cows. A rider came to Dustin's camp late one evening announcing Don Diego's cattle were being held just across the river and would cross in the morning. Dustin was very excited and made the necessary arrangements to receive them. As morning came, Don Diego himself rode to the rivers edge and was met by Dustin, the Colonel, and a dozen of the best cowhands.

"My dear friend, Dustin Thomas, here are the cows I promised. I trust you will be pleased with their quality." Turning to his men Don Diego signaled for them to start the cows across.

The Colonel said, "Wait, we'd better pass them through some men for a count!"

Don Diego raised his hand to his men for a halt.

"Bring them on, Senior, I'm sure they've been counted already. Please forgive my companion, Senior. He is accustomed to dealing with Americanos," Dustin said in way of an apology for his associates unintended slight to Don Diego's honor.

Don Diego again motioned for his vaqueros to start the cows across. As they passed across the river, Dustin sent the cowboys over with them and were met on the other side by many more others than were necessary.

Colonel Gibson sat with Dustin and Don Diego silently for a while then commented, "These cows are of a far superior quality than ours. I am very pleased and impressed Senior Augustina."

"That is fine. It is, however, not important that you are pleased. It is only important to me that my friend, Dustin Thomas, is pleased," the bad blood showing again in Don Diego's voice.

"Very much so, Senior. Your word has been more than honored, my friend. These are the finest cattle in our drive. I thank you for them and all of your help. Your friendship is a valued treasure I will always hold dear. I'll see you again when I return, my friend," Dustin said, extending a hand to this Mexican nobleman.

"My young friend, you have handled yourself with great dignity and integrity. I am proud to have become your friend. You'll find an extra one hundred cows in this herd. I want you to have them as a gift for the trust you extended freely in our transaction. God speed my friend. I look forward to your return and our next meeting," Don Diego, said then turned and rode away with his men.

"Damn, Dustin, I stepped in it didn't I?" the Colonel said.

"You did fine, Colonel. Don Diego is from a different world than you are is all. It's all right. Let's get these girls branded and start going over everything one last time. We leave in less than a week. How's the calf crop doing?" Dustin asked.

"We had a lot more than I thought we were going to but everything is under control. I've got several of the oldest ranchers overseeing the operation and I think it might even work. What the hell are we going to do with all the goats when they wean the calves?" Colonel Gibson asked Dustin.

"Give the children who raised the calves, the job of tending them. They can push them onto the high rocky canyons too rough for the cattle to graze. Hell, some day those angora goats might even be worth something. They'll get a lot of good out of country you are not using now and we won't have to worry about them until we get back," Dustin declared.

Everything was ready. Colonel Gibson had spoken with every man participating in this drive personally. Most of the hired men didn't even know Dustin was anymore involved than as a scout or guide. Dustin liked this arrangement just fine. The day before the drive was to start, Dustin went in to Del Rio and settled his account with the hotel, restaurant and livery stable. He then went to the bank with a disturbing letter he'd received at the hotel. It was from Mom Morton. She'd enclosed a letter Cindy had sent her from Europe. Cindy had run out of money and was in desperate need of help. She wanted to come home to join Dustin and settle down and begin life anew. This thrilled Dustin to no end. The part that disturbed him was Cindy was amassing more debt daily. Her need was desperate. He could travel overseas and rescue her but that would take far too long. The banker could wire funds in a fraction of the time. He was about to become very wealthy but it would be meaningless without Cindy. He told the banker to send the three thousand dollars he had held in savings and be prepared to sell the thousand dollars in stock if he notified him from the trail that Cindy needed it too. He would make this drive and Cindy would be waiting for him when he returned. She'd made some mistakes but he didn't care. She was coming home now. She'd return to Dustin and become his wife. He'd make enough on this drive so that they could live anywhere she wanted to live in a style befitting her taste. Arrangements were made for her financial rescue and return. Dustin signed a power of attorney over to the banker, Mr. Rogers, to handle all of his affairs.

He went to the Gibson ranch with a renewed vigor that was obvious to everyone around him. On this last night before the drive, he met with Colonel Gibson and all his captains for supper and a last opportunity to field any questions they might have for Dustin. All were excited about getting started. The most important thing for Dustin to go over with everyone was the contracts for his part of the profit. Dustin went over every detail of his agreement to make sure everyone understood and that all was in writing and binding legally. There had been changes made as to the expenses when it became necessary to purchase the Mexican cattle. This change was very essential to the cattlemen for the success of this drive. It was also a very lucrative change for Dustin for now the largest expense, that of the extravagant labor force, was to be paid by the cattlemen. After explaining fully the tremendous amount of money Dustin was to receive upon the successful delivery of this herd, several of the cattle owners complained some and tried to hedge a little. They were quickly reminded Dustin was getting them fifteen dollars a head for their cattle that were worth absolutely nothing now. Each one of them would cash in on Dustin's connections and organization to an end result of not only saving their ranches and way of life, but becoming wealthy above their wildest expectations in doing so. The fact that Dustin would share in this wealth was not only proper it was absolutely inconceivable to consider otherwise.

The Colonel was adamant in his clearing any disputes on this subject. Going so far as offering to buy the cattle from any association member who wished to back out on his signed word to the agreement with Dustin. There was no time left at this late date to cut out anyone's cattle. One smaller rancher who had been controversial the entire time took the offer of two dollars a head cash from the Colonel for his five hundred head. The rest of the association agreed to purchase these cattle out of the common fund to save the Colonel from trying to raise an additional thousand dollars when all knew well he'd contributed his entire fortune already. It would also allow them to share in the thirteen dollars a head profit they were to receive.

Upon handing the money over and receiving a signed bill of sale from this shirker, Colonel Gibson said, "Since you have just proven your word and signature are of no worth at all, I feel this bill of sale is of little value as a binding document. I will keep it in our lock box if the need to show a judge our rightful ownership of these cattle. A man in this country is only as good as his word, Sir. Yours is worth nothing. I suggest you take your cowards reward and buy yourself a new life elsewhere. I am sure you'll find no place around here for a man who would go back on his word this far into the game. You had numerous opportunities to pull out while we still had time to make the necessary arrangements. You, Sir, are a cur and have no further business at this meeting of honorable men. I hope to never see your face again. Good day!"

The man took his money and left. He started once to return to the Colonel's desk as if to recant his withdrawal. The Colonel stopped his attempt with, "Show this deserter the door!"

The rest of the meeting was festive and positive. The Colonel, true to his nature, produced some fine aged brandy and filled every glass.

"Gentlemen, a toast to our success and to this young man who made it all possible. May he enjoy his new fortune as we will the renewal of our own! Drink up boys, this is the last we'll have for a long time. Unless, that is, you've reconsidered the rule against whisky in camp, Dustin?" the Colonel finished good naturedly.

"No sir, we'll be better served if we all stay sober. I know you good gentlemen can handle your liquor in a civilized manner. What we have to think about is the nearly two hundred wild cowboys we're taking along with us," Dustin declared making good sense easier to accept.

"Here, here! Enjoy this last one boys! We're heading north in the morning," Colonel Gibson said to a round of cheers from the excited men.

Chapter 8

The morning sun rose on an assembled mass of activity so large yet so well organized that even the famed Gingus Khan, who conquered the entire known world with his traveling army, would be jealous. The detail and extravagance of this confederation of ranchers, teamsters, cooks, blacksmiths, cowboys, riflemen, horses, wagons and cattle, joined by a troop of cavalry was overwhelming even to Dustin who sat on a ridge near the lead herd. Colonel Gibson dressed in his finest and riding his favorite horse sat beside him. Dustin watched everyone moving into position for the start. He finally gave the signal to the Lieutenant in charge of the cavalry troop who would accompany them for several days. They would then be relieved by another from Fort Stockton and so on all along their drive. Dustin then asked Colonel Gibson to please fire a shot as the official signal to head out. The huge assembly moved as one and in a moment the entire valley seemed to be crawling along. Dustin would spread the five sections out a little as they traveled on their way. There were as many towns people and family members cheering on the start of this historical venture as there were men participating in it.

Following the Rio Grande west to its juncture with the Pecos, then northwest along its course, provided a constant water source and a satisfactory camp ground need but be selected from most any site.

The first night found the herd some fourteen miles on their way. There were very few bugs to work out at the camp. Dustin had the cooks and wagons in service for some weeks already and had them moving from one location to another to develop a routine. The horse remudas had been separated long before hand and held together by wranglers. They were also moved from grazing ground to grazing ground and were well adjusted to the regimen. The cattle had been held in the five herds long enough for them to establish a pecking order and were accustomed to the riders who's constant control they'd been under long enough to accept willingly. Only the first herd containing the bulls was any grief. A few fights broke out and upon loosing, the runner up would run out of the fray with such haste as to be a real danger to the cowboys nearest the action. The men on the lead herd had to stay alert. All the captains knew their men and the men knew the cattle. It was as close to no effort for Dustin as he could possibly have imagined.

The first evening a surprise awaited him. The Colonel had arranged for each of the five head cooks to hold an on going contest as to cooking proficiency and economy. Each started with the exact same supplies and were to feed the same number of hands. The Colonel will be the judge, of course, and a large bonus awaited the contest's winner.

Colonel Gibson invited Dustin to help in the selection of the champion chef among these pot slingers. Dustin gladly accepted the invitation and appreciated the Colonel's making his judgeship official with an announcement at each of the chuck wagons. This added to the already extra special treatment Dustin received from the cooks.

The trip progressed smoothly and all went as Dustin had planned. Once near the junction of the Pecos and Rio Grande a large band of Mexican banditos followed the herd at a distance for several miles. The cavalry lieutenant sent a patrol to the rear to dissuade any foolishly aggressive actions on the part of these would be cattle rustlers. The show of force was adequate to ward off their thoughts of evil doing.

Further north after the changing of the guard, a small group of Indians approached the herd. The new soldiers from Fort Stockton started to drive off these potential beggars but Dustin asked that they be allowed to come close and be invited to join them that night at camp, much to Colonel Gibson's pleasure. The old gentleman intended to study the various tribes they encountered on this pilgrimage. This invitation provided the first close at hand meeting with a savage native for the Colonel to start his examination of these primitive people. The Indians were treated as royalty instead of the beggars they were. Dustin introduced them to all the five captains and without being asked Dustin offered the Indians three head of cattle for the privilege of passing through their land. The Indians accepted Dustin's offer very graciously.

After a big meal, and with Dustin translating in grand fashion, they told stories about life before the white man and of great battles fought in years gone now. They blessed the drive and young Dustin with prayers few white men had ever heard before, then retired to the beds the men had rolled out for their guests. Colonel Gibson captured every moment, every word for all posterity in his journal.

The morning came early as usual in cow camp and after a hardy breakfast Dustin had three old steers cut out and started off toward the Indian's village. Before they rode off, Dustin gave them a small bag of coffee and another of tobacco and again thanked them for allowing him to cross their land. They assured him he was welcome and the word would be sent ahead to all the Indian nations that this young white leader who spoke many tongues was a friend to all men, red and white alike. He would be made welcome along his entire trip. They rode away driving their three steers ahead of them.

"Why didn't we just run them off, Dustin?" asked the Lieutenant.

"It seems to me we've already run them as far as they can go. They were once great hunters ranging over this whole country taking what game they needed as they found it. Now they're begging for cattle and waiting for hand outs from a government they don't understand and that understands them even less. I figure we could at least leave them a shred of dignity while we're taking everything else away from them," Dustin said, still watching the Indians ride away.

"Well said, Dustin. Well said indeed!" Colonel Gibson said while placing a hand on Dustin's shoulder. He was also watching them ride away.

There were similar encounters as the herd moved northward. The Colonel's journal was already an impressive volume in both size and content. Colonel Gibson was documenting everything that happened, especially Dustin's handling of the Indians. The Colonel was extremely interested in how the decent, fair treatment elicited a favorable and civilized reaction from even the most hostile individuals.

Dustin never gave the Indians anything as charity. He always gave as payment for the right of passage or simply as a token of respect. The Indians responded to his kindness in like manner. Once several recipients of Dustin's fair treatment followed the herd for several miles just to bring Dustin's camp three large deer they had killed especially for that purpose. These were received with such elaborate celebration as to stop the herd early for the day and prepare a feast featuring the Indians gift as the main course. The Indians stayed and the next day when they left they took with them the first real taste of self respect and pride they'd experienced in a long while. This too, all went into the journal.

The cooks talents were surprising to both Dustin and Colonel Gibson, who both had considerable experience cooking and eating out doors.

These wagon bound, culinary engineers took pride in their gastronomical delights that would please even the most finicky gourmet. One of Dustin's favorites was a fellow who demanded he be called Mr. Harris. Most cow camp cooks used to be cowboys. They had either gotten too old and stove up or an injury or infirmity of some sort retired them to the pans. Mr. Harris on the other hand had never sat on a horse. He was quite proud of that fact. He had been a Gentleman's gentleman. Mr. Harris had been employed in London and brought over by ship. He'd worked for and taken care of one of the richest men in New York City. Several years he answered the needs of this fine tycoon. Then one day the tycoon returned home early and unexpectedly to find that Mr. Harris was also taking care of the needs of Mrs. Tycoon, her most basic needs in fact. A row ensued and Mr. Harris shot the fellow during the fray. He was forced to seek exile in the west and found his skills behind the ovens was his most practical talent. He'd found refuge at the Miller place several years ago. Miller was often quoted as saying, "If I loose every cow and every dime I have, I'll find a way to keep that pastry making son-of-a-bitch, Mr. Harris. If I have to, I'll make beds in a whorehouse to earn the money to pay him. You see, I like me sweets." Dustin agreed completely.

Mr. Harris could drive a team well but with all the extra help on this trip he had a swamper drive for him. He was a very well read fellow and brought along a carpetbag full of the classics. He read aloud every evening to the boys in his camp. He let his swampers clean up after him. He too enjoyed the excess of Dustin's plan.

The ample crew allowed everyone to actually enjoy this trip. Each man worked his assigned position diligently and the cattle traveled easily. They simply grazed their way north. There was always a water course close by, so long dry drives were unheard of on this excursion. The Army brought new stocks of supplies with each changing of the guard. This gave the cooks all the necessary ammunition for their on going culinary battle. It had become quite a fiercely fought competition much to Colonel Gibson's delight. These dutch oven dignitaries varied greatly in their styles and produce. The aforementioned Mr. Harris had his strength in pastries and sweets of all descriptions.

Another pothook swashbuckler, Fighting Joe Johnston, his name alone telling quite a story, preferred the main course with which to exercise his special talents. Fighting Joe could turn out the most tender, succulent, tastefully prepared beef steaks ever to come out of a dutch oven. He hand cut his own thick steaks, rolled them in flour, added salt, pepper and a secret combination of chili powders and spices, then cooked them in a deep oven half filled with melted beef tallow at exactly the correct temperature. These mouth watering morsels of tender slabs of beef would satisfy even the most particular of tastes.

Another even more typical chuck wagon sovereign was Scotty Mc Dowell. True to his Scottish lineage, Scotty was as thrifty as any human being has ever been. If total utilization of supplies and complete lack of waste was the sole criteria used in selecting the champion of the chuck wagons, Scotty would reign supreme. Scotty's favorite offering is the butchers old time staple often called S.O.B. stew. Scotty was fond of saying when his meal was about to be enjoyed by an uninvited guest or a surly cowboss, "Come and get it boys! We're having a Son-of-a-Bitch for supper…and we're going to eat stew." He'd add smiling and looking straight at the intended insultie. Scotty feared no man or beast and allowed his feeling to show openly at all times.

Scotty was and had been the cook for Colonel Gibson since before the war. He took orders from the Colonel exclusively.

Scotty did not, at first, show much interest in this cuisine contest between the camps. He made suggestions that the cowboys of each herd hold competitions of a more physical nature. Scotty, himself an accomplished boxer, volunteered to organize a series of matches so that near the end of the trip he could hold a company championship. He also suggested roping and riding events would lend themselves more to the talents of this collection of social misfits. It was Scotty's opinion that these cowboys would eat the bark off of the trees they passed and enjoy it completely. A contest of the culinary arts would be wasted on this multitude of mongrel humanity who could be fattened on cowchips and sand and, if offered in adequate amounts and served with strong coffee, would be consumed without a complaint from all but the more sensitive cowbosses and foremen. Even with Scotty's apparent lack of interest in participating, Colonel Gibson explained that his was not a volunteer concurrence in this event. His performance would be judged by the officials selected to do so just as the other chefs would be. The Colonel added that he would be very proud if his own ranch was represented with at least a respectful showing. Scotty agreed a little hesitantly and Colonel Gibson placated his old attendant by agreeing to encourage the captains of each herd to pick a team for a more work related competition of riding and roping. He would take personal charge of the boxing matches. The Colonel also fancied his own prowess as master of the art of fisticuffs. Although his prime laid years in the past, his enjoyment of the sport thrived still. Satisfied by the Colonel's discourse, Scotty threw himself into the match with the tenacity known only to the Scottish. He prepared his S.O.B. stew from the throw away parts of a fat two year old heifer that had been swept up somewhere along the trail. He'd had her slaughtered especially for his first entry. He skillfully cleaned and cut up the sweetbreads; intestines, kidneys, liver, and added the brains and heart. A variety of vegetables some seasonings and a little flour for thickening finished this S.O.B. stew to a delightful perfection. It was so well received and enjoyed by all who partook of this magnificent treatment of bovine by-products that Scotty's involvement in the contest became so enthusiastic as to raise his standing to a front runner.

Dustin had a secret favorite among the camp cooks in the personage of Big Bill Dixson. Big Bill was a former slave that, like many others, fought along side his master during the war. His devotion to the land of the plantation he'd called home for many years was a reminder that the horrible war dividing this country was not a human rights issue. It was, as it always is, a matter of money. The south's textile industries had developed a tremendous market with Europe, France in particular. The government in Washington felt slighted and began raising taxes at an unreasonable rate. The southern textile states were outraged by these exorbitant taxes and aligned in a confederation of states protesting this greed inspired assessment. The slavery issue was just easier to sell the general northern populous and was not even brought up until well into the conflict.

Big Bill, along with thousands of slaves, stayed loyal to his plantation even after the war. Many remained on the property they'd lived and worked on their entire lives only leaving when the Yankee carpetbaggers of the reclamation sold off the land in pieces, forcing the tenant slaves to leave their homes, many with no place to go and no idea of how to make it on their own. Big Bill knew how to work and moved west, angered by the treatment of the southerners, who had been his only family, by the northern aggressors. Big Bill had worked as a cowboy, buffalo hunter, barman and dug graves for an undertaker on his way west. He was working in a restaurant as a cook when Colonel Gibson hired him to join this drive and take charge on one of the wagons.

Dustin enjoyed talking to Big Bill about the south that was and many other things about Big Bill's past not known to anyone else on the drive. Mostly Dustin enjoyed Big Bill's bread! Big Bill could make dutch oven bread like no one else in the world. He made good hearty meals of course but the principal event at the fire of Big Bill's chuck wagon was the ever present ovens full of fresh baked breads and yeast rolls that filled the air with a euphoric aroma that absolutely no one could or did resist. Big Bill took real pride in his breads and rolls but his biscuits were absolutely his life's love. No one has ever made lighter, more delicious breakfast fare than that which came from the ovens of Big Bill Dixson. Dustin, regardless where he'd slept, found himself more often than not at the chuck wagon of Big Bill come breakfast time.

The contest and trip agreed with Dustin. He was getting stronger and growing steadily. Already a large lad, he was becoming even more massive as the trip progressed. The excursion was having the opposite effect on the Colonel. He had been steadily thinning down. He had been a little too lethargic a little too long, he was fond of saying now he spent almost no time riding in the wagon. He'd get horseback soon after breakfast and only dismount to eat or to change horses until dark. He did sleep in the ambulance except on extremely warm nights when it was a little too stuffy inside.

Everything rolled along well. There were no stampedes, like so many wild west novelists write about. No ten days and nights in the saddle with only weak coffee and cold beans. No getting soaking wet and cold from unexpected falling weather. None of the sleeping in wet beds in muddy clothes and no freezing on night herd in the higher country. These obvious conditions of nature were all thought of and prepared for before the trip started. Dustin had left nothing to chance. Anything needed other than the stores on hand was merely sent for from the nearest fort.

The most difficult part of the trip for the cowboys was in the choosing which horses to match race against the other herd's best mounts. Many pre-race matches were held during the course of the drive. It was not at all unusual to see two or three riders traveling along side by side and suddenly race to some point in the distance. This done solely for the purpose of determining the most likely candidate for the forth coming races to be held each Sunday.

Another quite interesting sight was to be observed after supper at any given wagon. Several men would simply walk to the edge of the fire light and two would pair off and proceed to knock the hell out of one another. Several of the men watching, who had usually established themselves as expert judges of the manly art of self defense, would critique each fighter's style and power as to his potential as camp champion. There were to be three weight classes in the drive championships; heavyweight, anything over about one hundred seventy-five pounds; middle weight, from around one hundred forty-five to one hundred seventy-five; and light weight, anything under one hundred forty-five. All weights estimated of course. For now these preliminary campsite fisticuffs were catch as catch can. It was not unusual to witness a little bandy rooster weighing all of one hundred twenty pounds sparing with a hulk of a brute going near two hundred stripped. It was all in good fun and absolutely no anger or excessive violence would be tolerated, whatsoever.

This entire drive was for the most part self governing. On the rare occasion when a dispute arose the men could not handle by themselves, Colonel Gibson would hold court and decide the matter. His decisions were final and no appeal was available. This was seldom necessary as some sort of inequality or deprivation is usually responsible for civil problems. On this drive there was no prejudice or lack of anything that might stimulate unseemly behavior on the part of even the most uncivilized cowhand.

The closest thing to a criminal act occurred at near the midway point of the trip, and came in the form of an unexpected act of violence perpetrated by one of the chuck wagon sovereigns, Hank. Hank was in every aspect the typical camp cook. He looked and acted the part to the measure of perfection. He was a quite, proficient, potentate of the pots. In fact, Hank could do everything the other four meal monarch's could. Hank's aggravation was that each of his rivals had a specialty and he hadn't, as yet, come up with the one thing that set him ahead of the others.

Just above Fort Sumner, General Stewart, along with Captain Perron and troops, were to meet the herd and stay a few days with the drovers. Stewart was going to wait until delivery to take a look at this moving multitude on the hoof but in his excitement could not abstain. He'd sent riders south to intercept Dustin and ask if he would be offended by his visit. His message assured Dustin this was not to be an official inspection, rather a social occasion. The General added that if his visit would not be considered an intrusion he'd be delighted to bring along the company band and provide entertainment in way of a concert. Dustin sent return word by the messenger that they would all be delighted to have them. He briefly explained the approximate location the herd would be on the date the General would arrive. Dustin requested, if possible, that someone get word to the Morton family south of the Fort as to the herd's location in case any one of them wanted to ride out with the General when he came. Lastly, Dustin gave a list of store goods to give the Quartermaster to fill and send back out with the General's party. This all done, Dustin consulted with Colonel Gibson about the best way to fairly handle duties and social activities among the men and camps.

"By God, we'll just have us a juxtaposition!" Colonel Gibson said.

"Have a what?" Dustin asked.

"We'll just put everything side by side or maybe in a big circle with all the wagons in the middle. That'll work great. Then the ol' cooks can all throw something special together and the Army can set up in the center of the fires. The men can work short shifts and rotate often and won't none of them miss much. I'll get the word to the captains and have them work out a schedule so everyone can take part in the fun."

"What did you call it, Colonel? Adjustinposition?" Dustin teased the old timer.

"Juxtaposition! You smart ass. You'd think that before you learned to speak eight foreign languages you would have learned to speak your own properly," Colonel Gibson said jokingly.

The big get together was the talk of the drive for the next few days. Arrangements were made for horse races, boxing matches and of course the cook off.

This brings us back to Hank. All the men of the drive were making preparation for the General's arrival. Dustin rode ahead and found a likely spot to set the camp and night herd the cattle without mixing them. He choose a little knoll surrounded by long sloping shoulders running to the river on one side and far off toward the horizon on the opposite. When Dustin had it all laid out, Colonel Gibson ordered the captains to move the cattle around. This hold up was in the configuration of a wagon wheel with the chuck wagons in the center as the hub. The country was filled with tall grasses and being near water Dustin could hold his cattle for close to a week if necessary. It would not be, as General Stewart was due to arrive the next afternoon. Dustin had Colonel Gibson organize all the fun and games to be held for the benefit of their soon expected company.

The Colonel was really in his element; horse races, boxing matches, chuck wagon cook off, a cutting exhibition, roping events and an accidental encounter with a herd of wild mustangs added a bronc riding. The bronc riding was going to be omitted for want of any real bucking stock, but these wild horses would provide ample excitement for even the most reckless natured cowboy in camp. By this point in the drive all the saddle stock was broke and riding well, much to the disappointment of the more accomplished bronc busters in the crew. This find of a small herd of wild horses was the delight of the boys to an extraordinary extent. So much in fact, many volunteered to work their off shift keeping the wild ones gathered until they were needed for the bronc riding exhibition.

This brings us back to Hank once again. Now old Hank, our fifth chuck wagon cook, had chased wild horses many years before and had more first hand knowledge of the ins and outs of handling the spooking rascals than any man in camp. He of course offered a great deal of advice on the subject to those of his camp actually involved in their capture and containment. The real trouble started early the next morning, the day General Stewart was to arrive in camp. The boys intended to separate the horses they would use in the bronc riding contest from the main herd of mares with small foals. Contrary to the stories the boys had heard, there were several young stallions in the bunch along with the obviously dominant stud, a mousy colored gruilla about ten years old. These young, wild, strong juveniles were to be participants in the main event of the camp meeting. Other than being held under a rather loose guard by an exorbitant number of horsemen, the entire herd of wild ones were left unmolested until they would be needed.

Hank was officially declared consultant major for the handling of the wild horse herd. He took his honorary position very seriously and dedicated much time to the instructing of procedures necessary to accomplish the desired outcome with these frail nerved creatures. The push came when Hank was late returning to his chuck wagon from checking on the wild horse herd. He returned to find Scotty, the Colonel's personal cook, digging around in his chuckbox. Hank didn't let anyone prowl through his wagon. He'd not have stood still for even the Colonel rummaging around in his things like this damn fool Scotsman was. The closer Hank got the faster he walked. As he passed the fire he grabbed a long, heavy pot hook.

Just as he reached the table of the chuckbox, Scotty who was on his knees on the thing asked, "Hank, where in the hell do you keep your spices? I need to borrow some and can't find them."

Hank never said a word but laid poor Scotty out with the pot hook, striking him a terrible blow across the back of his head. Scotty fell as if dead. He was bleeding profusely from the open wound left by the bludgeon. Several witnesses ran to Scotties aid and restrained Hank, preventing him from applying a second dose of his peculiar remedy for meddling in his private kingdom.

The Army medic who had been with the current military guard traveling this leg of the drive, was called to assist Scotty by sewing his head wound closed and to help him regain consciousness as well as his sight. Colonel Gibson was also called to see what should be done with or to Hank. The Colonel was at first livid, then being the consummate leader and official judge of the drive calmed to a controlled vexation. Once the Colonel had everyone seated in a very judiciary manner he began his discourse.

"The wrong which has been committed here must be punished and expeditiously so. This is a crime, which because of its severity, mandates summary discipline of an equal severity. Do you all agree?" Colonel Gibson addressed the assembly and waited for a response to his question.

The entire gathering agreed something should be done to discourage such behavior. Colonel Gibson started speaking about the kind of punishment that should be rendered in this case when Hank suddenly stood and spoke clearly and deliberately to the simulated court.

"I appreciate your support, gentlemen but I've been thinking that poor old Scotty has probably learned his lesson already. I gave him a right smart blow with that pot hook. I don't believe he'll be misbehaving no more. We should just let him go." Then he turned and just walked away leaving everyone speechless.

The Colonel spoke up, "Now that my friend is a prime example of self delusion, I do not believe that any punishment we could legally prescribe would have the desired result on that gentleman. Court adjourned."

Scotty eventually got better but had to miss the big festival held in honor of General Stewart. Scotty sat on the sidelines and instructed his swamper who did an admirable job filling in as wagon cook. Scotty or no one else ever impugned the sanctity of Hank's mobile kitchen again. Except for the slightly unnerving appearance of Scotty sitting around staring off into space with his head wrapped up like a Hindu holy man, all was fun and games for the festival.

General Stewart arrived on time and in a grand manner of military splendor displayed a magnificent exhibition of precision drill work, cavalry style. Having been made aware of the festivities to be held, Captain Perron organized a team of participants for each event and also brought several top marksmen and sharpshooters to put on a demonstration and compete against any of the cowboys who might be interested in testing their skills with fire arms against the United States Army's finest.

Much to Dustin's disappointment, Ned didn't come along nor did any of the Mortons. Ned had apparently become moody and short tempered. He was even having a little problem with liquor. He was currently spending thirty days as a guest of the government in the stockade. Ned had gotten drunk, again, and started shooting the pictures of the President and his staff that hung in the post Officers Club. He'd been getting steadily worse since the encounter at Raton Pass. Captain Perron could only hope Ned was able to pull himself together soon.

The bright spot among the General's entourage was his heavy weight contender, Sergeant Major Michaels. Dustin, very much out of character, ran and jumped into the big man's arms and hollered like a nut, embarrassing Big Mike much to the pleasure of both General Stewart and Captain Perron.

"What you doin' here Mike?" Dustin asked as Big Mike finally got loose from the kid.

"I came to participate in the events representing my company," Big Mike said proudly.

"Damn Mike, you better reconsider. We got some pretty good cooks with us on this drive," Dustin joked.

"I didn't come to cook, you damn fool kid. I came as a pugilist!" again very proudly.

"I don't think we got none of them, Mike. At least none that would be near your weight category," Dustin said still being quite silly and poking Big Mike's ample middle section with his finger.

"What weight class you in now big fellow? Percheron?" Dustin couldn't keep from thinking himself very clever.

"Captain Perron, sir, did you happen to notice anything resembling a wood shed here abouts? Me and the Lad here are going to be needing one quite promptly," Big Mike asked as he kicked the smart aleck kid's behind with an enormous booted foot.

Everyone present participated in at least one event. Even General Stewart entered in the pistol competition and placed very highly. Captain Perron ran a horse in one of the many races and won. Big Mike only had two men who would accommodate him in a boxing match and everyone is sure they'll both be all right again, eventually. The cooking was splendid for the entire event and all the chefs were honored by declaring the contest a draw. Colonel Gibson made it clear that this little competition in no way influenced the out come of the on going contest among the cooks. He would determine the over all winner at trails end.

Dustin had a wonderful time and entered several events. He didn't fare too well in any of them but he had a great time anyway. His timing had been poor and cost him dearly. He had signed up for the middleweight boxing matches and promptly got his eyes both beat shut by a horse soldier with hands of steel and the speed of a cobra. Dustin's next event was the target pistol shoot in which he'd placed much hope as he was an expert shot. His vision was so impeded by the thrashing he'd just taken he was unable to compete to any standard of proficiency acceptable to his liking so he was forced to forfeit. Next, he tried his hand at the bronc riding. His draw was a good one, a large barren mare about eight years old. She was roped out of the hold up and stretched out, blind folded and saddled. Dustin stepped on and pulled the blind fold. This mare went crazy. It looked like Dustin was making the winning ride when things went south in a hurry. The mare in one wild effort to shake this unwanted passenger from her back, kicked madly while in mid flight. Her hind hoof kicking Dustin's right foot out of the stirrup causing him to nearly fall off. He was trying to maintain his seat and gather the stirrup with his foot when the mare hit on her front feet and sucked backwards. This threw Dustin down over her head and as he was going down, she threw her head upwards striking Dustin squarely in the face with the poll of her head. He wasn't knocked out but he was knocked off, disqualifying him from this event also. He roped well and did place in one heat of the horse races but mainly Dustin was simply an also ran. He had as much fun as anyone there and except for the mare breaking his nose and loosening several teeth, added to his already blackened eyes, he never felt so good or so happy.

Colonel Gibson and General Stewart had a shoot off for the championship in the pistol contest. Dustin was absolutely amazed at the proficiency with which each of these two men handled their weapons. The contest eventually rose to the next level and had moving targets. Still each man continued without a miss. Finally it was suggested that the men get horseback to finish the contest and perhaps break the tie. This suggestion was made by a cavalry officer who knew General Stewart was as at ease mounted as standing and thought to gain an edge.

Colonel Gibson smiled widely and agreed saying, "My young friend, you too quickly assume that an old man such as myself would not be as at home in the saddle as your beloved leader, General Stewart. Still I will in no way take your suggestion as a slight toward myself. I will accept your proposal even though it will be greatly to my advantage. You see, young man, I learned to fire this fine Virginia made pistol while riding a wonderful Georgia bred stallion pursing northern intruders I was driving off my families land. I can only assume and hope many of whom were relatives of yours!"

General Stewart spoke up apologetically, "Colonel Gibson, I beg your forgiveness for my young officers indelicate manner. I'm sure his intention was innocent enough. Let us continue our contest in the proper spirit."

"Certainly General Stewart. After you, Sir," Colonel Gibson responded.

The contest continued with one of the most impressive displays of pistol mastery ever seen. The contest went steadily for another thirty minutes without a miss by either marksman. The difficulty level had been increased to a ridiculous extreme which had the contestants galloping in a large circle shooting at moving targets on both the inside and outside of the circle. They shot for a total of two hundred sixty three rounds each. The last shots were fired in groups of six by each man as he circled in a fast lope. On the last turn, General Stewart's horse stumbled as he pulled off the sixth round and he missed the target.

The horse had not fallen completely down and General Stewart regained his balance and reined his mount to a stop next to the judges and Colonel Gibson and then said, "The field is yours, Sir. Good shooting."

Colonel Gibson not to be out gentlemened answered, "Sir, your horse misstepped. Please feel free to repeat your last turn."

General Stewart always a master of diplomacy said, "I'll stand by my effort, Sir. Luck alone has carried me this far. I would feel foolish showing contempt now that my luck has weakened. Please proceed."

"Very well, General Stewart. Before I do, I would like to say that you, sir, are quite possibly the finest pistol shot I have ever seen. It has truly been a pleasure watching you perform," General Gibson declared then started his circle.

He fired five rapid shots without a miss. The crowd was silently watching in awe the finale of this wonderful contest. Suddenly and very unexpectedly Colonel Gibson pulled his horse to a sliding stop and reared him almost perpendicular to the ground and giving a rebel yell fired his sixth shot into the air straight above his head, paused a poignant moment then declared, "You men have witnessed quite a shooting exhibition that has just officially ended in a tie. There will be no tie breaker held. Congratulations, General Stewart, you sir, are truly a winner."

"Thank you Colonel. You sir, are a gentleman and a hell of a shot as well. Now let us go see how the cooks are doing," General Stewart said and everyone applauded the two men's efforts.

The cooks, except for Scotty, held a pow wow right after Hank's trial, which he still thought was Scotty's. Hank and Fighting Joe had a large pit dug and slaughtered a three year old steer. They cut the beef into large chunks or roasts, added salt and pepper, wrapped the roasts in burlap and placed them into the pit on top of a deep layer of hot coals. Then they covered the pit with an air tight seal of dirt. They had put the meat into the pit the evening before the party and when removed from the ground the roasts were as tender and succulent as any ever offered. While Hank and Fighting Joe were busy with the meat, Big Bill and Mr. Harris were equally active with the preparation of the bread and pies for the feast. The cavalry cook, Sergeant Riggs, enlisted the aid of Scotty's helper Manuel and used Scotty's wagon as a base to prepare the rice and stewed tomatoes and the more recently introduced pinto beans and green chili, grown locally and finding an ever more popular place in the military fare.

The three teams of cooks prepared one unified banquet of culinary delights usually unknown on this wild frontier. Everyone ate in shifts and the band played continually after completing their meal on the first shift. As soon as everyone had eaten, General Stewart had his orderlies retrieve many cases of fine Bourbon whisky he'd brought along with him from the fort for this special occasion.

Dustin felt awkward for a moment until Colonel Gibson spoke up, "Our executive officer has proclaimed this a dry drive, General. I feel that do to the festive nature of this occasion we might persuade him to make a singular exception in honor of the evening at hand."

General Stewart spoke up instantly, "I'm very impressed, Dustin. That is without a question the most intelligent policy I've ever heard of being implemented with a group of little boys masquerading around in men's bodies. If in fact the Army could invoke and enforce such a rule, we could run the world. I leave the consumption of this gift to your obviously superior judgment, Dustin."

"I can see that you two orators have conspired against me. I surrender to older if not wiser minds and remove the injunction for the remainder of the evening. General Stewart please take charge of dispensing the libations as you see fit, and Sir, please do not overlook me. I do occasionally enjoy a good stiff drink even at my tender age. Remember gentlemen, that just because I know the dangers of liquor to the success of this drive, does not mean I'm opposed to its recreational consumption," Dustin stated.

"Well said, well said indeed," said Colonel Gibson.

"Yes, quite so, young Dustin," added General Stewart then had his men open the cases and lay them in a small circle just outside the huge fire located in the hub of the wagon wheel shaped camp.

The band played and everyone sang along. Shifts were taken often so that all could enjoy the music and imbibe a little. This was the first alcohol these men had consumed in several months. This was difficult for some of the cowboys as they were practicing alcoholics before this drive began.

Dustin was enjoying himself as was everyone else and had two rather large drams of the General's private stock. Dustin developed a warm feeling inside and was glad to see the men having even more fun than they had been having daily, if in fact that was possible. It did seem to Dustin that too many men were at the concert and not enough out with the herds so he decided to make a circle around the entire hold up and make sure everything was all right out there. Dustin was becoming a little melancholy anyway thinking of his darling Cindy, hoping she was well and wondering why she had not returned home. He was also a little sad and surprised his foster family hadn't made the short trip out to see him. He'd liked to have seen little Wesley and Matt and to see Kathy again.

The cattle were resting well after having been grazed all day and watered off well before being bedded down. Dustin's only concern was there was only a few men keeping the herds separated from one another. They had been pushed closely together in order to allow less men to encircle them than normally were necessary. Dustin thought this was a sorry display of judgment on the part of the captains of each herd as all were very short handed. The men could have taken shorter turns riding herd and still had ample fun while not neglecting the responsibility of the cattle. Even the remuda of saddle horses and wagon teams were under the watch of just two men both of whom had obviously already been into camp at least once by their state of insobriety. Dustin would take each captain aside and make sure they fully understood his concern and took the proper precautions to avoid a crisis with the cattle.

Dustin continued his circle and found everything uniformly unacceptable. The bull herd had mixed with the cow herd which had been far behind it until the wagon wheel was laid out. Dustin was so mad at this oversight he headed straight back into camp. He knew they'd be two day's sorting out the cows and the bulls. As he got closer to camp he calmed some, realizing it was late enough in the year to let the bulls run with the cows anyway. The boys were due a little blow out and nothing had really gone wrong. The two herds could just be divided in half and no harm done.

When Dustin got closer to the camp, he heard quite a row. As he rode into the camp itself, someone pulled him off his horse and hit him square in his already broken nose. Dustin jumped up and faced a drunken cavalry corporal quite on the hook. Dustin tried to ask what the hell was going on but before he could, he saw that the entire camp was in turmoil. It was in all appearance a riot! Everyone was participating in a brawl the likes few have ever seen. It was all very civilized as no one was using or attempting to use any weapons. It was simply fisticuffs except for the cooks who were wielding skillets and of course old Hank's pot hooks.

Dustin ducked another blow thrown recklessly by the inebriated Corporal and dropped the gentleman with a powerful right hook of his own. Dustin then tried to make his way toward the officers. He was quite worried about their safety and was hurrying to where he'd left them. He was overwhelmed to see upon his arrival, General Stewart and Colonel Gibson exchanging punches while Captain Perron was futilely trying to keep them apart. The most remarkable sight of all was Sgt. Major Michaels and the huge black cook, Big Bill standing toe to toe delivering blows to one another that would have killed lesser men.

Dustin ran over and grabbed Colonel Gibson and Captain Perron then took hold of General Stewart.

"Colonel, look at Big Bill!" Dustin shouted.

Captain Perron parroted his excitement when he saw the ferocity of the fight transpiring near at hand.

"General! Quit fighting and look over there. Sgt. Major Michaels may have met his match, Sir."

"What? Hell Captain, he only had two challengers and their both still unconscious!" Stewart said.

Things started to settle down as more people stopped their own minor fights to observe these really super human specimens physically abuse one another in an unbelievable manner. Soon every man that could stand with or without help was gathered around the two pugilists, watching this fight to end all fights.

After a few moments, Dustin asked Captain Perron what the hell had happened here.

"After everyone became a little more than slightly inebriated, someone started proposing toasts. One followed another and soon some damn fool toasted the Union. It seems Colonel Gibson took offense and toasted General Lee. What you see before you is the result of those toasts," Perron explained.

Several more minutes passed and all had become absolutely quiet. They were all enthralled at the spectacle before them. These two giants were settling the differences between all these men in a manner so absolute as to hold sway over all the little insignificant disputes previously on going between individuals. These representative combatants were debating opposite sides of an issue that had caused a civil war. They were doing so in a manner befitting kings. General Stewart and Colonel Gibson, friendly again, communally decided that all wars should be decided in such a way. The entire assembly was huddled around the fighters and after almost an hour, Big Bill suddenly stepped back and extended a huge black hand and Sgt. Major Michaels reciprocated in like manner.

"What the hell's going on here, Sgt. Major?" General Stewart demanded.

"Well Sir, me and me new friend, Big Bill here could see things were getting a little out of hand," Sergeant Major Michaels said and then Big Bill continued, "We couldn't see no other way to get things calmed down so we just figured

83

we'd cause a little row of our own and show you how it is supposed to be done so's you'd all see how silly you looked poking at each other like little children."

Sgt. Major Michaels then added, "It looked to us like you amateurs were having a little trouble with your liquor, Sir and the whole thing was a pitiful display, indeed just pitiful."

Then Big Bill again, "Come on my big Yank friend. I'll buy you a proper drink. I've got a pot of good strong coffee boiling at my chuck wagon."

The two Titans were joined by both commanding officers and their staffs following as the two walked away arm in arm apparently no worse for the wear, leaving everyone present a little stupefied.

Dustin gathered as many nearly sober cowhands as he could find to go back out with him to the herd. Things were a little hard to evaluate at night but Dustin didn't think they were as bad as they could have been. Two of the herds had no guards at all and had wandered off a ways but not too far. Dustin told his half drunk, half beat up crew to just hold everything until good daylight. After breakfast they could separate out five herds and get on the move again. At least that was Dustin's plan.

When he rode in at daylight, the camp was astir with excitement. There were new soldiers there talking to General Stewart. Dustin rode directly to the gathering and heard that Nacatan had resurfaced and was on a spree of murder and terror worse than ever before. He'd somehow put together misfit renegades from several tribes to follow him. This was the most disconcerting news of all. One of the main reasons the military had held sway over the many Indian tribes of the frontier was that they would not join their forces. Many tribes had fought each other for generations. They had the same language barriers and even cultural differences as separate nations normally do and no desire to unite against the white man, at least not so far. This new band of Nacatan's could prove to be a very dangerous experiment indeed. General Stewart ordered his men to be ready to leave within the hour. Nacatan must be stopped immediately. He had already raided the village near the fort and was even more savage in his treatment of his victims than a civilized nation could imagine.

"Sir, is there any word as to the well being of the Morton family?" Dustin asked General Stewart.

"No but their place lies directly in the path Nacatan came north on. It wouldn't surprise me if they'd been visited by him this time. We'll check on them and try to get word back to you," the General said obviously worried.

"General, I'm a scout and speak most of the languages of these renegades. I'd like to go with you. I believe I could help," Dustin said.

"We'd love to have you, Dustin. What about the drive? This is very important also," General Stewart reminded him.

"Colonel Gibson can keep everything running smoothly while I'm gone. I'll catch up to them farther north. You'll be all right, won't you Colonel?" Dustin asked.

"We'll be fine, Dustin. You've got us all lined out here. I've got the maps you marked and plenty of provisions to make the trip. We'll stop by the forts along the way just like you have and I'll treat the Indians fairly as we go," the Colonel assured Dustin.

"Colonel keep your battle eye open. Watch out for this band of fighters. You have enough weapons and ammunition to hold off a full scale attack if you can see it coming. It will be your good judgment that gets these cattle through now. You don't want to make enemys of the friendly tribes and don't want your throat cut by the renegades. Good luck Colonel, I'll catch up as soon as we've got Nacatan killed or caught," Dustin said and rode off with Captain Perron who would be in command of this operation.

Colonel Gibson decided to hold the herd on these wonderful grazing grounds until he had them put back into traveling order. He had the men commence cutting the herds back into shape by classification and only then did he give the order to head on north. This unexplained delay may have saved the lives of the entire company. Two days north the scouts Colonel Gibson had riding point came running back into the herd with rather disturbing news. A huge band of Indians all mounted on unshod ponies had crossed their course just ahead. The scouts estimated their number to near six or seven hundred. Must be some kind of war party or a council being held somewhere. No women or children, no one walking anyway. The scouts sent a man to follow the trail at a safe distance to see where they were headed. They appeared to be traveling fast to the east, northeast for some distant point.

"I hope it's real distant!" Colonel Gibson said at this news.

The Colonel sent a pair of riders to tell General Stewart what they'd seen. He kept thinking how if the herd had been moving instead of stopped regrouping the cattle, the dust from the drive would have given them away. It was unsettling to say the least, how close they came to sure disaster. He had all the perimeter men start carrying the rifles Dustin had obtained. They were heavy and awkward but were necessary. After crossing the deep trail the Indian warriors had left in the soft earth, not a man complained of the weight or inconvenience of the weapon. Not another sign of an Indian was seen by the drive except a few beggars about a week north of the big trail they'd crossed. Colonel Gibson offered these poor indigents a beef but they settled instead for a good meal, some coffee and tobacco. They were apparently just vagabonds without a village to support and had no need for an entire beef. These were the only Indians the drive came into contact with, Dustin was not so lucky.

Chapter 9

Once back at the fort Dustin went directly to his old home at the Morton's. They had not been assaulted by Nacatan or even seen him. They had been nervously watching out for him and had lost some stock from the end of the ranch that had been Dustin's fathers. Jim Morton had suffered a mild stroke, leaving him quite limited in what he could do. Matt had taken on the responsibility of the place and was trying to sell out and move into town. He had his eye on the cantina near the fort. He felt his family would be safer in town and he would be happier working indoors.

"Is the cantina for sale, Matt?" Dustin asked.

"Yes it is, to me anyway. Old Juan and I made friends. I worked with him before Dad got sick. If I could sell this place, I could buy the cantina and the little house behind it. With all the Indian trouble we're having, I can't give this place away let alone sell it," Matt confided.

"Look Matt, I've got real lucky and have some money and a lot of credit with the Army on those cows. I'll sign the note. You go buy the house and cantina. Give Old Juan what he wants for them and I'll leave a letter of credit at the fort for you to help with expenses until you get it fixed up the way you want," Dustin stated very adamantly.

"Hell Dustin, I can't let you do that after all Cindy's done to you already," Matt said apologetically.

"You can't stop me from helping you, Matt. If it'll make you feel better I'll just buy the ranch from you and you won't owe me anything. How's that sound to you?" Dustin asked trying to spare Matt's pride a little.

"Damn it Dustin, this place is half yours already. I can't sell it to you," Matt protested.

"Hell, I'll buy the other half. Now quit arguing and I'll help you move into town."

Dustin was pleased with how little Kathy was helping her mom with her dad's care and little Wesley and all the chores too. She was quite a girl. She told Dustin she thought Cindy was stupid for not coming back to him. She thought he was wonderful and Cindy didn't deserve him.

"Well she's got me anyway, Kathy. She'll come around someday, you'll see. She is just seeing the world a little, I guess. I'll be waiting for her when she decides to come back," Dustin said with a hope only known to those deeply blinded by love.

"I still think she's stupid! She should be here with you, Dustin. I would never treat you like she did," Kathy said her young girlish crush showing quite openly.

"Thank you, Kathy. I know you wouldn't. You will find the right man someday and he'll sure be a lucky guy too. Come on I want to give you something."

Dustin led little Kathy, now near sixteen and not so very little at all, out to where his horse was tied.

"Kathy, I want you to have Peso. He's a sure enough good horse and you'll need your own mount so you can ride out here once in a while and check on my place for me. I'd like you to make sure it's still here for me if I ever need it, O.K.?" Dustin said more as a reason for her to need the horse than really caring if the place got carried off or not.

"Oh yes, Dustin, I'll watch it closely. I was going to miss it awfully. I love it here. It's the only home I can remember. I wasn't sure I could ever leave it but now I can still come out and see it for you. Thank you Dustin, thank you so much for the wonderful horse and for, for, ... well for everything!" Kathy said eyes full of happy tears.

She gave him a big hug and kissed him full on the lips.

"Holy shit!" Dustin said. "Oh, I'm sorry Kathy, I meant to say, Wow! You been doing some growing up while I was gone. Matt and your mom are going to have their hands full with you that close to the fort and all them young soldiers around," Dustin said still a little out of breath from the passion in Kathy's kiss.

"I don't care about them soldiers. Nobody's going to have to worry about me. I'll behave myself until the right man finally figures out he's come along," Kathy said very womanly.

"What? Damn it Kathy, sometimes I hear your words but have no idea what you're saying! Now tell me again, do you like Peso and will you watch my place for me?" Dustin asked teasingly.

"Yes and yes! Now did you understand that Mr. Dustin Thomas?" Kathy said and again gave Dustin a quick kiss, on the cheek this time, and then ran into the house telling everyone about her new horse.

Dustin went in also and sat by Jim Morton's chair where he spent most of his time just staring out the window. It looks as if he was looking at nothing but Dustin knew he was staring

back through time at a life hard but well lived. Dustin and Jim Morton always had understood one another better than anyone else in either family had been able to. Now was no different. Dustin sat silently next to his father's old friend and gave what comfort he could by just being there.

After a while Jim looked at Dustin and with tear filled eyes spoke with great difficulty and much effort as clearly as he could manage, "Thank you for helping Matt. He never liked the ranch. He'll do better in town. I'm very sorry about Cindy. The way she's doing you breaks my heart. I wouldn't have blamed you if you never spoke to us again and here you are helping us out one more time. You are a good man, Dustin Thomas. Your father would be very proud of you."

Dustin patted the man's shoulder and said, "You all are my family. I will always do anything I can for you. Cindy has done nothing to me I have not allowed her to do. I'll do more until she returns home to me. She is going to be my wife and I'll not stop helping her or you ever," Dustin stated then turned with a start at the sound of sobbing and someone running out of the room.

He hadn't seen her but Kathy had just entered carrying little Wesley. She heard Dustin's declaration about Cindy as she entered, it was too much for her to hold in.

"Damn it! Seems like I'm always hurting someone's feelings," Dustin said more to himself than to Jim.

"Dustin, Kathy cares for you very much, probably more than any of us knows. She's young, she'll be all right," he replied and weakly placed his hand on Dustin's and smiled the half smile the stroke left him with.

Dustin took the Morton family into town and helped set up house. He then had to get to work as he was greatly needed to help find Nacatan and his warriors. He reported to Captain Perron ready for duty and was distressed by the report of the large movement by the Indians.

"What do you think this means, Dustin?" Captain Perron asked.

"I am a little afraid to guess, Captain. For several years I've heard about an Indian Messiah coming to unite the tribes and lead them to victory against the whites. I hope like hell they haven't come up with one. It will change things considerably," Dustin speculated.

"Yes, I'm afraid it would. Go to the Indian villages where you are known and see what you can find out. Get word back to me a.s.a.p." Perron ordered.

"Yes sir, Captain. I'll be gone about two weeks. Here, I'll draw you a map of my approximate location in case you need me sooner," Dustin said as he drew out the lay of the land and his approximate route to the villages.

Dustin visited many villages and only saw a handful of braves of fighting age. He'd made friends long before with these bands of friendly Indians and was well received. No talk was made as to the whereabouts of all the men. The first three camps Dustin went to were with the same results. The fourth encampment was different. They were packing everything up. A young buck had just returned to bring the village back with him. The Indians had gathered in large numbers in the Dakotas. Thousands of Indians from numerous tribes had come together to throw themselves against the onslaught of the white encroachment.

All the great chiefs were in agreement as to this being the only way. The warriors needed their families to join them. There was no telling how long this action would last. Dustin helped his Indian friends roll up their lodges and prepare for their journey. He feigned no interest or concern in their destination or motivation for their trip.

Once they were on their way, Dustin cut short his tour and proceeded, with great haste, back to Captain Perron. Dustin made a full written report and turned it over to Perron. The Captain realizing the importance of this information had Dustin go with him to confer with General Stewart.

"Well done, Dustin. Well done! I'll send runners to the telegraph and we'll put this into the hands of those high profile, political wannabes in the north and let them deal with it. I'll get word to Washington as well. They'll need to reconsider their whole policy in dealing with the Indians. We might get this whole mess settled now. Dustin, the government will have to deal with these people as a nation now," General Stewart declared.

Dustin was surprised at the sympathetic nature General Stewart showed toward the Indians. Most military men felt all the Indians should be annihilated.

"Has Nacatan joined the others, Dustin?" Captain Perron asked.

"I don't know, Sir," Dustin answered shortly.

"What do you mean?" General Stewart asked.

"I have no positive information as to Nacatan's whereabouts. My source has not seen him or his band. I just don't know, Sir," Dustin explained.

"Can you find out where he is?" Captain Perron questioned.

"I'll try, Sir. I came in with the news of the joining of the tribes thinking it was most urgent," Dustin explained further.

"Certainly it was. Well done, Dustin. It would be of great assistance if we could locate Nacatan. If he's still here, people are at risk. If he's going to join the counsel, he might have an even more damaging effect on the outcome of the meeting of the Great Chiefs. His will not be a vote for peace," General Stewart finished looking far out across the distance toward the direction of the Dakota's feeling some foreboding feeling in his soul he could not fully explain, nor did he try.

Dustin left immediately after talking to his friend Big Mike, about how to find a little camp he'd once showed Dustin. Many bandits and renegades laid overnight at it's reliable fresh water source. It's location also offered a clear view of the approachers to this hidden refuge. Dustin thought he might gain some information by laying out and watching who came and went from the little refuge. He got his instructions and a large telescope from Big Mike. Dustin had known how to get to the camp but needed to know how to get near enough to watch it without being seen himself. Big Mike came through as usual with enough detailed description of the area to not only refresh Dustin's memory as to its location but enough to familiarize him with the area as to give him the confidence necessary to attempt this dangerous mission.

Mike had volunteered to go along with Dustin immediately. Captain Perron felt Big Mike's presence would be too risky. Dustin could blend in with the desperate crowd if he needed to in order to gain the necessary information enabling him to locate Nacatan and his warriors. Big Mike, on the other hand, was relatively famous in the area. His value undercover would be limited at best. Captain Perron said he might be able to send Big Mike undercover someday, if he ever needed an undercover preacher, because the church house would be the only building in town he wouldn't be recognized in.

Dustin took with him the intelligence offered him by his big Irish friend and headed out. Three days hard ride placed Dustin on the ridge over looking the camp. Big Mike's help had already paid off. The camp was occupied and Dustin's approach would have been surely noticed, possibly with fatal results. From his vantage point atop this the highest ridge, Dustin was able to see down into the canyon where the spring and camp lie. The powerful telescope he'd borrowed allowed Dustin, while at a safe distance, to look down into the camp and clearly identify its occupants. Big Mike had warned him of possible detection from the suns glare on the lens so Dustin was extremely careful with the scope and was able to watch undetected until dark. This group was just a bunch of common thieves and probably not privy to any real knowledge of importance. Dustin relocated for the night, just on the chance he'd been seen during the day so he would not be vulnerable to an attack while he slept. The few short hours Dustin required on even a normal night were shortened even more by the potentially perilous situation he had place himself in.

Dustin heard movement early in the morning from the camp below. He eased back to his former vantage point and saw a blood chilling sight. A gang of Comanchero's had come into the camp taking the occupants captive and summarily executing them. There was nothing Dustin could do but watch as these cold blooded butchers tormented these small time crooks and thieves and then placing them on their knees, fired single shots into the backs of their heads. The most upsetting and unbelievable thing was one of the two apparent leaders of the Comanchero's looked like Ned. Dustin knew that Ned had been undercover before but he'd never have stood still for this kind of heartless killing. Dustin could see that Ned may have had little choice in the killing of these not to be remembered men. Maybe he's got himself in too deep and could use some help. Ned was a friend and Dustin was damn sure going to try to help him.

Just before sun down, Dustin eased in close to the camp. He'd gotten a good look at the location of each of the Comancheros from above. He'd seen where they had drug the bodies of the thieves who had been shot. Dustin rode boldly up the trail to the camp, the first guard had fallen asleep. Normally a fatal mistake. In this instance, Dustin wasn't going to shoot first.

"Easy there friend," Dustin said just loud enough to wake the guard but not anyone else.

The guard, a Mexican, jolted to a sitting position and reached for his pistol.

"Easy amigo, I'm just hungry not dangerous. You boys got anything to eat?" Dustin said real casually with his own pistol noticeably out, ready and pointed directly at the Mexican.

"My friend, don't shoot! We got some food. Don't shoot, mister," the Mexican said.

"Hell, I aint a gonna shoot nobody, friend. I just don't want to get shot myself. OK?" Dustin explained.

Just then they heard voices from camp. "What's going on, Marcus?" a voice asked.

"Nothing, Alanso. We got some company, he's a friend. He says so," Marcus proclaimed.

"I'm just hungry is all. We don't need to have trouble over this," Dustin assured them.

"How do you know this place?" Alanso continued as he approached.

Several other men came up on both sides of Dustin. He had shifted his pistol to point dead center of the approaching Alanso who had noticed the pistol shift and stopped his approach and told his men to do likewise.

"Hold up boys, that pistol's pointing at me. I asked you how you knew this place, friend," Alanso repeated.

"I came here with Sanderson a time or two. He said this was a safe place to lay over," Dustin said convincingly.

Just then Ned walked up and looked Dustin in the eyes.

"Hey Ned, you ran with Sanderson. You know this kid?" Alanso asked.

"Yea, I know him a little. I saw him with Sanderson a time or two. I sure as hell don't know what he's doing here now!" Ned answered.

"When that stupid Sanderson got his self killed a while back, I went to Mexico. Things got thin there and I decided to work my way back north," Dustin answered.

"Well, put that damn gun away and let's get some breakfast. These boys left us some good food. They won't need it no more," Alanso laughed.

Dustin tried to make eye contact with Ned but he seemed to be avoiding Dustin's glance.

He holstered his pistol but was not asked to relinquish it. This crew of outlaws, eight in number, prepared a big breakfast of jerky gravy with hard tack and boiling coffee. A real frontier feast.

During the lull, while some were finishing their morning repast, Alanso asked Dustin, "Did you say you were with Sanderson when he got it?"

"No, I didn't say that. I said when he got killed, I went to Mexico," Dustin answered not revealing any more than required of him.

"I did not think so. Little Red Dickens was with him and never mentioned no one else. Did you know that damn fool Sanderson had a fortune on him and got hisself killed stealing a damn horse? Don't make sense," Alanso said pondering.

"Sanderson never made much sense, my friend," Dustin added and then poured himself more coffee, even though he didn't need it, then offered Alanso more and then Ned.

Ned took a little and while Dustin's body was blocking Alanso's view of his face, Ned

mouthed the words, "Get the hell out of here!"

Dustin sat back down looking as relaxed as if with close friends or family. Alanso continued a barrage of questions trying not to appear too suspicious of this new comer. When the subject of Armstrong came up, Dustin started to answer that he'd heard of him but was just a kid and never got to see him.

Then a revelation came to him and much to his surprise and Ned's, "Yea, I knew the Colonel well. I was there when he was arrested."

"Bull shit! My young friend I think maybe you are a liar," Alanso said menacingly.

What he hadn't counted on was that as always Dustin was thinking way ahead and had eased his pistol out of his holster unnoticed. With just the lifting of his hand and no noticeable rush at all, Dustin was pointing it directly into the face of the shaken Alanso.

"Sir, I implore you never call me a liar again. Trust your life to the fact that I never point my weapon at anything I don't intend to kill, unless given proper and hasty reason not to. I was with Colonel Armstrong when he was arrested like I said. It was at our headquarters in Magdalena, Mexico. Ned was there. He saw me before he got away with a handful of others. The army just let me ride off. I was just a kid then. It has been several years now. Please now my new friend, tell me you were mistaken in your assessment of my verity so I may spare your life and return this heavy pistol to its proper place," Dustin eloquently stated.

"Damn it young fellow, you are going to have to stop pointing that quick pistol of yours at me. It makes me a little uneasy," Alanso said.

Ned spoke up, "Was that snotty nosed little pain in the ass kid you? I'd not of recognized you all growed up. This kid was there when the hide out was overrun, Alanso. I saw him clear. You are a little touchy to be out here by yourself. Maybe you should tag along with us for a while," Ned suggested.

"Yes, I think he should, Ned," Alanso said.

"Anyone that can get the drop on me twice in one morning might be good to have around. Besides I'd kinda like to keep an eye on him awhile anyway. The day after tomorrow we'll meet up with Little Red. We'll see if he knows this good friend of Armstrong's," Alanso sneered.

"No, I don't know the man. I only seen him once. I heard he ran and let Sanderson get killed. I'm looking forward to seeing him again," Dustin said without hesitation or fear.

"Bueno!" Alanso said. "We'll stay here one more day and rest the horses then we'll pick up Little Red and his men."

Dustin was wondering what this group of murderers were planning but showed no interest. While lying around the camp close to the middle of the day, Dustin by chance perhaps, caught a split second flash coming from the ridge he'd occupied the day before. He was sure he'd seen it and that no one else had. He stood and stretched his back looking directly at whatever had made the flash to let whoever it was know he knew they were there.

Ned was watching him when occasion allowed, which was not often because Alanso kept up a constant vigil aimed at Ned and Dustin who were both very evidently suspect at the moment. Without being noticed or at least not trying to be, Dustin would look under the brim of his hat at the ridge. He never saw anything else and was questioning if he'd actually seen the flash or had imagined it. Once Dustin thought he saw Ned pick up on the fact that he was looking at the ridge for something. This made Dustin stop any and all glances that direction. If Ned suspected something, Alanso surely did also or soon would.

That evening Alanso was talking to his Comanchero's in Spanish. He laid out the whole arrangement of how he and Little Red were going to join forces with Nacatan's warriors. The Indian had been in hiding long enough now that the soldiers thought he'd gone to the Dakotas with the other chiefs for the big conference. The government would pull many soldiers from the western forts to send back and help the cavalry around this large gathering of the Indian nations. This would leave the western frontier vulnerable to Nacatan's braves. He would drive out the remaining soldiers and reclaim his home land for his people. The Comancheros could loot and pillage for their part in helping Nacatan. What Nacatan hadn't counted on is that even though the government pulled the soldiers from the frontier during the war to strengthen their forces against the south, no such order would ever be given to aid the cavalry's units trying to govern the Great Plains. This was a near catastrophic error in leadership and a fatal one for many brave if not cautious cavalrymen.

Dustin lie there listening to the conversation, wondering what part Ned was playing in this. Was he there on behalf of the Army or had he gone bad like most people at the fort suspected? If he had turned renegade, why hadn't he told Alanso who Dustin really was? Dustin was also wondering if he really saw something on the ridge. He had been guessing that it was his friend Big Mike and maybe others. If Mike had been watching them at camp he could have picked a safe time to signal Dustin with the lens flash. For now this was all speculation. What was for sure was he was with seven cold blooded killers and Ned, whom the vote was still out on. The day after tomorrow they were going to meet the man who saw him kill Sanderson. Things were going to get lively then, no doubt.

The morning came and Dustin had rested well thinking he'd need to be fresh for the action ahead. Ned seemed relaxed and even friendly this morning. It was good to see him joking around like old times but it was also a little unsettling for Dustin. After all, this wasn't a Sunday school picnic. Here they were out numbered seven to two or was it really eight to one. That apparently remained to be seen. Maybe Big Mike was out there somewhere waiting to make his move, or maybe not. Regardless, Dustin had to be ready for anything when he encountered Little Red. If Red recognized him, he'd have to kill him or be killed himself and maybe get Ned killed too. If Red didn't remember him or was not reminded by Alanso's questioning him about Sanderson's demise, Dustin might be able to continue on with the charade until Nacatan was located. He'd just have to be ready either way.

The ride out was a little tense. Ned and Alanso rode in the lead then came Dustin with Marcus beside him. Ned started talking to Dustin as they approached the proposed meeting place. Little Red was not there yet. Alanso and the rest of his men started setting up camp as Ned and Dustin led the horses to water.

Ned without looking at Dustin asked, "How's this going to go down?"

Dustin in return said, "Depends on what role you take in it I guess. Are you here officially or have you really gone nuts?"

"I guess a little of both. The Army didn't send me if that's what you're asking. I am here on their behalf, they just didn't authorize it," Ned explained.

"That's what I was afraid of! I'll probably have to kill this Little Red fellow. I'm sure he'll recognize me. Do you know where Nacatan is now?" Dustin asked.

"Yes. Don't worry about..." Ned stopped short at the approach of Alanso and two of his men.

"Need help boys?" Alanso asked.

"You bet. Take a couple of these horses over to the other side. They'll water off faster with more room," Ned replied.

"Hey boys, here comes your old friend Little Red Dickens. I'll bet he'll be glad to see you again," Alanso chided.

Little Red rode into the camp like a general returning from a victorious campaign.

"Howdy Alanso! I just left Nacatan. He's all fired up. Got over a hundred warriors. The bloodiest bunch of renegades I've ever seen. Hello Ned, who's the new man? I don't like surprises," Red stated.

"He's an old friend of Colonel Armstrong's and Sanderson's he says, and Ned vouched for him," Alanso said.

"By god it's the kid from Magdalena. What the hell you doing here? It's plumb good to see you again. I never expected to after they got Sanderson in Texas. I just barely got away myself. I'm glad to see you are all right," Little Red carried on like he and Dustin were best friends.

"Yea, it's real special to see you too Red," was all Dustin said.

"I'll be damned, I thought this kid was running a bluff," Alanso said.

"Bluff my ass! This kid's seen more action than you have, you silly bastard. You're lucky he hasn't shot you dead. He must be in a good mood," Red said.

"Hell Red, I didn't mean nothing by it. I was just being careful like you said to be," Alanso apologized.

"Never mind that now. Let's get to work. Hey kid, we're going to throw in with Nacatan for a while. You in or out?" Little Red asked Dustin like he was inviting him to a dance.

"I ain't got nothing to do. I'm in! Lay it out for me," declared Dustin.

"We're already in, kid. All we got to do is show up for the ball. He's got a simple plan. He wants to take over the frontier and give his people back their homeland. What do you think about that?" Red asked.

"What's in it for us?" Dustin demanded.

"Loot and lots of it if he wins and a huge reward if he looses and we kill him and take in his body to the fort. All we're risking is getting killed before the end," Red said excitedly.

"What if someone talks him into returning to the reservation?" Dustin asked.

Red shot a quick look at Ned then back to Dustin, "Same reward, no loot! Let's go, we got some miles to go before dark. Kid, you ride with me. I want to ketch up on where you been since Sanderson got killed."

The men packed up camp and rode out. Ned talked to Alanso almost nonstop in what seemed like a diversion to Dustin. When they all got lined out, Little Red started talking softly to Dustin without looking at him so no one else could hear or see what was said.

Red started, "You did a good job keeping your head back there with Sanderson. I was afraid you'd move and I'd hit you accidentally. You are a cool hand. I put that in my report to General Stewart."

"I'll be damned!" was all Dustin could say.

"Are you looking for Nacatan?" Red asked.

"Yep, Captain Perron sent me to find out where he is. He never mentioned you," Dustin explained.

"Perron don't know about me. I'm General Stewart's man. I'm an assassin. As soon as I kill Nacatan and get out alive, he'll be no more problem. I've had to do a lot of things I'll be sorry for the rest of my life to get close to him. I don't know how you feel about Nacatan's murder but I can't or won't let you stop me. That's what Ned's doing here. He came out here unauthorized to stop the assassination of that murdering savage. He thinks it is his fault Nacatan went wild. Ned don't remember Nacatan had already killed the Indian agent before...well before his mistake."

Red paused when Dustin interrupted him, "I was there at Raton. It wasn't Ned's fault but it was a terrible thing."

"I know Dustin. He might not ever get over it. That doesn't matter here. I've got a job to do and I'm going to do it. I've had to be a part of things much worse than slaughtering innocent women and children. Ned will just have to get over it," Red stated matter of factly.

"Good Lord Red, what could be worse than that!" Dustin asked in disbelief.

"Son, there are things worse than dying or being killed out right. Take my word for it Dustin, much, much worse," Red said with his voice trailing off into a silence brought on by great sorrow kept deep within the man's soul.

"Will you let me try to talk him in, Red? Nacatan I mean?" Dustin asked.

"If you can get him in before I get my shot, go for it," Red said and kicked his horse into a trot marking the end of the conversation.

Dustin rode along in silence trying to imagine what this little man had been through in the name of military duty. Alanso seemed eager to talk to Little Red about Nacatan, so Dustin fell back and switched places with him and rode along talking to Ned. Ned had seen Red Dickens meeting secretly with General Stewart at the fort even before the undercover mission to Magdalena. Every crime Nacatan committed, every murder, every raid, Ned felt responsible for. He did not want to see Nacatan killed for crimes that he himself was responsible for. Ned was hoping to talk Nacatan in, get him back to the reservation and allow him to live in peace the rest of his life. Dustin reminded Ned that Nacatan had murdered the Indian agent before Raton Pass. That's why they were there in the first place, looking for Nacatan for murder.

"All I know is this has got to stop. It's all my fault, Dustin. You were there, you should understand," Ned pleaded his position to young Dustin.

"All I'm supposed to do is locate him and report his whereabouts to Captain Perron. I think Big Mike is out there somewhere. He could help get us out of here if he don't get himself caught and killed," Dustin said.

"I thought you were looking at something back there," said Ned. Then he added, "Have you ever seen Nacatan? Will he recognize you?"

"Yes, to both. We've talked a lot. I learned to speak Apache from a young buck in his village years ago. He thought it was a good thing a white boy took the time to learn his language and gestures. We were kind of friends," Dustin said proudly.

"Good, if you get a chance, I want you to interpret for me. I need to tell him I was responsible for the murders. Promise me you'll do it!" Ned almost begged his old friend.

"Yea, I'll interpret for you, if he don't kill us on sight tomorrow," Dustin said absolutely serious.

"I thought you two were friends," Ned quizzed.

"We were. That's a little chancy to bet your life on. That's just what we're doing. We'll have to take it as it comes, Ned. That Red covered for me good but he's a little spooky. I think this assignment may have gotten to him," Dustin confided in Ned.

"Don't count that little man out just yet, Dustin. He's seen things that would make a lesser man gouge his own eyes out to keep from seeing more. He'll take care of his business the best way he knows how. I've got a chance to try and make things right. I'm not mad, Dustin like most people think I am. I know I may not even get to talk to Nacatan, let alone get him to return to the reservation in peace. I have to try. You understand, don't you? I just gotta try," Ned said.

"That's my plan too, Ned. We'll make a run at the old drunk if we can. If the shooting starts, I'll watch your back and will expect you to be watching mine as well," Dustin proclaimed.

"I'll be there for you, Dustin. Remember to stay out of Red's way once he starts shooting. He won't have time to be very selective with his shots after Nacatan goes down," Ned advised.

"Let's hope it don't come to that, Ned. These damn cut throat Comancheros could go either way in a fight. We might be in pretty deep," Dustin said not able to hide all the concern he had about a fight against Nacatan, his warriors and these Mexican bandits too.

"Little Red will be there 'til the end, Dustin. Trust in that. Maybe Big Mike brought some help with him. This might not turn out too uneven," Ned said and laughed a little.

"What the hell you laughing at Ned? I believe maybe you have gone mad," Dustin scolded.

"I'm not mad, I was just thinking you still have a way of showing up when something is about to happen. I'm a little worried it's a habit that's going to get you killed someday. I hope like hell it is not today," Ned explained.

"Damn it Ned, what a thing to say. I'm a little worried myself. There's likely to be a lot of shooting and we're liable to be providing the targets!" Dustin said with just a hint of humor.

"Yes sir, we're sitting on them right now," Ned joked almost back to his old self.

The men soon rode over the last ridge before the long well hidden valley Nacatan called home in between raids. The sun burnt brush covered hillside shone a dull brown orange from the last rays of the late afternoon sun setting, ending another day the same way it had done for millenniums. This days end held no cause for celebration. It was, as always, a courier with the potential of bringing an ominous message of disaster and finality with it. The outcropping of rocks, left undisturbed for millions of years, seemed almost alive. They looked as if they were actually moving, turning slowly as the riders passed. In fact, they were watching, or rather the warriors Nacatan had posted as sentries were studying each riders every move as they passed through the little saddle harboring the only trail into the sanctuary of the outlaw chief. A sight that would torment Dustin the rest of his life awaited him just over the ridge. The shouting and yelling of war cries were near deafening and certainly blood chilling.

As Red, Alanso, Ned, Dustin and the now thirty Comancheros dropped into the little haven of pagan hostels, Dustin's worse fears unveiled themselves before him. A display of sadistic, vicious savagery he'd only imagined in his worst, most horrifying, hellish nightmares were awaiting as he approached ever near. Unable to look away, yet wanting to with all his heart and soul, he could do nothing but press forward trying to believe what he saw was somehow just a distorted image, an illusion brought on by anxiety and apprehension. It was no mirage, it was real. There providing the substance for the jubilation of these heathenish murders were three men. What was left of three men would be more accurate.

The first Dustin saw had caught his attention with his screams of pain and fear. He was stripped and had virtually been hacked to pieces. He had been tied to a post surrounded by brush and an Indian warrior was about to set the death circle on fire. Behind him at a distance of less than one hundred feet, also tied to a post, was the second poor victim of these fiendish, bloodletting ghouls. He was already dead. Bled white through wounds too numerous to attempt to count. As the fire was being set under the already dying first sacrifice, a squad of archers were viciously shooting arrows into his body trying their best not to inflect an immediately fatal wound which would cut short their targets anguish.

At that moment Ned took hold of Dustin's arm and said, "Good Lord, Dustin, look over there. That's Big Mike."

Dustin turned to see his friend of these last several years tied like his companions to a post. Unlike his companions, Big Mike had remained silent much to the displeasure of his tortuous captors. He'd stood there mute, taking his death as they saw fit to deal it out. The more he refused to cry out, the more heinously they dealt it. He'd been so mutilated and disfigured by these proficient creative executioners that no one but a close friend or member of his immediate family could have identified him. He stood as erect as his arrow riddled body would allow him. Nacatan himself was inflicting the last fatal abuses to this noble martyr.

Dustin loped ahead and jumped off his horse next to the knife wielding murderer Nacatan. Dustin had his pistol out and looked his suffering dying friend in the eyes and Big Mike gasped almost silently, "Please Laddie, end this."

Nacatan shouted something Dustin did not clearly understand. Still looking into the pleading eyes of his dear friend he raised his weapon and fired, ending the suffering and life of Sergeant Major Michaels. Then without a thought fired a second shot and then a third. The second of these dropped Nacatan striking him full in the face. The third ending the agony of the now burning first soldier. The dance now commenced.

Dustin's concern about the Comancheros was soon answered. These half breed bandits who had no apparent allegiance to anyone or thing were the fightingest bunch of bastards Dustin had ever seen. Nacatan had sent a scouting party of about thirty warriors north several days ago. This still left seventy battle hardened warriors against thirty of Little Red's Comancheros, hardly an even fight.

After just moments, Dustin realized the odds were against the Indians. As bravely as the warriors fought, the skill of the Comanchero butchers surpassed all efforts made by the relatively primitive savages to take advantage of their numbers. The most impressive display of all was that of Red Dickens. When Nacatan fell, everyone stood motionless until the second and third shots rang out. Then in one mass movement everyone was firing simultaneously. Men were falling everywhere. Ned fell with the first borage. He was seriously wounded but not yet fatally. Dustin knelt by Ned's side and fired carefully and exactly into the warriors while the Comancheros, most of them still mounted, dashed crisscross through the assemblage of combatants. The Indians having all been a foot participating or watching the torture of the three recently captured soldiers, either fought where they stood or ran for their horses.

In the busy middle of all this was Little Red standing with one foot resting on his fallen horse like a stone sentinel. Everyone was rushing around or hiding behind something except this lone centurion who remained motionless except for the alternate rising and lowering of his pistol filled hands. With twelve shots fired, ten warriors lie dead or dying at his hand. Red then stepped to the nearest fallen man and picked up two more weapons and resumed his position and commenced dropping Indians at the rate of almost one per shot. Red stood his self appointed post at great peril and extreme risk. He was shot through the side, once in the thigh, twice in the meaty part of his upper arm and was grazed on the side of his head, knocking his hat off and sending it sailing yards away. He never flinched or faltered except when retrieving new weapons, then only briefly.

Dustin too was actively in the fury. He had been shot in the back of his left shoulder at the first volley. He received two more wounds neither serious, one low on his side the other below his armpit, before things started settling down. Ned wasn't quite so lucky. He'd tried to stand for a better aim and was shot through the heart for his effort. He fell dead at Dustin's feet.

Shortly after things had gotten started Dustin saw two braves drag the still withering body of Nacatan away. He'd fired a shot in their direction but had received one of his wounds at the same moment and never knew if he'd hit one of the would be rescuers or not. All he knew was they were gone when he was able to look again. Dustin had been rendered semi-conscious by a blow from a primitive hatchet delivered by a valiant but foolish warrior, who finding himself out of ammunition, standing surrounded by Comanchero's, ran directly at Dustin wielding his ancient artifact of battles long past. Dustin was able to fire his pistol dead center of his noble assailant bringing death instantly but not able to stop the momentum of the forth coming blow to his own head.

When Dustin was able to clear the cobwebs and again rise, the encounter was ebbing slowly to an end. A victorious end at that, if in fact one could consider the loss of two thirds of his force a victory. The body count was twenty-one dead Comancheros, Alonso included, Ned and sixty-one of Nacatan's warriors.

Nacatan's body could be found nowhere. This count meant that close to a dozen braves had escaped. Some more than likely wounded, a few probably fatally. These survivors would still reach the scouting party soon and there would be an attempt at redemption. Red told the last of the Comanchero's to head back into Mexico and lie low for a while. He'd come gather them and others again as soon as things settled down some.

Red turned to Dustin and said, "Come on Lad. We'd better get out of here pronto, too. These Nacatan boys ain't gonna take too kindly to the way you greeted there old chief."

"We gotta bury Big Mike and Ned first, Red. Hell! We just can't leave them for the animals," Dustin argued.

"Lad, the animals already got them. What more could a few birds and varmints do to them now. You can stay and dig em graves if you want to. Be sure you dig one extra. I'll come back by here in a day or two and throw you in it if you like. Do what you will, I'm headed out of here now!" Red finished and removed his saddle from his dead horse.

Some of the remaining Comancheros had gathered many of the loose horses and Red saddled one that looked good to him.

"You'd better pick one for yourself Dustin. Your horse took a bullet in the butt. He won't be much good for a while. Pick one without a brand or Indian sign on him. It might save our necks later."

Dustin did as suggested and got a fine mount saddled. Marcus wanted to join him and Red but was assured it would be better if they split up for now.

The Comancheros, quite happy with their loot of guns and horses and apparently unconcerned about the loss of twenty of their comrades, rode off toward Mexico, driving a sizable herd of horses ahead of them, most of whom still carried the saddles of their fallen previous owners.

Dustin took one last look at Ned and what remained of Big Mike and said, "Ain't much left to be leaving, is there Red?"

"We ain't leaving nothing, Lad. Their souls have done been released. Them there is just the carcasses. Let's get!" Red said comfortingly.

The two rode off in a north western direction for a long time then due east and then on northwest again. Red had survived out here running with the worst the frontier had to offer these last four years and Dustin wasn't about to question him in his route.

Late the second night out Dustin asked Red, "What now? I mean what are you going to do now that Nacatan's dead?"

"What makes you think he's dead? We didn't find his body. Indians wouldn't likely have taken him away in the heat of battle if he was already dead. They might have come back later for his body but not during a fight. I think he's alive or at least was when they took him off," Red speculated.

"Damn Red, I shot him full in the face. The bullet hit him just below the nose and knocked his mouth wide open. I was looking straight at him when he fell, "Dustin defended his shot.

"I ain't saying you missed him, Lad. I've just seen bullets do some strange things, that's all. I was in Kansas once and seen a fellow real drunk loose his last dime gambling. This old boy walked outside and put his pistol to his temple and decided to end it all. He pulled the trigger and killed another poor bastard who was standing behind him. That damn bullet grazed off the drunks skull and traveled around above his ear and came out from under the skull at the back of his head and killed this unlucky S.O.B. for just being in the wrong place at the wrong time," Red explained.

"He ain't gonna be very happy with me if he's not dead! That's for sure," Dustin said like it was funny.

"No and he ain't going to be too damn thrilled with me either. Remember I brought you to him. How are your wounds doing, Lad?" Red added.

Dustin looked at the blood soaked rags he'd stuffed in the holes and replied, "Not too bad, Red. I'm more worried about you. Hell, you're shot to pieces. How are you?"

"I'm fine, Lad. We'll both need a little cleaning up and rest before we go after Nacatan," Red said meditatively.

"Go after Nacatan! Hell, Red, wasn't three to one odds enough for you? You want to make it thirty to one for your grand finale? You are kidding me, ain't you?" Dustin challenged.

"No, I've never been more serious, Lad. You and me won't be safe until ol' Nacatan's dead and gone permanent. His braves might someday forgive us but the old Chief is going to think of us every time he feels his blown off jaw. I can't live looking over my shoulder. We've got no choice. We've got to get healthy then try and find out for sure about the Chief's condition or we'll never be able to rest again. We started something we have to finish. Do you know a safe place we can get some help?" Red inquired.

"Yes, but it's close to the fort. The Mortons are like my family. We'd be safe there if no one sees us arrive," Dustin assured him.

"No good. We can't go to the fort. I'm in too deep now. I know a Mexican whore that's got a place south of here. We'll go there," Red decided.

They rested awhile and then headed south. Dustin was feeling a little weak from the loss of blood but remained silent. He could hardly complain when his companion had suffered twice the damage he had and remained strong, even good natured. Little Red Dickens was probably the toughest man any weight Dustin had ever seen. His being absolutely fearless had won Dustin over but his blatant disregard for pain was much more than impressive, it was supernatural.

They rode on for what seemed to Dustin and eternity and finally Red pulled up. It was pitch black and Dustin wondered why they had finally stopped. He was so glad they had, he asked no questions.

"Hold my horse and keep still, Lad," Red said and slipped into the darkness.

Seconds later he reappeared and said, "It's all right. Take the horses around back and come on in the house," then he disappeared again.

Dustin found the shed and little make shift corral originally used for goats. He could tell by the smell of the place. He unsaddled the horses and put their gear into the feed room by the shed, threw the tired horses some hay and checked their water. He then headed for the back of the house. He was hurting badly and his shoulder was bleeding freely again. As Dustin walked toward the house, he ran into Red coming to check on him.

"Damn boy, are you all right? I was worried about you," Red said and then led Dustin toward the door and into the little adobe house.

"Dustin, this is Senorita Teresa Delgado. Miss Delgado, this is my friend Dustin Thomas. You'd better take a look at him while I clean my wounds up, Teresa. I think he might need sewing up a little. He's lost some blood too."

Red went over to a pail of hot soapy water and stripped to his drawers without the least sign of modesty. Teresa, a beautiful young Mexican girl not much older, if any, than Dustin, didn't seem to notice this mostly naked man standing at her sink. She helped Dustin out of his shirt and started to remove his pants.

"Everything down there is fine, Ma'am!" Dustin exclaimed a little panicky.

"Oh, I'm sure it is Senior Dustin Thomas. I just want to tend to your wounds, right now," giggled the Senorita.

Red was laughing out loud over at the sink.

"That's what I mean Miss, my wounds are all up high," Dustin still embarrassed tried to explain.

His shoulder wound was the most serious but the bullet had gone clear through just under the collar bone and would be fine shortly. The one in his side and under his arm were sore and ugly wounds but just flesh and meat were involved, no real threat. Dustin's head hurt more than anything right now. Teresa gave him some kind of homemade concoction to drink for pain while she tended to Red's wounds, the least of which was worse than Dustin's shoulder by a great extent. Even the bullet that had grazed Red's skull had torn loose a patch of scalp as big as a large man's open hand.

Teresa had obviously done some amount of repair work on this man or others like him in the past. She cut away some hair and took close to fifty stitches in various lacerations on Red's body. He used no anesthetic more than that same wonderful potion she'd given to Dustin. Taking ample doses of this prescribed fluid had Dustin feeling so completely rejuvenated as to feel it necessary for him to offer his services and advice on the doctoring of his companion. It seemed the more of this mystical elixir he ingested, the wiser he became. His newly attained intellect was of the most verbose nature. The knowledge literally flowed from his lips, great questions of scientific import, theories of philosophic inquiry plaguing mankind for centuries. Even strategies of battle no matter how complex were solved on the spot by this mind so highly stimulated by this simple medical miracle which the lovely and gracious Teresa Delgado called Mescal.

Dustin had only thought his head hurt last night. This morning he was sure it was going to explode and quite possibly blow down this little adobe hovel with it. He needed to get outside and puke his liver out but was absolutely sure his head would not fit through the doorway. He decided to just sit there and die as proudly as one could sitting on a dirt floor in a Mexican shack with no clothes on. That's right, not a stitch. All he wore were the bandages Teresa had covered his wounds with the night before. As Dustin sat, naked, trying to lift his heads enormous weight from against the dirt wall it rested on, straining hard to try and think of what should be thought about at a time like this, and not able to have and hold one clear idea, the door burst open. It was Red with Teresa following him, both holding pots of something delicious smelling for an instant then suddenly putrid. It was certainly more than Dustin could take. Still unable to move he just let nature have its way and as he apologized proceeded to cover himself in vomit.

"Good Lord, Dustin. Drag your sorry ass outside. Damn it man, people are trying to eat!" Red scolded as he drug Dustin, enormous head and all, out back in the yard.

"Bring Romeo here some cool water, please, Teresa. I'm afraid he's going to live," Red said smiling and then returned to eat his breakfast.

Dustin woke up with the hot sun boiling his brains and burning his skin. He opened his eyes then shut them again against the glare of the sun. He grimaced from the noise they made as they slammed shut.

Then unexpectedly the roar of a thousand lions accompanied by the blast of ten thousand trumpets rang out with, "Are you all right, Lad? You look like hell. Can you stand up long enough for me to put your pants on you? You are becoming a tourist attraction. Remember, we are supposed to be hiding out," Red said so solemnly Dustin once again attempted to open his eyes.

He managed to get one to remain partially open enough to see Red kneeling by him holding his drawers and pants out toward him apparently being foolish enough to believe that he could in fact get them put on even if he cared to do so. Dustin looked away from Red and saw standing just behind his booming voiced friend, six small children of various ages from around three to about six. Each properly impressed with the subject of their stares. Dustin managed the slightest of smiles for the benefit of these little urchins then closed his eyes and thought of how he'd always liked small children,… and the color blue and the smell of a new saddle and poultry.

103

Then once again the ear piercing screech of his friend's fiendish howl, "Damn it Dustin, open your eyes and sit up or I'm going to just leave you out here!"

Dustin pitifully tried to nod, trying so very desperately to explain that was exactly what he wanted to happen. No nod came. His body still refused to obey even the slightest command. Then surely straight from heaven, an angel touched his brow then his lips and returned once again to his throbbing forehead. A simple rag, a rag torn from a discarded gown of a whore. A lovely rag worn and tattered but wet. Yes wet, wet and somehow in this primitive inferno, cool. Cool as the first snow fall of the year. Cool as the melting streams in spring. Wet and cool, truly a gift from God. Life saving cool moisture. A salve for the soul as well as the body. Best of all this was being administered by this lovely Mexican angel, softly, gently and most importantly in absolute silence.

Red shook his head saying, "Pitiful! Plumb pitiful."

Within the hour, Teresa had Dustin standing, with a little help and dressed to the waist. She moved him into the house and sat him at the table. He laid his head on his arms folded on the table top while Teresa bathed his neck and head with more of this cool liquid of life. Mere water had never before or maybe since been so enjoyed or appreciated as it was now by Dustin Thomas. Men who had died of thirst on the deserts of this planet and had eaten sand in a disoriented state of dehydration would by comparison hold water in great contempt. The only thing keeping Dustin from believing he was in the paradise of heaven itself was that every few moments his stomach would ram itself up into his throat so violently that it would bring him back into facing the trials and tribulations of his circumstances in this earthly existence. That and the constant beating he was taking from Red's droning conversation. Dustin, in moments of coherency, wondered how a man so small could talk so loudly. And how a tiny dirt dwelling could stand up under such an earthshaking bombardment of oratory and not be shaken to rubble.

About noon Red offered Dustin a warm beer from the nearby cantina where Teresa worked. It wasn't really beer but it damn sure wasn't that hellish mescal. By evening Dustin was able to eat a little. He wasn't able to keep anything down but was at least able to get outside before it came up. By nightfall he had consumed a full meal and several more beers and for the first time in just over twenty four hours Dustin thought there was a fifty-fifty chance for his survival.

The next few days were more pleasant than one would expect under the circumstances. Red spent days sleeping, getting better as he put it and nights at the cantina drinking or paying attention to the girls, Teresa included. He called this gathering information. It looked more like getting drunk and lucky to Dustin but some mornings Red would share some tidbit about the renegade Indians from someone passing through. Days, mainly afternoons, Dustin spent visiting with Teresa and several of the other ladies. He abstained from doing any business with them even though it was tempting as several of the girls were quite beautiful. Just visiting with these ladies in their off hours, you would never suspect their night time occupation.   These were mostly just girls although referred to as ladies during the evening and nights. Most were not as old as he and had already seen the worst this life has to offer.

Dustin really enjoyed watching the girls down at the creek doing their laundry. The girls were all Mexican except for two half Mexican Indians and a full blooded Apache girl who had been orphaned in a Mexican raid on her Indian village and raised communally by the little village of Mexican peasants where the cantina was located. Speaking fluent Spanish endeared Dustin to the girls greatly. Almost immediately the girls let him know he had a free pass on any of the rides at the Cantina or for a private session if he so desired. Dustin explained that he was engaged to be married and even though he very much appreciated their more than generous offer, he would respectfully decline. He enjoyed the evening meal with Red and Teresa and watching her get ready for work, which usually amounted to no more than brushing her hair and putting on the same time worn dress every night.

One day, or actually one night, Red came busting into the house.

"Get your stuff gathered up, Lad. We've got work to do. An old friend of mine had dinner two nights ago with our boy Nacatan. The old bastard is real sick but looks like he might make it. We've either got to kidnap or kill the old gentleman. Let's go! We'll let him decide which one," Red said excitedly.

"All right Red, I'm getting a little antsy sitting around here," Dustin said as he started throwing his few things into his saddle bags.

"The reason you're antsy Lad is you aint lurn to take advantage of the opportunities nature provides us to release the pressure through pleasure," Red said very philosophically and still quite drunk.

"I told you Red, I'm engaged. I'm going to be married as soon as she gets back from England," Dustin explained.

"I don't know how someone in England could catch you fooling around way out here!" Red reasoned.

"Come on Red, we got an old Indian to catch and he is way out here too!" Dustin scolded.

Dustin and Red rode into a canyon surrounded by high rough mountains that looked out of place there in the desert.

"Dustin, I should ease up close and get some idea of the set up down there. He's supposed to be in a cliff dwelling left abandoned hundreds of years ago. Might not be too easy in or out," Red suggested.

"Red, let's just ride in and shoot the old bastard. It's the middle of the night and by the time those damn dogs they always have with them give the signal, we could kill or scare off most of their guards. If we take him alive we'll have to baby-sit the sick old fool all the way back to the fort. I don't fancy being too damn kind to the ghoulish old murderer after what he did to Big Mike," Dustin proclaimed.

"By God, Lad, you ain't short on guts. I'm with you. How many pistols you got?" Red asked.

"Four, Red. I've got my dad's old gun and my own and I picked up Ned's and another I think was Big Mike's," Dustin answered matter of factly.

"Fine, Lad, fine. Break 'em all out an' load 'em up. I've got three pistols and this old double barrel and of course my little belly gun. It's a sissy looking little thing but has saved my ass more than once. How do you want to play it?" Red asked.

"We could spread out and make them aim twice to get us both and meet at the front door of the hold up," Dustin said while making sure everything was plumb loaded. "Hell Red, I got my saddle rifle too. It's a dandy. It's one of them Springfield lever actions Lincoln rejected for the Union army. It's mostly for long range but in a pinch it'll do some damage up close too," Dustin added.

"That could be the difference we need. Has it got a sling?" Red asked.

"Yep," replied Dustin.

"Good, hang it around your neck and left shoulder upside down so you can just swing it up and fire it from the waist if it comes to that and it damn sure could. I can't believe this is your idea. These are the odds we been looking for, to avoid that is," Red joked as calmly as if they were discussing what color shirt they were going to wear to the dance Saturday night.

The two assassins could barely mount their horses from the weight of all their weapons. Red had his shotgun hung on a leather thong around his neck for easy access and dug a shot shell cartridge belt out of his roll and put it on as well.

"Well Lad, if they give us enough time to run out of ammunition we'll kill all the bastards!" Red said very matter of factly.

"We'll ride in as far as we can before we shoot. Big Mike and I played it like this years ago down in Magdalena going after Armstrong," Dustin said.

"Yea, I remember, don't seem like over four years now. We'll not shoot 'til they do, Dustin. If they let us ride in and get the old man, that's what we'll do," Red proclaimed.

"Yep! We'll just ride right in and saddle the old boy's horse and the three of us will ride right back out. Nothing to it!" Dustin said mockingly while cocking his pistols and started ahead down the long canyon to whatever fate held in store.

Chapter 10

The large group of men gathered around staring at their fallen leader. Colonel Gibson lie still and silent on the cold, grass covered ground. His broken neck, now straightened by Mr. Harris the cook to a more natural angle, still told at a glance the cause of the demise of this fine old gentleman. His beautiful gray mount having broken a leg in the fall as well, was shot and would be buried along side his rider. A huge association this size had little trouble with the graves. This was a great show of respect and unity. This honor was reserved for chiefs among the Indians but seldom was an animal ever buried by whites at this period in time. It was bad luck that could come to anyone on the range, a horse loping along easily, suddenly stepping into a prairie dog hole. Many fatal falls have occurred in this manner. Few if any were as history changing as the one of Colonel Gibson.

With Dustin just over a week gone and now unexpectedly Colonel Gibson dead, the five captains held a conference about how to continue. Each felt he should lead the herd on to Montana and receive the lions share for his efforts. No agreements could be arrived at and a fight broke out ending in near gun play. Scotty, the Colonel's cook and friend, hid the old gentlemen's journal and all the documents of the drive it contained from the five bickering captains. They, in their thirst for more power and money, had forgotten its existence and contents. The five angry men broke up and decided to separately continue to Montana only to pool the cattle together again upon reaching their delivery point. Until then it was each herd for themselves.

Two of the captains secretly conspired to throw together and move as one unit. These men, Brant Wilson and Timothy Mullen had been neighbors for many years and were in partnership on the cattle they had provided for the drive. Theirs' were two of the mainly steer herds and the most valuable cattle on the trip. They had Big Bill and Mr. Harris as cooks and after Colonel Gibson's untimely demise, started their cattle north east to pick up the rivers which would lead them eventually north west to Montana.

At first each of the other herds traveled along well. All were constantly on the look out for Indians. Since the late migration of warriors toward the Dakotas, the Army had been sending less and less escorts to watch the herd. Now that the cattle were spreading out and in one case actually taking an alternate route, all the military could do was send a small patrol to check on the general well being of the drive. None of the captains spoke much Spanish and none even a word of any sort of Indian. They each relied on some of the Mexican vaqueros to interpret for them when the occasion arose. Poor judgment and greed brought on some real problems for the ill fated cattlemen.

Being the slowest traveling, the cow herd now mixed with bulls was the last in the procession. As was an Indian's habit, if he was up to honorable business, he would ride directly into the front of whatever he wished to encounter. When up to no good, he'd way lay the tail end of his intended victim cutting off the last of a wagon train, military scouting party, or in this case cattle drive. This particular band of ne'er-do-wells had passed their chance to join their country men in battle against the forces of the white horse soldiers on the great plains in favor of remaining home and accepting reservation life. A wanderer happened to see the large herds of cattle passing through what was once their land and they, having nothing else to do, decided to investigate. They sat hidden, silently watching the first large herd pass, then another.

The third herd, under the command of Richard Epps, had already headed east out on the plains to follow the buffalo trails north. Epps, thinking this would save them the effort of fighting the mountains, figured the buffalo had to eat and drink as often as cattle so there should be ample grass and water on the well marked trail. Epps was driving the remainder of the cows and bulls and had a few steers as well. The herds had mixed again during the funeral and subsequent conference about leadership. Epps' easterly route kept him from being the recipient of the visit of the Indian welcoming committee. A stroke of good fortune not to last long.

This little package of Indians decided to send just three of its membership into the camp and discuss a fair charge for the right of passage across their lands. The rest of the Indians would remain in the edge of the forest until needed to help drive off their ill gotten gain. They presumed they might even receive as many as three or four fat cows or even a crippled steer or two. The orator for the group, Behachew, a large fellow that thought himself very chiefly even though if one traced his lineage he would not find a single chief or even council member among the names, approached the camp of these white intruders without the slightest show of fear. His two companions rode just slightly behind, flanking him on each side. They did not do this out of respect but simply because Behachew would kick his horse into a jog each time one of them rode beside him. Riding a jogging horse with just a blanket between your butt and his back is unpleasant at best. The two companions succumbed to his pretentiousness and allowed him the lead to avoid a ridiculous head long race into the white man's camp just to see who could get there first. Not very dignified behavior they thought for official toll takers.

Behachew always carried a huge, large bore musket across his lap when he went anywhere. This was purely decoration as the old gun hadn't been operational in many years. Behachew felt it lent an air of authority to his already grand presence. He used it like a wand in his speeches, waving it one direction or another and pointing it to emphasis a point he'd made. He loved the show of important conversation. Having never been allowed to speak at council meetings or any other time much, he was prepared to show the world what a great leader he could be.

As they approached the camp, the men gathered nervously around Captain Miller who was near the fire. They had seen glimpses of Behachew's friends remaining in the trees and had over estimated their numbers and misunderstood their intent. These men, already uneasy about being the last herd on the drive and not having been in contact with the others for quite sometime now, were getting very jumpy. These dozen beggars hiding in the woods had been counted by several normally dependable hands at a number of not less than one hundred fifty warriors.

Miller told his men as the great war chief Behachew approached, "Men if a fight breaks out, start the cattle running north and then it's every man for himself. We'll try to get back together up the trail later and gather what cattle we can. Right now it's live or die boys!"

This comforting speech of Miller's had an effect like that of telling a man in an outhouse that the hole was full of rattlesnakes. These poor, misled cowboys were needing to get their butts somewhere else and pronto. It's amazing how fear can turn large and dumb in to big and bold. That is the mistake Miller made concerning Behachew.

Miller had a man who spoke good Spanish come forward to interpret for him. Miller's apprehension spread like wild fire through his men, all of this unnoticed by old large and dumb.

When Behachew pulled his horse to a stop, he was just feet from the obvious negotiators, Miller and his interpreter. Behachew's two companions rode up beside him. He felt this lowered his esteem and eased his horse even closer to the cattlemen. This was not interpreted well at all. Miller counted this close proximity as aggressiveness on the part of these representatives of the native war mongers.

Behachew addressed Miller in his best 'I'm in charge voice', with no response at first. Then one came back in Spanish which might as well have been Israeli as far as Behachew was concerned. He just barely spoke his native tongue. He certainly could not have mastered another as well. Behachew repeated his greeting. Still nothing. With this last failure to gain a response, Behachew did as all truly intelligent men do when not understood. He said it again, just louder! Still no response he could understand. This time Behachew shouted his greeting and waved his useless old musket to stress his joy at being spokesperson for his band of beggars. This display got a response. Not the one Behachew wanted or expected but still a sure enough reply. It came from the barrel of Miller's handgun. The bullet struck the big, harmless fellow square in the center of his forehead. In the split second before Behachew fell dead, the look on his face, had it not been such a sad mistake killing him, was almost comical. Total surprise and confusion swept over his face then death took its place.

Behachew's two companions turned and raced away under a borage of fire and shouting. They were unable to even return the shots as neither of them even owned a fire arm. As the two were fleeing for their lives, the cattlemen were in full panic, Miller heading the insanity. Men were rushing for horses normally gentle, now spooked from the atmosphere of eminent disaster. The Indians previously lurking in the woods, all twelve of them, rushed out to meet their retreating comrades. This obvious attack by a vastly superior force was more than these already over excited cowboys could stand. Full chaos ensued.

The first mounted men got the cattle moving and then running wildly by shooting above their heads with reckless abandon. Scotty, who was the cook for this outfit, had seen much action in every kind of battle. He had not, however, seen a mess such as this. He tried to calm the men down but to no avail. Poor Scotty stood helplessly on his wagon seat watching his team run off along with the rest of the remuda and all the cattle as well. The cattle were boiling around the wagon and tearing up the camp unbelievably. Scotty was so worried the wagon was going to be tipped over by the on slot of rampaging cattle, he began shooting his old pistol in their faces trying to turn them away from the wagon. This was somewhat effective momentarily. He grabbed his double barrel shot gun when his pistol ammunition ran out. Things turned bad for Scotty at this point. His first shot from the twelve gauge struck a large steer in the face blinding him. The steer not only did not turn away, but ran head on into the front wheel of the chuck wagon knocking Scotty and his shotgun out. When they hit ground, after bouncing off of the steer, the shotgun discharged striking Scotty in the throat nearly severing his head, killing him instantly. Just one more tragedy caused as a direct result of the needless hysteria. There was more yet to come.

Only about half of the thirty-five men belonging to Miller's herd regrouped and this was at the ridiculous distance of nearly twenty-five miles north. Miller finally regaining some sense, organized three groups of five man details to ride carefully southward gathering any of the cattle they might find. He sent two men to the nearest fort to report the latest Indian uprising.

The Indians remained hidden for some time before venturing back to retrieve poor Behachew. They rode cautiously up to the wagon and took Scotty's shotgun and vest. Then dug through the wagon looking for and eventually finding more twelve gauge shells. The harness was all still neatly hanging on the wagon, as was custom, so one Indian suggested they hook up and take the whole thing home. They'd be heroes to their village. The Indians loaded Behachew's body and all the dutch ovens and miscellaneous cooking paraphernalia into the wagon box and hooked up four head of their gentlest ponies. Not knowing exactly how the harness worked made quite a task of this. The ponies were just strong enough to untrack the wagon but were able to maintain motion, once established, with relative ease. The triumphant dozen, minus one, had taken Scotty's scalp before they left. An error of etiquette never breached by a true warrior. A combat brave would not consider taking a scalp not from his own kill. These were after all just reservation Indians and a scalp was a scalp to them. They headed toward the village, at times helping the ponies by pushing on the wagon in steep places. When they arrived home, the village went wild! There was now truly a reason for celebration and enough food stuffs to put on a good one. Singing and dancing and telling the tale of the brave and mighty Behachew and how the poorly armed old rascals had driven off over one hundred of the white demons. They would go out tomorrow and gather some of the cows left behind by the cowardly white men and have another celebration.

The fort was reached by late the next day through hard riding. When told of this large scale attack on these poor cattlemen, Captain De Laquote, the fort commander, rose to the occasion. He mounted a full scale assault on this murdering band of rabble. Surely it was none other than Nacatan himself. No chances were to be taken that anyone would escape. He ordered a score of field artillery to be made ready to move within the hour. Captain De Laquote led an entire company of men on a three day forced march to the spot of the attack. Upon arriving he found the tell tale wagon tracks a child could follow. Nacatan was either setting a trap for him or was getting careless. Most likely his need for supplies outweighed his good judgment in the taking of the wagon. The first three miles above the attack were a gruesome sight indeed. Cattle injured or dead were everywhere. Some having been shot by the excited cowboys themselves. Many signs of fresh butchering of several animals told Captain De Laquote he was close. Evening was coming. He wanted to attack at first light in the morning. He sent a detachment of scouts to locate the village and return with the details of the enemy camp. To his complete delight, the scouts returned with favorable information in just under four hours. He had the men fall out and rest 'til midnight, then moved them up into place surrounding the village. An hour before sun up found all of Captain De Laquote's company, including a full compliment of artillery, in place and ready. The men were concerned because there didn't seem to be enough horses in the meadow or wigwams in the village for a force of one hundred fifty warriors and their families. Captain De Laquote wasn't going to let this opportunity for fame and advancement go by through being overly cautious.

He told his men when they brought the shortage of horses and housing to his attention, "We'll take what we have, gentlemen and get the others later. Prepare to fire!"

"Excuse me sir, would you like me to see if they want to surrender first?" asked a Lieutenant standing close by the Captain.

"Return to your post Lieutenant or I'll have you placed under arrest," snapped the Captain.

"Thank you, sir," then turning to his fellow officers, "Make a note of that order gentlemen. It may come up in a court martial trial someday soon!"

The Captain was livid, "Stand down, Lieutenant! Sergeant place the Lieutenant here under arrest and take him out of harms way. We'll see who gets court marshaled here!"

The Captain resumed his commands to his troops. The orders were to open fire on his signal shot eliminating the village.

"You don't wait for a lion to attack you, then shoot. You fire first and measure his teeth afterwards," he told his officers in justification of his actions.

The moments passed slowly by, then the time came and De Laquote fired his pistol. The first resident had yet to even appear out of their home. The forest came alive with the roar of heavy cannon fire. They fired endlessly into this tiny village leveling every domicile in it. The cannon killed every living thing in the circle of fire without missing so much as a dog. The Captain waved his signal of cease fire and sent in his horse soldiers to clean up any possible survivors. None were found but the body count of only eighteen men older than thirteen, twenty-six women over the age of thirteen and twenty-two children, disturbed everyone including Captain De Laquote.

"Are you sure, Sergeant? There must be more men. Maybe some of those children you counted are small adults. Count them again!" the Captain demanded.

The Captain turned white when a Corporal came running up with the information that during the night the Captain had led his men across the reservation border. They had, in fact, just destroyed a village located exactly where it was placed by the United States Department of Indian Affairs.

"Good Lord, men, what a disaster. May God forgive me. Lieutenant take command. I'm placing myself under arrest, but before I do, may I please suggest you send a detachment to bury those poor children," the Captain said weeping openly.

Another disaster resulting from the foolish panic of Miller and his men. Many other foolish decisions were being made about this same time.

Epps and his herd had several hard drives trying to reach the trail of the great northern buffalo herd. When they reached it near the Kansas border, while still in the area known as the Nations, he was relieved of his herd and his life by one of the notorious Kansas border gangs. These bloody thieves let hard working cattlemen drive their herds across the dangerous Indian nations from parts south as far as Mexico then they just rode out with a superior force of heavily armed men and take the herd away to deliver them at the rail head themselves. Epps and his men not being familiar with the country had no idea how close to the border terrorists they had ventured until it was too late. When Epps refused to relinquish his herd, he was simply shot dead. His men put up the best fight they could but the border bandits were seasoned veterans at this game. They had been doing this same thing since the herds started coming to the Kansas rail heads. They had simply eased in and surrounded Epps' men and when Epps fell, their fates were sealed as well. In less than thirty seconds, thirty men lie dead. The Kansas raiders left them where they lay and drove their still saddled horses into the remudas, jumped a man into the wagon, pushed Fighting Joe's body to the ground and drove off toward Kansas City. Many times if the numbers were too great or the cowmen too ready, the raiders ran the cattle off during the night and gathered all the cowmen couldn't find. They had become more and more bold as time went on. This mass murder of Epps' men was the boldest yet.

The other herds weren't fairing much better, except one. Robert Bliss had the third herd in the original order and was following Dustin's plan exactly! He made every move as if Dustin was there advising him and it was paying off. His trip was not trouble free but as close as it could possibly be. Hank, the all round best camp cook of the bunch, had gone with Captain Bliss on this stick to the plan excursion. This herd was the most mixed up of the whole bunch and probably the largest by count. Close to six thousand five hundred head of steers, bulls and cows being watched over by forty of the steadiest most dependable cattlemen ever assembled. This herd would get through!

The combined herds of Wilson and Mullen were traveling fast being mainly steers. They reached Denver where an Easterner, Horace Taber, had struck it rich mining east of the fledgling city and was building like a mad man. Mullen and Wilson ran into Tabor's agent while in town looking for a market in the mines for a few beefs to sell for cash. Horace Tabor had millions of dollars and bigger plans than the two Texas boys. He offered the two captains fifteen dollars a head delivered in Denver or seventeen dollars delivered to the mining camps in the mountains. Here the boys fell apart. They agreed to sell but Wilson wanted to leave them all in Denver, Mullen wanted to make all the money and go to the mountains. He'd always wanted to see a gold or silver mine.

"Hell, Wilson, with all the money we're going to make on these damn cows, we could buy us a mine of our own," Mullen said as excitedly as a child on Christmas morning.

"I don't want no part of no damn mine! Gold or Silver! Damn it Mullen, we're going to have more money than we'll ever need to start our lives over. Why would we throw it away on a mine?" Wilson reasoned.

"Why would we have to start our lives over? We came north to sell our cattle. Now we have. What's the problem?" Mullen asked.

"The problem is, all these ain't our cattle and this many short is going to blow the whole deal for everyone else. We'll never be able to go home again. We'll have to send for our families and change our names!" Wilson explained.

"Who gives a damn what we call ourselves. We're going to be rich! Very rich. I'm feeling lucky, partner. Let's try and get us one of them mines in trade for cattle," Mullen suggested.

113

"We have to have enough cash to pay off the men. And how do you think we're going to operate a mine without cash?" Wilson reasoned.

"All right, we'll get cash enough for the men up front then the mine will take care of itself. Look at that Horace Tabor. He's a millionaire from these mines. I'm gonna make the deal. Just watch me work on that tin horn Tabor! I'll show him how we do things in Texas."

Before midnight Horace Tabor owned the cattle and had lent the boys enough to pay off their men, some of whom were also hit with the fever and stayed to try their luck. The rest returned to Texas to try and find someone who could still afford to pay cowboys back home.

Wilson and Mullen traded all the cattle to the tin horn Horace Tabor for forty-nine percent of the Holly Varden silver mine and were now Horace Tabor's partners in this venture. What they hadn't thought of was this one mine was about as big a part of Horace Tabor's holdings as a single cow had been of theirs not long ago. In less than six weeks, Wilson and Mullen were working in another of Tabor's mines. The Holly Varden had run out shortly after being invested in by the two Texans. Now they were completely penniless and unable to return home. They would be hung as cattle thieves if ever caught. All they could do is go down underground, both literally and figuratively.

The only two men out of this whole bunch that came out of this with a little profit were the two cooks, Big Bill and Mr. Harris. Mr. Harris met Horace Tabor in one of Tabor's fine dining halls and the two men hit it off instantly. Tabor hired Harris to be his assistant at an unbelievable wage and allowed the romantic fellow free access to the ladies at his less glamorous establishments to avoid future problems with the millionaire's wife.

Big Bill had tried to talk Mullen and Wilson out of their illegal and potentially disastrous plan but was paid no heed and only a small part of the wages due him. Bill took some of his pay and turned it into a small fortune at the tables located in one of Tabor's palaces, as it seems the mining towns were color blind and Bill was not only allowed but encouraged to gamble.

With the freedom his newly acquired windfall provided, Bill thought he'd just ride south and see how the other herds were doing and let them know what Mullen and Wilson had done. Maybe he could help keep the deal from falling completely apart. He liked the kid, Dustin, and didn't like what Wilson and Mullen did to him and the others. Hell, they didn't even give the cowboys their bonus. They'd borrowed enough for their wages, but just enough. The boys could have stayed home and made wages. A few did seem excited about being near the mines. Several tried the tables, some lucky, some not, so much so they had to borrow from those winners to get home. Big Bill had considered traveling across the mountains and go see San Francisco then take a trip on a ship around the cape, maybe even to Europe. In the end his loyalty to Dustin surpassed his love of travel and trying to help the young cowman save the drive won out over touring the world.

Chapter 11

There was a panic at the Morton household. They had received a letter then a wire from Cindy. The letter said she had returned to New York. The wire was to Dustin. It simply stated, Dustin: Have come home. Need surgery. Very urgent. Must have money. Two thousand dollars. Sister of Mercy Hospital NY, NY. Cindy.

The Morton's hadn't seen Dustin or heard from him in months. Matt had a little money, almost a thousand dollars equity in his cantina, but it would be hard to turn into cash. He wanted to help his sister but he didn't. He knew that somehow Dustin would show up and send her another fortune just in time to save the day. He wasn't jealous of Dustin. He loved him as only a brother can, unconditionally. It was just a fact that Dustin had a way of always showing up when things were happening. When Cindy was involved, he'd never not shown up sooner or later. Matt often dreamed of being like Dustin. He spent countless hours staring off into space, running some scenario or another about he and Dustin riding side by side going after bad men or being chased by a thousand Comancheros or wild Indians. Always he pictured the two of them being famous frontier heroes. He was always embarrassed when someone would catch him standing there behind his bar staring off, or eyes closed, thinking what it would be like if he had gone with Dustin. He wanted to, he just hadn't.

Chapter 12

Big Bill traveled from the Horace Tabor owned hotel in Denver toward the hostile plains where he hoped to encounter Robert Bliss' herd. He knew even if he missed the Bliss herd, Epps and then Miller would be close behind. Bill stopped at a little stage stop along the route the cattle were to take on their way to the Platte River. He helloed the house and was invited in. Bill tied his tired horse to the hitching rail, after watering him off and headed toward the little house. He was met by the aromas of meat cooking and coffee boiling, two of his favorite things. He was also met by a shot gun and a madman, two of his least favorite things.

"Hold it boy!" this gun wielding fellow hollered.

"Easy there, mister. That thing could go off," Bill said calmly.

"It damn well may. What the hell you sneaking around my place for?" continued the man.

"Sneaking around? Hell mister, it's still broad daylight and I hollered a greeting from way down the road. My horse was thirsty and I could use a little something to eat. I got a little money," Bill offered in his own defense.

"Where the hell did you get any money, boy?" the old nut asked accusingly.

"I got it picking cotton, masser. Where else could a poor ol' black boy get some money?" Bill said in his best slave voice, as he stepped forward and grabbed the gun away from this cranky old fart.

"Now, old timer, let's get some things straight. First my name is Bill, not boy. Secondly, I sure don't like having a shot gun pointed at me by anyone and last, do I get to come in and have supper or not?" Bill said very instructively, yet still extremely friendly.

"What? You ain't agonna shoot me?" the old man asked Bill.

"Shoot you? Why in hell would I shoot you?" Bill questioned.

"I don't know. I thought you was gonna shoot me is all. My name's McNabb, Ray McNabb. Glad to meet you Bill," McNabb said like he'd just met the president.

"Nice to meet you too, Ray."

Bill ejected the shells and handed them and the shot gun back to McNabb. They walked into the house and the food smell was even better inside than out. They ate and Bill cleaned up the dishes. The two men sat outside after supper. They visited and told of lives very similar in many ways.

At bedtime, Ray said, "Ain't no stage due through here until tomorrow noon, Bill. You're welcome to stay the night on the extra cot if you want to."

"That would be great, Ray. Thanks," Bill said and the two men turned in.

In the morning, Bill made biscuits and Ray was overwhelmed.

"Damn, these are the best I ever eat! I almost hate to see you go," Ray said sincerely.

"I've got to find a cow herd, Ray. It was good to meet you too."

Bill got his horse from the pen and saddled him. Ray stood talking to Bill the whole time.

Bill mounted to leave and Ray hollered after him, "Come back sometime Bill. You're the only black man I ever knowed. If all of them can make biscuits like you do, I may never talk to another white man again!"

Bill rode on and eventually came to the fort formerly commanded by Captain De Laquote. The Captain had left to stand trial in Kansas at Fort Dodge. No replacement had been sent to the little out post yet and the Lieutenant was temporarily in control. Bill asked about the drive and was shocked to hear about Miller's herd. He was worried that there was no word of Epps herd but was relieved to find out Bliss had passed safely and right on schedule.

Bill was torn between riding ahead trying to catch up to Bliss or heading east to find Miller and what men he had left to try and put the herd back together. Bill had never liked Miller but he knew he'd need help and Bliss was apparently having no trouble. The word was Miller was holding a small bunch of cattle east of the fort a few miles.

Bill was surprised how few cows Miller had gathered in two weeks time. It was true he had a short crew but not that short.

Bill asked what he could do to help and Miller answered, "You can cook, is what! We ain't had a fit meal since Scotty got killed."

Bill asked, "Where's your outfit?"

Miller, a little mad and embarrassed answered, "The god damn Army blew it all to hell is where it is. We've been using that bunch of dutch ovens over by the fire. The supplies are in those pack boxes there by the bed rolls."

"Fine, Miller. How many men you got out there?" Bill asked.

"These five with the cattle and twelve out looking for more," Miller answered.

Bill fell right into building a big fire. He'd need plenty of coals to cook with. Things weren't really any tougher than with a wagon. Packing up and moving would be harder but the cooking was the same. Bill rigged up some pack boxes and built a table like work surface. He had supper ready when the men came in. Everyone was thrilled Bill was there. They had been sharing cooking duties and no one seemed very handy at it. Bill explained that it was the wagon itself missing that was the problem The chuck wagon on a cattle drive was much more than a conveyance for pots and pans. It is the center of camp society. The wagon to camp was like the hearth to a home. Bill's pack saddle table would have to take the place of the wagon and seemed to be an adequate substitute. After supper Bill talked to Miller and the men trying to gain an approximate count. The general consensus was just over five hundred fifty head.

"Total?" Bill asked unbelievingly.

"Yes, totally. We're having hell watching out for Indians and looking for cattle at the same time!" Miller said defensively.

"Don't worry about no damn Indians! The Lieutenant at the outpost said De Laquote killed every man, woman and child left on this part of the reservation. A patrol came in while I was there and confirmed the fact that there ain't but a hand full anywhere near here. Anyway except for a few they might kill to eat, the Indians ain't got time to mess with your cows or you for that matter. The Lieutenant said there had just been a horrible massacre up in the Dakotas. Some hot shot named Custer got his whole damn company killed riding into the main council camp unaware of its being there. The worse loss yet by the cavalry. The Army's put all its energy into stopping the Indian resistance and getting them all killed or on the reservations. They pulled General Stewart back to the plains to head up that operation. He took Captain Perron with him. They're sending out some young Brigadier General named Montclair from back east as temporary commander of the frontier forts until things come under control a little better. If I were you Miller, I'd send me two fast riders north to find Bliss' herd and ask him to hold up and wait for you to catch up. Maybe he will send some men back to speed things up a bit. You still have more than forty-five hundred head loose out there!" Bill reasoned.

"I know damn well how many cattle are still unaccounted for, Bill. I don't need no damn cook telling me my business. You just make bread and I'll run this herd," Miller said rather arrogantly considering the poor job he was doing.

"Good then, since you asked my opinion," Bill continued unfazed by Millers statement, "I'd send a large body of men, maybe everyone except the few needed here to hold this pitiful little bunch together. Send them south back over our trail. You may have started them north on the run but they'll go right back south as soon as they realize you're not pushing them north any longer. I just came down from the north and saw no cattle sign at all fresh enough to be your cattle. I'll bet they're in those ridges and canyons to the south and west of the trail. Our cows kept wandering west into the foothills as we came through here. I'll have breakfast ready early so you can take the men before it gets good light. No need looking close to camp. I'll bet this area has been checked pretty good already," Bill finished.

"I been staying here with the gather to make sure we don't lose them again," Miller said his fear showing plainly.

"These men need a leader, Miller. You go with them and get your cows back. Me and four of them can hold this bunch and I'll still have supper ready."

That was all the conversation. Next morning, shamed into leading his men, Miller rode south with eleven cowboys following him. He'd left four with Bill and sent two ahead to try and find Robert Bliss. Not far south of the spot where the encounter with Behachew, one of the men picked up cow tracks. The farther

119

they went the more sign they saw. Just before noon, as the cow hunters rode over a little ridge that over looked a long green valley, the tracker pulled up.

"Hey Miller. Here's a bunch of em! They're grazing their way south like the cook said," he shouted.

"I'll be damned," Miller exclaimed almost exasperated. "Well let's get around them and try and head them north," Miller added.

There were close to nine hundred head in this one group. The feed was so good and water plentiful they had only traveled a few miles southward in two weeks. It got dark before Miller reached the hold up and he was getting nervous again.

Finally the point man on the other side from Miller shouted, "I see the camp! Bill's got a big signal fire going to lead us in! We're off course to the east quite a way, Miller. Head toward me some."

The next five days netted thirty-two hundred head total. With the five hundred Miller already had, they had around thirty-seven hundred head. The real problem was they had not recovered a single horse. Every man had the one he had ridden off on the day of the panic. Up until the last five days, those horses were holding up well. Now that the men were actually working hard gathering cattle, their mounts were worn out.

That night around the fire Bill said, "Miller these horses are played out! The cattle still out are too far south to gather from here. It don't make no sense to move these we have back down the trail to try and catch up with those so I suggest we rest our saddle stock a couple of days then drift these cattle on north. We'll have to move real slow and easy or we'll all be afoot. Another problem is how did you get all these packs out here?" Bill asked Miller.

"The army packed all these supplies out to us and left them. I figured we'd catch the remuda and would have plenty of stock to use as pack animals," Miller replied again defensively.

"I can only cut down so much and still feed you boys so I'll tell you what we'll do. We'll rest tomorrow and then the next day, you and your boys ease out to the herd and catch me the five oldest, fattest, laziest steers you can find and bring them in close. Rope them and hobble them tight. We'll break them to pack. If you boys hadn't gotten your bed rolls blown up, it would take twenty. When we get close to a town, we'll have to trade some cows for horses and new beds. It's getting kinda late in the year and we're going to cold country. A blanket on the ground won't do. We'll need good heavy rolls," declared Bill to the looks of men who knew he was right, about the beds anyway. The vote was still out on the pack steer proposition.

The next day came and went without any excitement except for one of the men had gone for a walk in the foot hills and shot a huge deer. He came back and had no trouble getting volunteers to help carry it into camp. Only eight horses were saddled and being used holding the cattle. Tomorrow the others would work and these would rest. Bill prepared a real feast that night of venison steaks and fresh bread with rice and canned tomatoes.

The next morning found the chosen steer selectors among the cattle, who were so used to

men horseback they had to be kicked out of the way to get through the herd. In less than two hours the picks were made but no steers were caught until Bill rode out and approved each prospect. Five were chosen as perfect for packing. They were cut out and driven toward camp. These gentle giants were all close to ten years old and should have never been allowed to make this drive in the first place. They were too old and tough for most anyone to eat. They were, however, exactly suited for this purpose. They were all roped, hobbled and cross hobbled then tied together head to tail and let stand until after the noon meal.

The afternoon was spent adjusting pack saddles to fit steers. It was surprising to everyone how little adjustment was necessary. They weren't a lot different in size and shape than a horse. Not one even flinched when the heavy packs were placed on the Sawbuck pack saddles. After all were loaded and the packs were secured tightly with the lash ropes, Bill had the men turn them loose and drive the old gentlemen around some, then back up to camp to unload. Bill had made several dozen biscuits extra and had saved them for this moment. When the steers were driven back up to camp, Bill had five men each rope a steer. He then walked up to each one petting him some and scratching his head. Bill also fed each one four or five of those delicious biscuits as he scratched them. He then had them unpacked, unsaddled and turned back into the herd. The old fellows just walked slowly away and started grazing rather close to camp. This routine was repeated for the next two days including the scratching and feeding of the biscuits. By the fourth morning, the morning they were to start north for real, the steers neither had to be roped or tied to be saddled and packed. They came to Bill when he called the men to breakfast. He kept biscuits ready for when they came to him and made sure he always had a sack full for emergencies. The steers were all named and became great pets and pests in short order. Often during the day you would see one or two of the old beggars heading over close to where Bill was riding just in case he had an extra biscuit handy. They were seldom disappointed. Bill was generous with those biscuits and seemed to be genuinely fond of his "gang" as he called them.

During the next two weeks the herd passed several stage stops and outposts and were nearly always able to trade a couple steers or a cow or two for a horse. They had taken the Big Sandy River course by mistake and missed Denver by many miles. This led them straight to the Platte near the new Fort Morgan. They were able to trade cattle for all they would need here. Bill refused to trade off his gang and rented pasture for them from a settler near the fort. He paid the man very well from his gambling winnings and told the Captain at the fort, in front of the settler, to make sure no harm befell his boys.

121

With this attended to, Bill proceeded to furnish the new wagon with a chuckbox and supplies. They traded for a trailer for the large bed rolls, which all wouldn't fit in front of the chuckbox in the main wagon and went with a six horse hitch which was more than ample power for wagon and trailer as there was not much weight to the bed rolls just a lot of bulk. Since they were short on hands this saved having an extra man driving a team and wagon. Before they left the fort, they sent word out by the Army of their location and route in case the other herds inquired about them at another fort somewhere. They were sure they'd missed Bliss and his outfit who would be farther west. They might overtake him or Epps, who they still didn't know they would never see again. Bill checked on his gang one last time and felt confident they had a good home. As he drove away, he saw the settler's child, a young girl, feeding one of the old fools a biscuit from her small hand and all the other old fellows standing close by waiting for a hand out.

Chapter 13

Dustin and Red could hear chanting and see a light from a fire down the canyon a ways. Red took the far side and Dustin went straight down the canyon wall. Below the fire he could see the cliff dwelling. As he rode along anticipating hearing the first shot or feeling the first arrow, he hesitated briefly and grinned big. In the process of his mind running in a thousand different directions as he anticipated the quickly approaching eminent doom, he had just realized this was his birthday! He was twenty-one years old today! He could hardly believe how much had happened in these last few years. It seemed only yesterday he was with his Dad and Mom coming west to a new land and then the mess with Armstrong, Big Mike surprising him in his room at the Morton's barn, Cindy's troubles, the cattle drive and now this mess with Nacatan seemed to have happened in the blink of an eye or had it taken a thousand years. Dustin couldn't be sure. He was just thinking of how wonderful it was going to be to see Cindy again. She would be home waiting for him when he got back. That's when the first shot broke the silence.

Dustin couldn't tell exactly where it came from. Ahead and to his right he thought. He rode more quickly yet still carefully. He only had to wonder for a fraction of a second where the shot had come from as it was followed shortly by dozens more. The warriors had been performing some kind of ceremony around this big fire when one had apparently seen Red and grabbed a gun and fired. Dustin didn't know if Red had been hit or not. All he knew for sure was all the Indians had their weapons now and were using them freely. No shots had been at him so far and he was sure he'd not yet been seen. He pressed his horse into a lope and broke into the clearing. Red's horse lay floundering on the opposite side of the canyon from a soon to be fatal wound. The Indians were all crouching down behind some cover, shooting at the wall opposite Dustin. They were totally exposed to Dustin's position. He remained mounted and began firing, trying to draw some of the pressure off of Red, if he was still alive. Dustin's vantage point and deadly accuracy with a pistol began to even the odds some instantly. He emptied his fathers old black powder 44.40 and Big Mike's army colt killing or critically wounding eleven braves. Dustin thought to himself during the heat of battle while dropping both weapons and drawing Ned's and his own forty-five's, how he'd done even better than Red had in their last encounter with Nacatan's other warriors. Red had only hit ten of twelve.

As he pulled his reserve arsenal, his horse fell dead from multiple wounds, both bullets and arrows. Dustin, in his excitement to take advantage of the Indians vulnerable positioning, hadn't thought of his own when they turned to return his fire. He was close to the door or opening of the cliff dwelling but not very damn close with a dozen warriors shooting at him. As his horse hit the ground, Dustin pushed off backwards so as to be behind him for cover and to make sure he wasn't trapped or hung up underneath him. The Indians rushed toward Dustin and he started firing as they came, knowing full well he could not stop the impending onslaught. When the braves were in the middle of the canyon floor, Red again opened fire. All he had left was his shotgun and it was not effective at this distance. It did stop the charge on Dustin for a second and allowed him to dispose of a few more of the Indians. They were also running out of ammunition and were scattering into the darkness.

Dustin had no idea how many more were left. He did know he'd been shot through the same shoulder as before, and on his damned birthday to boot! He made a dash for the opening in the dwelling and the Indians sent up a howl for real then. Arrows came through the door so fast and furious they almost blocked out the light from the fire. Dustin had taken an arrow in the thigh that was in deep and one down low in his calf that just tore stuff up a little but hurt like hell. He lie still for a moment trying to feel if he'd been hit anywhere else. Sometimes in the middle of a skirmish like this, you don't actually ever feel the one that eventually kills you.

While he surveyed his injuries, Dustin felt the presence of someone in the dark little room with him. He listened and he could hear breathing. He almost jumped back outside it startled him so. It was probably a good thing he was so shot up or he might have run out just to be shot even more. He looked hard, straining to see who or what was in there with him. As his eyes adjusted to the darkness, he saw old Nacatan himself propped up on his death rest, a chair back and bottom made of wood and rawhide with no legs. An Indian, especially a chief, doesn't wait to meet his death lying down and this device allows a sort of sitting up position to be maintained until the end comes.

Dustin spoke to Nacatan in his native tongue, "I'll bet I'm the last person you expected to see. Damn if it don't look like I'm going to be the last too. I'd heard you were getting better."

Shots rang out. Two of them, then a pause and two more. Dustin looked out the door and saw a brave moving to gain a better line of sight on him. Dustin squeezed off a shot and "click", he'd lost count and the pistol was empty. He panicked a little and fired the other pistol but it missed the mark being fired too quickly and not taking good aim. That was the last shot in it as well. He swung the rifle around and his heart sank. The stock had been hit and shattered to pieces. This large caliber rifle would be hard to shoot and impossible to aim from the hip. Two more shots rang out and Dustin realized they were shotgun blasts. Red was alive and fighting. He must be trying to get to the dwelling door. The shots were getting much closer. Dustin forced himself to his feet and to the door. He saw nothing for a moment, then the brave who he had missed before rose to fire an arrow. Dustin stood motionless and tried to take aim by holding the splintered stock of his rifle out from his torn up shoulder just enough so he could still sight the Indian brave. The arrow grazed his side but he stood still and pulled the trigger. The wound in his shoulder had weakened him even more than he knew and the tremendous kick from his rifle drove the splintered stock hard against the open bloody wound knocking him back against the back wall of what might be his tomb. Weakly he loaded another round into the now blood covered rifle and started out the door. He'd be damned if he was going to die in this hole with this old, mutilated face having Indian. He looked down at Nacatan, who Dustin could see clearly in the fire light now that he was standing. Damn if he couldn't see a little compassion in the dying old eyes. The old man was proud of the way Dustin was facing the end. Dustin thought he saw a little pleasure in the eyes to the fact that he, Nacatan noble chief of his tribe, was going to out live the man who had killed him.

Dustin started out, rifle ready and said, "So long old man. See you in hell… tomorrow," and ran out the door.

He didn't make it outside. He was knocked back in and down by someone coming in. It was Red.

"Where the hell do you think you're going? You look like hell again, Dustin. Sorry I took so long. I had to run the last two down. We couldn't have no witness left or we'd never be done with this," Red stated real short of breath.

"Is it over, Red?" Dustin asked relieved.

"Yes it is, Lad. Old Nacatan ain't dead yet but looks like he's soon to be. They sure thought he was about to go. They have his war horse all painted up and a travois hooked to him with all his stuff on it. They was just waiting for the old fart to die so's they could kill his horse and burn them up together. They got to die at the same time or real close to it or they can't find each other in the happy hunting grounds or some such bullshit as that. Let's shoot the old bastard and we'll take his horse to Teresa's place. We both could use her services again. I'll let you ride on the travois! How does…"

Red was stopped by an arrow coming clear through his back and out his chest, sticking out nearly two full inches. Red could not speak but looked pitifully at Dustin who could do nothing for his friend. When Red fell, the Indian stepped into the door apparently not thinking Dustin was still alive for he didn't have an arrow strung. A fatal mistake. Dustin stuck his big, broken rifle in the man's chest and fired blowing the surprised brave back outside. The recoil snapped Dustin's wrist like a twig and he lie back cradling his right arm in anguish. He pushed Red off his legs and drug himself outside. He still wasn't going to die in there.

It had been cloudy all afternoon and now a cold rain started to fall. This may have been what had saved Dustin's life. He drifted in and out of consciousness until morning's light finally came. He was able to stand but just barely. He looked inside at his friend, the fightingest son-of-a-bitch he had ever known. As he stood leaning against the doorway looking down at Red, he heard the breathing again. Nacatan was still alive. He was obviously very close to death and the breathing was erratic. He looked in the old man's eyes and they seemed to be asking for help.

"I'm afraid you're done old man but if you want me to, I'll take you to a place not far from here where we can get some help. I ain't as bad off as you are but I'm in real trouble. A couple of these wounds are worrying me some. You're hurt worse so you get to ride in the travois."

The Chief nodded weakly his approval of Dustin's plan. Dustin was too shot up to bury Red so he just recited Red's own words over him the way Red had over Big Mike and Ned. Dustin's left arm was still working pretty well. That was about all that was working. He limped out while his strength lasted and took his saddle off his horse and put it on the chief's.

Dustin hadn't really looked at this horse before now. He was a magnificent animal. Red, with a bald face and a blue eye, with four legs white to above the knees and hocks. Dustin had always preferred to ride plain colored horses but there was something about this big young horse he really liked. He picked up his pistols and got Reds shot gun and belt. He even put his old Spencer forty caliber on the travois, broken stock and all. He figured he'd get the stock replaced when he got to a fort. Besides it was a good gun and they were expensive. He was able with great effort to drag Nacatan out the door and onto the travois. He had to tie him in so he'd not slide off. Everything ready, Dustin stepped onto the big red horse he had been calling Chief and started toward Teresa's.

As midday approached, Dustin developed a high fever from the effect his wounds were having. Nacatan was riding painlessly now. Dustin didn't realize it but the old man died by mid morning. His fever growing worse Dustin was delirious and was riding in a large circle finally blacking out completely. He'd have fallen off to die alone along side the trail but for his foresight in having tied himself into his saddle when he began feeling light headed.

Chapter 14

Robert Bliss, having reached the point of delivery just before the appointed time, rode into Fort Belknap to notify the Commander of his arrival and see if any word of the other herds had been received. It had not. The Colonel in command of the two forts and of the two large reservations, a man named Lovell, was relatively new, having just recently been sent out from Washington to this wilderness as punishment for some politically incorrect act or another. He was bitter about his new assignment and it showed in all his actions, or lack of them would be more like it. The Quartermaster's storehouses were full at both forts with goods for the reservation Indians, yet they were freezing and starving to death for want of food and clothing. This herd of cattle shows up, that he knew nothing about, along with news that even more are coming was all very disturbing to Colonel Lovell. Cattle were a commodity he couldn't very well just ignore. They would require some action on his part once he received them. He decided that was the answer, he'd just not receive them, at least until he'd seen the proper paper work for their purchase. Bliss assured the Colonel all the paper work was in order and with the cook of the last herd. Bliss hadn't known for sure Scotty had the journal and its contents but he hadn't remembered seeing it at the burial of Gibson. He explained to the Colonel that if he would get word to General Stewart or Captain Perron they could explain the details of the purchase. Bliss was dumbfounded by the news Lovell told him next and especially by his pleasure taken in its affect on him.

"Both Stewart and Perron along with six interpreters and nine other officers and government officials were savagely killed by the Sioux and Cheyenne at a meeting held to relocate reservations previously given to these people on land the United States was going to need back. The Indians refused to sign the new treaty and insisted that the government stick by their word in the original one. The officers and officials explained why that would be impossible, because the land the Great White Father had given them was too valuable to the white settlers to waste on Indians and that the new land would be plenty good enough for their reservation, but the ignorant savages still refused. The officials demanded the Indians sign the new agreement but the chiefs refused saying there was no need to sign. The Great White Father's treaty and word weren't true anyway. The officials threatened to place the chiefs under arrest and send them to prison if they did not sign and when they attempted to arrest them, the Indians watching the proceedings over powered the government representatives and killed them all. A small group of the guards were allowed to get away to tell what happened to liars from Washington," Lovell finished his oratory with a swollen pride having dashed Bliss's chance for support in his ridiculous story.

Bliss was told to hold the cattle until all arrived and he would decide what was to be done with them then and not before. Bliss rode back out to the herd as dejected as a man could be. As he approached, he sat up straight and would not let the men suspect the gravity of the situation.

"Men, we need to just graze these beasts awhile here, at least until the others arrive. I'm a little concerned about Mullen and Wilson who were ahead of us. They may have met with some bad luck. Let's scout around and find us a valley near here with good water and deep grass that will hold us through the winter, if need be," Bliss said as cheerfully as he could.

A beautiful spot was located midway between the two reservations and allowed the cattle to graze under a very loose guard for the first time in eight months. Shortly after their arrival, Indians from both reservations came to see the cattlemen. These were different from any Indians the cowboys had ever seen. Their language was very different. They spoke French instead of Spanish as a second language. Whatever language they spoke it was plain what they wanted. They were starving. Their children died daily from hunger. They had not been allowed to hunt off the reservations for many months and there was no game left within their boundaries. Both tribes suffered the same slow sure death of starvation. Bliss had the men cut a dozen steers out for each tribe and drive them to the villages immediately. The representatives from both tribes insisted the cattlemen come join them for a feast. A year before this would have caused a war. The two tribes had been sworn enemies for years and choosing one tribes feast to attend first would have offended the other to the point of causing blood shed. Because of the shared hardships and starvation these two warring peoples had become compatible and even friendly toward the needs of each other. It was decided to have a long feast and everyone would attend both. The cattle would still be driven straight to both villages as quickly as possible so they could be put to the life saving use of sustenance for the villagers. The cattlemen and chiefs would just start at one party and finish with the other. This ritual was repeated so often in the next few weeks as to become routine.

The weather was turning harsh and log shelters and dugouts were built for the cattlemen to live in. Several of these were fairly substantial structures. The Indians showed the cowboys how to build fireplaces out of a certain type of sod lined with river rock of a particular type so as not to explode when they got hot from the fire.

It was shortly after the first hard snow of winter that Miller's herd showed up near the fort. They were minus Miller along with many more cattle than they had previously lost. This came when they were preparing to cross the Mussellshell and it was rising from fall storms. Bill suggested they cross quickly because it would be dangerous with quicksand for days after it went back down. Miller didn't agree. He held the herd and waited four days for the water to subside then against Bill's warning started the herd across. By midday over eight hundred head were bogged in the Mussellshell. With half the herd on each side they didn't have enough men to watch two herds and still have men to pull out the bogged cattle. Miller was unable to get the cows that had already crossed to go back to the larger group still on the original bank so he forced small bunches into the mire until nothing remained on the south shore. At one point near dusk, the men estimated twelve hundred head were bogged simultaneously. It was too dark and dangerous to try freeing the cattle that night. They would have to resume their efforts in the morning. A heavy rain to the northwest saved Miller the trouble. By morning the water had risen again, drowning or washing away every animal previously stuck in the mud of the Musselshell.

Proceeding on, the herd had only the Missouri to cross just east of its joining the Judith. Miller had Bill ride with him to check out the crossing. It looked exactly like the Musselshell had, it was rising steadily.

"We should hurry across now to avoid the same thing happening, right Bill?" Miller said sure he'd receive an affirmative answer.

"Not this one Miller. It's fast and deep. We'd all drown for sure. I think there's enough rock and gravel along here to maintain a good bottom. We'd better wait till this one goes down then try," Bill offered.

"Bull shit! The last time we waited we lost a third of the cattle! I'm not going to let that happen again. You drive that damn wagon across and I'll bring the herd in a run," Miller scolded Bill like the last crossing had been Bill's fault instead of his own.

"I don't believe I will, Miller," Bill said as he climbed off the wagon seat and untied his saddle horse from the rear of the trailer, then continued, "You want this wagon across, you drive it across. I've had all of you I can take! If you live to see Dustin, tell him I came back to help," Bill finished in a tone that did not encourage debate.

Miller jumped off his horse and onto the wagon and as he headed toward the embankment hollered back at Bill, "Good riddance! You've been nothing but a thorn in my side the whole time you've been here!"

The point men and cattle had drawn close to the raging torrent and had witnessed the last of the disagreement. They all watched silently as Miller's team splashed into the water. The current began washing the horses down stream instantly but they were past the point of no return and had to try to cross. When the wagon hit deep water it was just a matter of seconds until it rolled over and over dragging the horses and Miller down with it. A more horrible sight is hard to imagine than that of those six poor horses restricted by harness being pulled down that raging torrent getting ever more tangled until their struggle was finally over. The water was so strong and fast that the wagon never washed to either bank. Bill had two men follow the river to retrieve Miller's body if it washed up but it too raced on seemingly forever.

Bill shared his recommendations with the men and all agreed. They spread the cattle out and in just two days the water receded to where a man's feet did not get wet when he rode across it. The far bank was a little soft and a dozen cows now very heavy with calf bogged down but all were recovered without instance except for one of the cowboys lost a boot in the deep mire and try as he may, could not retrieve it. The one bare foot caused him much grief and concern. Luckily for him, they were near the end of the drive.

A similar reception to the one Bliss received awaited them from an ever more unpleasant Colonel Lovell. The cold weather and rough conditions did not suite him at all. Bill was hurried off without even the small amount of explanation Bliss received. A soldier told Bill where he could find his companion's camp.

There was a big celebration when Bill and his herd arrived. Bliss had his new Indian friends come and to everybody's surprise, Bill spoke fluent French. When he was a child, he worked in the garden by the big house of his master. The master's little girl was being taught her lessons, including French, on the porch overlooking this garden. Bill picked up the language and he and the little girl talked in French to one another their whole lives. The Indians were very curious at what Bill had to say. They learned all about the original size of the drive and its intended purpose. This caused a little trouble but was settled shortly. The Indians decided that if the cattle were intended for them, they should have them and it took some amount of deterrent to make them realize that they would not be theirs until the cattlemen they belonged to had been paid. Bliss had Bill remind them that he had given freely all the beef they could eat since his arrival here and that because of this, their people no longer starved. He also had Bill remind them that the other items like flour and coffee and blankets Bliss had given them, he had traded cattle for with the quartermaster of the fort. These had kept them warm and full. Bill told them Bliss had saved their lives and they were acting more like whites than Indians and he was ashamed of their behavior. His scolding them in French seemed to add more strength and venom to his reprimand. It was because they had learned French from the missionaries and they considered it the sacred language. They apologized for their poor behavior and excused themselves. They would return after they had prayed for forgiveness for their covets.

Bill and Bliss talked all night about all that had happened and what could be done about any of it. Epps was a big worry to both men. They had no way of knowing he was far past worrying about. The twenty-five hundred head Bill had arrived with were mainly cows and bulls and the cows were bred to calve in the spring. The two men knew that now the snows had started there was nothing else they could do until spring but dig in and concentrate on survival.

Chapter 15

Dustin came to hearing the laughter of children playing and dogs barking. He was lying on a buffalo skin rug on the ground in what must be a teepee. He had no idea they could be so warm and pleasant. He looked across the fire, which was in the center of the area and saw an old woman sewing something with a bone needle and gut thread. He lay still watching her ancient fingers nimbly plying the needle and thread, producing a beautiful row of perfect stitches in what appeared to be a pair of buckskin pants.

In her own tongue Dustin spoke to this elderly seamstress, "Those are beautiful, young lady. Are they for your lover?" (Apache's have no word for boyfriend), Dustin teased.

"Why yes they are. They're for my most recent lover. They're for you. You have no idea what we've been to one another since you've arrived... You disrespectful one." (There's no Apache word for smart ass either), the old woman said slyly, a hint of remembrances long gone in her tired old eyes.

"Thank you very much, ma'am," this time a little more respectfully and he continued with, "I'd bet if you help me sit up I could eat a little."

His nursemaid rose and started to leave, tossing the finished garment to Dustin smiling and said, "Here you might as well put these on, no better than you were with them off!"

She giggled at her cleverness and Dustin encouraged her by looking grievously hurt by the implication. She hurried out of the teepee doorway very young girl like and still giggling.

In a moment the teepee flap flew open and a large, bronze, young warrior, his face painted, stepped in. Dustin lay speechless for a moment then thought, what the hell, if they had wanted him dead they would have just let him die. More than likely they probably wanted to make him confess to shooting the old chief. Dustin wondered how Nacatan was doing anyway.

Then figuring if he was to be tortured, they might as well get it started and said, again in Apache, "Did I sleep through the ceremony? I see you're in your best clothes. I didn't think you could start without me. Help me up and I'll come out and join you. I don't want you to do this with me not there," he said very solemnly from the pain and prospect of even more too come but not wanting to show any fear of knowing how much more there could be.

He kept picturing Big Mike's torn, mutilated body and remembering how nobly the big Irishman had met his end. Dustin silently prayed he could die as well. The young man, not too much older than Dustin, stood looking deep into Dustin's eyes. An ever so slight smile of approval came to the corners of his mouth.

131

"So be it!" the man said and turned to motion to someone outside. Two other men, a little older than the first, entered along with the old nursemaid. The men lifted Dustin not too gently but with total absence of the malice which he had expected. The old woman knelt down in front of his nakedness, his new buckskin pants in her hands and slipped them on him giving him a little wink while she tied the waist cord. She then pulled the most beautiful, buckskin blouse, with long fringe the length of each arm and all across the back, over his head, being as careful as possible not to open the horrible shoulder wound which was now neatly bandaged. Lastly, she fetched from her side of the teepee a new pair of very high top, lace up moccasins with the heaviest souls he'd ever seen.

It all fit perfectly and he commented so to the nurse who said, "Of course it does. I made it all especially for you."

Dustin asked, "Why?"

The old woman looked down and said, "For the funeral."

Dustin simply stood erect as possible with his right leg hurting so terribly he was hoping to pass out from the pain and miss the rest of this dance.

He said, "Thank you," very softly to the old woman.

Once Dustin was dressed, the first warrior said, "Come, I'm sure my father will be glad to see you again."

That removed any doubt left in Dustin's mind as to what was next. He walked with less help than he really needed now. He had decided to die so bravely that these noble warriors would weep with shame at the mere mention of his name for generations to come

He walked outside into the light saying, "Take me to the Great Nacatan. I wish to see him again also."

Dustin had conviction in his voice and it commanded respect from all those around him.

"Here is my father," said Yoshela. Dustin hadn't recognized him before. It had been years since he'd seen Yoshela and never in ceremonial paint. Dustin stood speechless looking at the burnt ashes of a funeral pyre. He remained quietly studying the burnt bones of man and horse trying to remain conscious. The pain had him very light headed and he wanted this over now. His passing out would only delay the inevitable.

After a few silent moments, Yoshela spoke to the gathering, "This is our friend, Dustin Thomas. He came to our village many years ago as not much more than a boy. He learned our language and our ways. He has returned to us as a man bringing us home the body of our Great Chief Nacatan, my own father, in spite of his own wounds so serious we thought he too would surely die. We welcome you to our home, to your home, Dustin Thomas. I know my father welcomes you as well, for I know he is looking down from above and smiling on us all here today."

Dustin shed tears as sincerely and abundantly as he ever had before. He too looked toward the heavens and silently thanked his father then succumbed to the pain and dizziness and slipped into deep unconsciousness.

Chapter 16

Cindy left the telegraph office again from her weekly trip to wire Dustin for money for the operation she needed. The surgery wasn't for Cindy herself but for her husband. Yes, for her husband, Louis De Larinso. She'd met Louis while on a trip to Rome when she first arrived in Europe and had been taken with his grace and elegance. He was different from any man she'd ever met. Very dainty in manner and delicate in stature. He was a gambler and being the son of a wealthy, politically powerful family from Sicily, could afford to play win or loose.

Cindy loved the flippant way in which this pretty young fellow tossed large sums of money around. He was quite taken by her as well. She very obviously was new to money and he very accustomed to limitless amounts of it. After a short period of time, as fate would have it, the political mood in Sicily changed considerably leaving the De Larinso family outside the circle of power and wealth. Much of their land was seized, and most all of their fortune as well, for being sympathizers to the old regime.

Louis without mentioning his families situation to Cindy did the only noble thing and married her as quickly as he could for her money. The political environment in Sicily grew to a violent state of military aggression and many enemies of the new government were arrested and assassinated, Louis De Larinso's father and his two brothers included. Louis must flee or be taken as well. He purchased two very first class passages on a ship to the states and told Cindy it was just a honeymoon excursion and that they would return after taking in what pleasures the Americas had to offer.

Cindy had relinquished control of the money she'd received from Dustin to her husband for him to add to his own fortune. Louis was very nervous and quite short with her until the ship sailed then he returned to his charming self again. This lasted for just over half of the voyage. Louis had been gambling in the ships plush casino and had not faired well at all. He came to Cindy late one night demanding more money from her. She explained he'd taken all she had already. He beat her in anger and took much of her recently purchased jewelry and then left. Cindy wasn't hurt badly. Louis wasn't a large man and she'd been beaten severely before by some very sizable ruffians.

Taking some of the jewelry to the Captain, Louis secured a line of credit for meals and drinks for the remainder of the trip. He was not, however, able to regain the freedom at the gambling tables he'd once possessed. The Captain was willing to consider a mistake had been made and funds left behind. He would be willing to wait until their arrival in New York harbor for payment of the notes Louis had written to the ship's casino. He'd hold the jewelry as good faith but was sure its value would not nearly cover Louis' debt.

Louis had taken a few of the simpler pieces from Cindy's collection below to the common passage section of the ship and financed one more night of gambling in much less plush surroundings. Louis not only lost her jewels but got his ass kicked for not being able to cover his last wager. He returned to their estate suite and when Cindy accidentally showed a slight smile when he told her what had happened, he shared his beating with her, this time blackening an eye that kept her in her room for several days. The more time that passed, the more violent and cruel Louis became. He would sometimes just stand in front of Cindy cursing her and her lack of funds as a plague he intended to cure.

One night after Cindy had gone to bed, Louis entered their suite with a fat, smelly, half drunk man of obvious wealth. The two men walked directly to the bed chamber she lay in. Cindy sat up startled by the intrusion.

Louis turned up the light and said, "There! I told you she was beautiful. Now give me the money. I'll be back in two hours. You be gone when I return."

Louis turned and walked out with cash in hand without even looking at Cindy. She was numb to her soul, was it the nightmare beginning all over? The fat man turned the light down slightly and stepped to her removing his clothes as he came. Louis said he'd return in two hours but he could have returned in fifteen minutes as far as the fat man was concerned. Her beauty was more than he had anticipated and he finished his pleasure quickly and left.

Louis had not returned in two hours as he said he would but it didn't matter to Cindy. Nothing mattered now. Louis came in early the next morning, freshly groomed, wearing a new suit of clothes and carrying a tray with a lovely breakfast on it. He never apologized or explained anything to her at all except for saying he had a better run of luck and things would be back to normal again shortly. Nothing changed. In a matter of days Cindy received another visitor to her bed chamber and then another and still another. The remainder of the trip passed in the same manner.

Finally the ship pulled into New York harbor and the passengers disembarked. Louis made a point to avoid the Captain as he could not pay the old debts owed the casino. Louis forfeited Cindy's jewelry as partial payment. It was all the payment he intended to remit. Louis and Cindy landed on the docks with their rather expensive wardrobe and enough money for a months rent in a mid priced hotel. This would not suit Louis at all. Instead he checked them into the finest hotel in New York for one night. He and Cindy dressed in their finest, minus her good jewelry and descended the stairs to dine in the hotel's fine dining room. Supposedly by accident, they passed a very well appointed room where several card games were going on.

"It's too early to eat. Let's step in and watch the action for a moment," Louis said to Cindy almost dragging her into the room.

There were four tables going and one had an empty chair.

A large man seated at this table said, "Good, De Larinso! You made it. We've been waiting for you!"

Louis didn't look to see if Cindy was mad or even surprised by the deception. He need not bother. She was neither mad nor surprised. She was once again numb. She stood silently for hours listening to someone playing classical music on a piano in another room. She loved the beautiful sounds and drifted away listening to it's soothing then invigorating movements. Soon Cindy was brought out of her musically induced trance by Louis accompanied by the gentleman who had greeted them on their arrival. The three walked upstairs and Louis returned to the table alone loosing his newly gotten gain quickly.

He'd returned to the room sooner than he had anticipated having lost so rapidly. The gentleman visitor was enjoying himself and getting full benefit in return for his investment. Louis demanded the fellow leave instantly. When he refused to go, a short fight ensued. The same result as always was forth coming. Louis got his ass kicked and later shared the whipping with the lovely Cindy.

They had to check out by ten the next morning with nowhere to go and no money either. They spent the day selling their trunks and what clothes they could and raised enough money for another game. Cindy hadn't said anything to Louis but her last visitor had given her a twenty dollar gold piece as a tip. She kept this hidden from Louis in case he didn't get them a place to stay. He hadn't surprised her and hadn't gotten a room. He had won a little money and was playing well. Cindy tried not to look at any of the games participants. She knew well enough she might see one or more of them soon enough. By the early morning hours Louis was broke again and playing desperately.

He won another hand or two and then suddenly the man seated to Louis' right reached and grabbed his hand and said, "Mister, I just threw that king you played here away with my discards. My friend, you are a cheat!"

Louis jumped up and declared his innocence while reaching for his vest pocket derringer. Louis didn't have the nerve to use the pistol and in fact had never fired it. He intended to use it to allow a get away. This move was too slow and predictable for a sleazy New York gambling hall. The man across from Louis drew a beautiful, little, thirty-two caliber pistol and shot Louis dead center. The bullet entered his sternum and lodged in his spine paralyzing him instantly. Cindy ran to Louis who could talk and move his head and arms but had lost all feeling and control of his body from just above his navel down. Louis was rushed to a hospital and stabilized. He needed surgery to give him any chance at prolonged survival. It would be very dangerous and even more expensive than it was risky. Cindy pleaded her case of poverty and homelessness to a nun in charge of something at the hospital and was found lodging and given a job mopping floors and cleaning up after patients; bed pans, dirty sheets, etc.

Cindy wired Dustin for more money immediately and continued weekly to try to get Louis the help he needed. She continued working at the hospital and caring for Louis who had become even more abusive than ever before. She had to physically restrain him one night after she came home from work exhausted as usual from the labors of the day. Louis had gotten some liquor from someone and was in a particularly good mood, complimenting Cindy on how beautiful she had remained and what a terrific body she had. He told her how much he missed seeing her in her beautiful gowns like she used to wear. He was so nice for the first time in a long time it made her feel pretty again. She finally agreed to put on one of the dresses they'd not been able to sell. She cleaned herself up, brushed out her beautiful hair, letting it hang down long instead of in the bun she wore to scrub floors in. She seductively teased Louis through the closed bedroom door.

"Are you ready, Darling? Here I come!" Cindy said very enticingly.

She opened the door and stepped into the room. She was wearing a tight, very low cut red satin dress with a slit up the side to mid thigh. She'd purchased this and many others with the money Dustin sent her to come home on. This dress was considered too scandalous even to wear in Paris where its designer lived. Cindy had worn it once when she was feeling particularly sassy one night in Rome and was the hit of the evening. Tonight as she stood there she looked even better in it than she had before. She'd lost some weight without losing any of her shape. She attributed it to the hard work and also thought she still looked good. The mood left her as soon as she entered the room. There by Louis stood the drunken bastard who had given Louis the booze.

Grabbing a kitchen knife she screamed, "Not this time you sorry trash. Not this guy or any other ever again, do you hear me?"

Then addressing the standing drunk still wielding the knife, "How much did you give him?"

"Half a bottle of good whiskey and two dollars!" the drunk said.

Cindy went to her purse and got four dollars cash and coin and handed it to the drunk and with one hand waving the knife in his face grabbed his shirt at the shoulder and manhandled him out the door threatening to cut his throat if he ever gave Louis any more liquor. She slammed the door and turned around walking straight to Louis wheelchair.

She placed the knife point under Louis' chin saying, "Not ever again! Do you understand me? Not ever! I'll cut your heart out and shove it down your damn throat and leave you in the street for the dogs!"

She walked toward her room, stopped and turned around, "Never again! Damn you to hell you sorry son-of-a-bitch! Damn you!"

She slammed the bedroom door behind her and finally let herself cry. She cried until she fell asleep, waking up still in her sassy gown, barely in time to get changed and to work.

Louis didn't speak to her as she left. It was best he hadn't. She was still in a volatile state of mind. She sent an extra telegram this week and just kept on working and waiting for Dustin to send help.

Chapter 17

Dustin came to and it was dark except for the glow of the coals burning in the fire located in the center of the circular floor. He was again on his buffalo hide rug and was very warm and comfortable. He drifted back off to sleep and was later awakened by the sounds of someone moving around him. It was his old nursemaid building up the fire against the cold of early morning. Dustin gradually was getting better and stronger. He could feel the steady improvement daily. These Apaches treated him like one of their own, not once asking more about Nacatan's death than Dustin was willing to tell them on his own. He told them of a Great Chief dying nobly in a fierce battle. That was good enough for them.

Dustin was eager to get back to the Morton's and be with Cindy. As soon as he could, he got outside and walked around. Soon he felt strong enough to ride only he didn't have a horse. He asked Yoshela if there was a horse he could use to go home on. His future wife was waiting for him and he wanted to get to her. Yoshela said he wished Dustin would stay longer but understood his desire to go home. Yoshela sent a man to get Dustin's horse. He returned in a few moments with the beautiful, red, bald faced, blue eyed horse that had been the chief's.

"I thought you buried him with Nacatan," Dustin said obviously pleased the horse was alive.

"We sent my father's old war horse along with him on his journey. This is your horse now as a gift from my people," Yoshela said and handed the reins to Dustin.

His saddle was already on Chief and he was ready to go.

"You will always be welcome with us anywhere we are, Dustin Thomas. Your name will forever be held sacred among our people," Yoshela said very officially.

"Good by my friends," then turning to the teepee he'd stayed in he said, "Take care of yourself young lady. I'll be back again someday to see you."

The old woman threw a kiss to him and giggled, then reentered the teepee.

Dustin, dressed in his new buckskins, riding Chief, the most beautiful horse he'd ever seen, rode home to Matt Morton's cantina, the Confederate. He had ridden too far and nearly fell as he dismounted in front of the saloon. He stood hanging onto his saddle and Chief's mane until he could bear his weight on his right leg. He walked into the front door and said hello to Matt who had been standing there day dreaming about a make believe time when he and Dustin were riding alone across the frontier avenging wrongs and punishing evil doers, as bold and famous as two men have ever been. They were noble and honest, brave and free, feared and loved by every man, woman and child in the west. He was a little embarrassed to be caught starring off into space by the very man he was dreaming about riding with, as if Dustin could actually read his mind and know what he was thinking. He could have rode off after adventure like Dustin if he'd wanted to, he just hadn't.

"Hello Matt! How's Cindy?" Dustin asked Matt first thing.

Matt was startled by this strange looking white man wearing buckskins and moccasins. It took several seconds for him to put the voice together with the face of his foster brother.

"She's in trouble, Dustin. Here I've got a box of telegrams from her. She's in New York and is real sick. She needs more money, lots more for a surgery," Matt explained as he showed Dustin the telegrams.

"Goodness Matt, these started coming months ago. Why haven't you sent her any money or gone to get her?" Dustin asked almost panicky.

"The surgery is not for her, Dustin. It's for her husband," Matt said both angrily and some ashamed of his sister.

"Husband! You're mistaken Matt!" Dustin said disbelieving.

"Read them yourself. I haven't shown them to the girls. Mom's still pretty sick over Dad's passing. I didn't want to upset her anymore over Cindy's damn husband. I knew you'd come along and know what to do," Matt explained.

"When did Dad die, Matt? What happened?" Dustin said sadly.

"He had another stroke and died on your twenty-first birthday. It was for the best. He was suffering pretty badly, Dustin. I sure do miss him."

I'm very sorry Matt. He was a good man," Dustin said reflectively.

"I'm sorry about Cindy, Dustin. What are you going to do?" Matt asked

"I'm going to send her money and go help her. That's all I can do. She asked me for help and I told her I'd always help her when she asked me to."

"I don't know why you would," Matt said angrily.

"Damn it Matt, because she asked me to. I hope it's not too late," Dustin said.

"Dustin, I thought it was you!" Kathy said and ran jumped into his arms not thinking he might be hurt.

In fact, he liked the way she felt in his arms.

"Damn girl, you're about to become a full growed woman. How's the place?" Dustin asked her as he sat her down.

"It's beautiful. We've got nearly four hundred head of 08 cows with calves on 'em."

"We've got what?" Dustin asked.

"Cows, you ain't so much an Indian fighter you forgot what a cow was did you?" she teased.

"Hell no! I haven't forgotten what cows are but how did we, I mean you get four hundred head?" Dustin asked her.

"They just wandered in and joined the hundred head we already had."

She went on to explain that one day while she was checking on the hundred head of 08 cattle, she found a few east in the foothills and kept finding a few more all the time until she'd gathered three hundred more cows and two hundred-fifty steers."

"That's wonderful, Kathy but if you had all those cattle why didn't you help Cindy?" Dustin scolded.

"Help Cindy do what? What's he taking about Matt?" Kathy asked her brother obviously surprised.

Matt said, "Cindy is back in New York and has a problem and needs two thousand dollars."

Instantly Kathy said, "Dustin, let's sell all the cows we can gather!"

"You are really all right, Kathy. That won't be necessary honey. I should have a fortune in a bank in Texas. I'll wire my friend Mr. Rogers, to get Cindy the money. Thanks for volunteering. You are very special. Why couldn't I have fallen in love with you first!" Dustin said to Kathy looking into her eyes deeply seeing what he always had wanted to see in Cindy's but hadn't.

"Kathy, you've done well with the cattle and even though I'm worried about how the cattle you found wandered away from the drive in the first place, I want you to be my partner in the ranch. I'm going to go get Cindy and bring her back here. I was going to go to Texas with her but I think she would be better off here with all of you. What do you say, full partners?" Dustin said sticking out his hand.

"All right, Partner. I've always wanted to share the ranch with you, but as your wife. For now I'll settle for being your partner," Kathy said very matter of factly.

"Damn it girl, you don't pull no punches, do you?" Dustin said.

"Nope! Hey, Partner, where'd ya get the buckskins?" Kathy kidded him.

"It's a long story, honey. I'll tell you when Cindy and I get back from New York. I gotta get. I have a long way to go. Take care of my horse for me, will you, Partner? His name is Chief and he's real special to me," Dustin asked her.

"You bet I will and if you call me honey one more time before you go, I'll shoe him and brush him for you too!" Kathy said.

"He's out front. Take him with you. Matt, take me to the fort so I can get a ride east," Dustin asked of his friend.

Matt took Dustin to the fort and let him out.

"Dustin, I'm sorry I didn't go get Cindy. I wanted to but just didn't," Matt said.

"I know Matt, I know. It'll be all right if I can get the money to her in time. See you when we get back," Dustin said and shook hands with his friend.

"You are going to bring them back here?" Matt said quite confused.

"Yep! If she'll come," Dustin answered him.

"What about her husband?" Matt pressed.

"I guess we'll have to wait until he's well enough to travel and bring him too. The climate will do him good I bet," Dustin said very seriously.

"You are the strongest man I've ever known, Dustin. She's got a husband! He needs some kind of operation, maybe that cost two thousand dollars and you send the money then run all the way to New York to bring Cindy and her husband, who may or may not be there when you get there, back to your ranch to take care of them both because you think the climate might agree with him. Good Lord Dustin, Cindy might just be trying to get even more money out of you," Matt tried to explain.

"You got a terrible attitude, Matt. You need to get out of this place for a while and see some of what life is like on the outside. Come with me to New York and we'll get Cindy together," Dustin said invitingly.

"I'd like to Dustin but," Matt stopped when Dustin interrupted, "You just can't! I know Matt. Someday you will be sorry you never did a lot of the things you could have done. You'll be a tired old fart just dreaming about a life you could just as easily have lived. See you my friend," Dustin finished.

"I already do dream about it, Dustin," Matt said too softly for his friend to hear.

At the fort Dustin tried to get some information about his cattle drive. None was available. There had been a wire run to the fort and Dustin being listed as a scout was allowed some time on it. He used it to ask his banker, Mr. Rogers, to lend him twenty five hundred dollars and have it wired to the Sister's of Mercy Hospital in New York City.

Dustin filed a report about the death of Nacatan and Yoshela's willingness to come into the reservation. Dustin answered many questions from the newest post commander, a veteran Cavalry Colonel named Joshwell, transferred from the plains. He had been placed here for his sympathetic view points in dealing with the Indians under his charge. Washington felt now was not a good time to have an Indian rights activist in charge of one of the forts on the once again hostile Great Plains. Colonel Joshwell was very happy to hear Yoshela was against the war with the whites and could see there was no chance of winning it. Yoshela was the only hope his people had, and if coming into the reservation would give them any chance for survival, he was going to take it. Colonel Joshwell would do all in his power to make the move as painless as possible for Yoshela and his village. The Colonel offered the reward for Nacatan to Dustin but he refused it. He asked the Colonel instead to split it three ways between the families of Red, Big Mike and Ned if they had any. He couldn't accept it after how good Nacatan's people had treated him.

This all taken care of, Dustin headed east on a fast horse leading another of equal speed. He would ride cross country to the railhead already being built westward from Kansas City. There he'd take a train all the way to Cindy. He didn't know how to feel about her having a husband. It didn't matter to him really. She'd wired him for help and he was going to do whatever he could do for her. No questions asked as always. He'd never ridden on a train for any distance. He purchased a ticket on a freight car and was perfectly comfortable. Dustin, being used to very few luxuries, found the box car ride quite enjoyable. The car he rode on was empty and he had the privilege of opening or shutting the big sliding side doors, as he pleased.

He spent much time sitting or standing in the open door looking at the beautiful country and thinking. He had even more to think about now than ever before. On one of the layovers on his ride he'd met a herd of cattle being driven across Kansas to the railroad. The foreman told him of the 08 herds sold in Denver by Mullen and Wilson. In fact, two of the 08 hands were on this drive with him. Dustin had dinner with these two punchers and learned of the assumed fate of Epps' herd and of Mullen and Wilson's foolish trade and eventual financial ruin in the mines of Denver. The cowboys were upset by the wages they'd received minus the bonus promised them. They also joked with Dustin about this drive not being as luxurious as his had been. They'd had a pretty rough trip. Short rations, long hours and rank horses made this one more typical than his had been.

After Dustin visited with the cowboys he checked the stockyard manager's records to see if a herd of 08 cattle driven by a man named Epps had arrived. Dustin was both relieved and angry with the report he received. Yes, a herd of five thousand two hundred fifty head of mixed 08 cattle were sold through the yard last fall. Not, however, by a man named Epps but by a Kansas based organization called Plains Cattle Corp. The bill of sale was signed by a fellow named Bowdry. Dustin could not acquire information about this Plains Cattle Corporation until Monday morning and he didn't have the time or inclination to wait. He had to get to Cindy now. He'd settle with the P.C.C. later. He traveled along, his mind spinning. He couldn't believe Mullen and Wilson had sold cattle not theirs and been fool enough to then loose it all on a mine. He was glad Epps hadn't sold out but knew some dreadful end had come to him. He'd heard about Miller's fiasco and subsequent horrible results to the Indians at the hand of Captain De Laquote. He'd heard that Miller had lost many of his cattle but had continued on north with what he'd gathered. He was in the company of a huge black man named Big Bill. Dustin was glad Bill was with Miller. That would increase his chances of completing his drive successfully. No word about Bliss arriving at Belknap was weighing heavily on Dustin's mind. He couldn't do anything about it now. He'd have to come back and straighten things out at another time. Now he had to think about what he could do to help Cindy. The tragic and untimely death of his good friend Colonel Gibson added to the turmoil in his emotions, making it hard to focus his thoughts in any one direction. He'd found a mentor in this man and would truly miss him. His memory would not be put aside.

The miles passed at the rate of twenty five an hour. Just forty eight hours of travel time would cover the twelve hundred miles. The lay overs and car switches, of which there were many, made it a five day rail trip.

Upon arrival in New York, Dustin acquired directions to the Sister's of Mercy Hospital. He had received so many ugly comments about his frontier garb he stepped into a haberdashery and purchased a cheap suit so he wouldn't look too offensive to Cindy when she saw him. It had been a long, long time since their last meeting. He was looking forward to seeing Cindy again, husband or not! Dustin showed up at the Sister's of Mercy admissions office and realized he had no idea of Cindy's husband's name. He asked the sister at the desk if she was familiar with Cindy Morton or her husband. The sister became solemn and asked if he was Dustin Thomas.

"Yes, I take it you received my wire of funds," Dustin answered.

"We did, Mr. Thomas. We have some to return to you," the nurse stated.

"I don't understand, ma'am."

"The bill was less than your payment. We have a little overage for you in the office. I'll get it for you, Mr. Thomas," she continued.

"Where's Cindy and her husband now? I'd like to see him," Dustin requested.

"I'm sorry, I thought you knew," the nurse apologized.

"I haven't seen anyone, Ma'am. I just this morning got to town. I pretty much came straight here," Dustin explained.

"Mr. Thomas, I'm sorry to tell you Mr. De Larinso didn't make it through the surgery. His condition had been getting steadily worse and we didn't get to operate on him as early as we would have liked to," the nurse said in defense of the hospital.

"I sent the money the minute I received the wires, Ma'am. I had been out and hadn't been in touch with anyone for several months. Where's Cindy? Is she all right?" he asked her.

"No, I don't think she is all right. She's taken this real hard. She'd been working here ever since just after they arrived in New York, but she hasn't been back in since the operation. She came to the funeral and I think she'd been drinking. Several of us went. We think a lot of Cindy. We're all pretty fond of her. She lives in one of the apartments the church owns. Here's the address and a map," she said as she handed him a piece of paper which she'd written the proper information on for him.

"Stop by the office and they'll have your money, Mr. Thomas. If we can help you with Cindy please let us know. Good luck, Mr. Thomas. Our prayers are with you both," the sister said as compassionately as Dustin had ever heard anyone before.

He picked up an envelope containing just over two hundred fifty dollars in it. He then went to find the apartments where Cindy lived. Once in the building he climbed the narrow, dark stairs to the floor Cindy's residence was located on and found her door. Dustin was very excited. He stood up straight and looked at his new town clothes. On the other side of this door was the girl he'd loved these many years. Fate had taken her husband and he had tried to save him for her despite his desire to have her for his own. She'd be very proud of him for being able to raise the money necessary for the surgery. He bet that even in her sorrow, Cindy would know he'd done all she'd ever asked of him and would always do so. He could almost feel her in his arms. He could see her beautiful face in his minds eye. This was the moment that was to be the one that started the healing process for Cindy. He would take her home and she would get over all the heartache she must have endured these many, many months. She'd be his someday. He would give her the time and support necessary to get her through this. Dustin reached up and knocked on the door.

Chapter 18

It was spring now and most all chance of snow was gone. Montana had an extremely wet, cold winter but the cattle had made it through well and the calves were coming steadily. Robert Bliss was standing out in front of a barn like pole structure they had built to house the horses. He was talking to Big Bill who was saddling his horse and loading a pack horse as well.

Bill decided one Montana winter was all he needed to see. Robert was trying to talk him into staying, fruitlessly. Bill had made his mind up early in the winter that if he didn't freeze to death before, he was leaving with the thaw. Robert had asked what Bill thought he should do about the cattle. Bill told him to just keep on supplying the Indians and charging the army. Bill would tell the boys back down in Texas where he was and what was going on. They could decide as an association what to do. Most of the boys were willing to stay with him. This Montana was a beautiful place, sure enough. A few men left during the winter, most of these never made it far. A few more were going back to Texas with Bill. There would still be more than enough good help for Bliss to build a ranch with. The one certain thing was Bill was leaving. He'd never liked the cold and liked it less now that he'd had a real taste of it. Before he left he'd taught Hank to bake good bread and biscuits and Bliss to speak pretty good French. They'd be fine without him. He was heading south with the five Texans sharing his opinion of snow.

One of these men was fond of saying, "I always figured it was the Lords fault when the first snowflake hit me and mine if the second one did. I been at fault a lot this winter. It might take me years to forgive myself."

The men left with the promise to get word to the association members that didn't make the drive as to the condition of Bliss and the cattle. They could work out whatever details they could all agree on and get their decision back to Bliss when they did.

Bill rode away as if he was traveling alone and the other men simply followed him. The first night on the trail Bill explained that he would cook but if he did the other boys had to cleanup, build the fires and generally make themselves useful around camp. He was glad to have their company but he had no intentions to take them to raise. With this simple rule established, the trip was very pleasant.

The one close call came when Bill and his little group were surprised by a large gang of riders traveling at night. This gang literally ran through Bill's camp late after the fire had died out. The leader of this huge gang of midnight riders was a mean fellow called Bowdry. He questioned Bill and the others about what they were doing traveling through the nations. Bill assured Bowdry they were just trying to get back to Texas. Bowdry made a big joke about them driving an 08 herd and said him and his boys had a little experience driving 08 cattle too.

Bill choked back his feeling the best he could, laughed and said, "I hope you all got more out of them than we did. We just barely got out wages!"

"We did a little better than that! Of course we didn't have too much in them either. Low overhead! That's the key to success in this cow business," Bowdry declared.

Bill talked for a while to Bowdry about the country ahead and the mind set of any Indians that might be in the area. A bunch of Indians from several tribes were returning from the Dakota's. The multi tribal conference broke up after the severe retaliation from the military after Custer's screw up. These stragglers were just wanting to return home safely. Some were still a little on edge from the army's attempted genocide of their race. These easily excitable natives could be a little quick to shoot. They had to be given a wide berth or left alone all together. Most would just keep riding if let be. A few had been pressed too far and the pushers had paid for their poor manners with their lives. Bill told Bowdry that he had no intentions of upsetting anyone especially a band of pissed off warriors.

The sun came up and the men were still visiting so Bill made breakfast and won approval of all present. Bowdry took a sack full of biscuits with him and let Bill and his company go unscathed. This was not his original intentions. Bowdry never left witnesses to his where-abouts. Bill may have suspected but his riding buddies had no idea that Bill's biscuits had just saved their lives. Bill packed up and left camp early and made as many miles as possible before he stopped again.

Chapter 19

Dustin heard coughing behind this door concealing his past and leading to his future. On the other side came a deep, fluid, hacking cough like the ones he'd heard coming from dying men. It came again just as rough and loud as before followed by a long wheezing gasp. He knocked, his heart filled with trepidation. Behind this door sat the only woman he'd ever loved. Surely there was someone else in there too. He knocked again! Cindy's husband must have other family staying here. That cough could not come from a small young woman. He knocked yet again, this time more loudly and called out her name.

"Come in before you beat down the damn door," came a voice from inside.

He smelled smoke from cigarettes and the stench of illness as he entered the room. He quickly searched the room for Cindy. The only person he saw was an older woman in a too large, red, very reveling satin gown. She was smoking a roll your own and drinking whiskey from a water glass that was nearly empty. The bottles, some empty, some not, on the table next to the cigarette makings and mess, showed there was and had been no chance of the glass staying empty for very long a period of time. Dustin stepped past the table and pushed open the door to the other room of the apartment.

"Come out of there you bastard! I've told you all I ain't doing that no more. Get outta there I said!" the woman screeched.

"I was told a friend of mine lived here," Dustin said to the woman who was still slumped over the table trying to regain her strength from the coughing episode.

"He's dead! There ain't nobody here but me and I don't want no damn company! Do you hear me, get the hell out of here or I'll shoot you dead!" the woman said wielding a little derringer Dustin hadn't noticed before.

He froze looking at the face! There was much he hadn't noticed here.

"Cindy? Cindy is that you?"

No answer.

"It's me, Cindy. It's Dustin. I've come to help you."

The woman stared up at the face of this intruder. She was coughing a little and showed no signs of recognition. Her eyes showed nothing at all. She sat starring into space, it just happened to be in Dustin's direction. He stepped closer to the table and she raised the tiny pistol.

"Hold it you son-of-a-bitch! I swear I'll shoot you," came the slurred threat.

Dustin moved just enough to grab the gun and laid it on the table by the whiskey bottles. He knelt down in front of Cindy and looked into her face, his hands on her shoulders.

"Cindy look at me! It's all right. I'm here Cindy, it's Dustin. I came as soon as I got your wire," Dustin said compassionately to this wreck of a woman who was once his beautiful, little Cindy.

He knew she was still in there somewhere. Time and loving attention would bring her back. He had to deal with the cough first. It was bad and she needed medical care urgently. He looked into her eyes trying to find some spark of what used to be a fire gleaming so hot it could melt his soul with a mere glimpse but he saw no ember of it. He spoke her name again, not to her really but to the room or maybe to the world just to identify her to it. A someone, someone who had been and would be again. A person, a soul, someone people had loved. Certainly someone that was more than this sick, drunken, shell of a human being sitting in this putrid hovel with her life's light flickering slowly, surely out. The slightest whiff of circumstantial wind would easily extinguish it forever.

He rushed over, took Cindy in his arms and held her tenderly to him. She struggled some, weakly at first, then succumbed to his strength and to his will. She relaxed for a moment and then went limp in his arms. Dustin rose with her and started toward her bedroom. He stopped and turned around, the sound of gurgling deep inside her chest sent a chill through him. He walked to the hospital with the near lifeless body of this woman he had loved for so long. He entered the same door he'd exited that morning. He was surprised by how little attention he was drawing. Here he was in a hospital, carrying a seemingly lifeless body and no one had more than glanced at him. Finally the sister who had helped him before spotted them and came hurriedly toward him.

"Please help us! She's very ill I'm afraid and she's burning up with fever. Please do something for her," Dustin pleaded worriedly.

Cindy came to now and again. She saw Dustin each time she opened her eyes. She did not speak to him for the entire first day. Then much to Dustin's anguish, what she did say was mean and apparently, intentionally hurtful to him. The nurse told Dustin it was just the fever and illness talking. He was sure it was all of the pain she'd suffered striking out. Her words hurt him but he knew she'd get over her anger or at least learn to channel it at something other than him. For now he would just sympathetically absorb anything she threw at him.

Then again, "There you sit gloating. Why are you still here? I told you that you were too damn late! Your money was too damn late and you are too damn late. Why did you come at all?" she would say cruelly then go back to sleep.

The words hurt Dustin tremendously but what really hurt him was the satisfied look on her face after she'd say these things. She sometimes would wake up and just lie there silently staring at him. He would tell her stories about Wesley, Kathy, Matt, her mom and even a little about her dad. He spared her anything negative or too thought provoking. She lay there ten days. Except for nature calls and one trip to close up the apartment, Dustin never left her side.

As her strength came back her mood didn't improve as he'd hoped it would. Her insults had gotten meaner. Usually kept to one venomous comment or another like, "I never have been able to count on you!" or "I can't believe you'd let him die!" or "What are you doing here? Do you think you can just hang around and take Louis' place? You think I'll just jump in bed with you now that you've killed him? I know that's all you have ever wanted! Don't you think for a moment you'll ever be able to take Louis' place, you'll never be half the man he was. You might live for a hundred years but you'll have to live every day knowing you'll never be the man he was and knowing I know it too."

Dustin could barely believe his ears. He became more and more nervous about what she might say next. At the end of a week a doctor asked Dustin to step out of Cindy's room to talk with him.

"Mr. Thomas, Cindy is very ill. Fatally quite possibly. She's developed tuberculosis most commonly referred to as consumption," the doctor explained solemnly.

"How bad is she, Doc? What can be done for her?" Dustin asked anxiously.

"Not much really, Mr. Thomas. She needs bed rest in a dry warm climate preferably," the doctor went on.

"We're from the warmest, driest climate there is Doc. She'll get better quick out there," Dustin said excitedly.

"Mr. Thomas, Cindy is not going to get well. She's dying. All you can do is try to make her as comfortable as possible 'til the end," was all he could tell Dustin about Cindy's condition.

"Dying! Doc you gotta be mistaken. She's so young," Dustin said in total disbelief.

"Why don't you make the necessary arrangements to get Cindy back home on the frontier. It's the best chance she has. Go slowly and do not let her over exert herself or get too upset. Make her stop smoking and at least reduce her drinking to a more tolerable level. I understand from the sisters here that Cindy's developed a little problem with alcohol. Good luck Mr. Thomas. You are taking on a tremendous responsibility. I wish you well. The sisters will give you some medication for Cindy now and something for her pain later. She'll need it before too long. I don't know what the availability of Laudanum is on the frontier. I'll send enough to last her until…well enough to last."

The doctor turned and walked away down the long corridor and out of view. Dustin signed a large stack of papers and paid an exorbitant amount for a large case of medication. There were many small packages of pills and powders Cindy needed now twice daily. Also several large bottles and two smaller more convenient bottles of the Laudanum to diminish her pain when it became necessary.

Dustin had purchased train tickets for a private room for Cindy as far as the line went. The trip was little more than perpetual anguish for Dustin. Cindy was either silent or critical the entire trip. She did willingly take the medicine, a fact which made Dustin believe she at least wanted to try and get well. The room had a good bed in it and Cindy was comfortable yet the movement and noise caused her to complain often. The further west they traveled the more stops and car drop offs they had, the more verbal abuse Dustin had to endure. He was holding up well but getting a little frustrated at not being able to keep Cindy content for more than a few minutes at a time. While she had a private comfortable room with a place to walk a little and a window to watch the world pass by, Dustin had a simple wooden chair sitting by the foot of her bunk. This passenger train took a much less direct route to the west than had the freighter Dustin came east on. The exclusive car containing the private rooms only traveled west as far as St. Louis. The trip on to Kansas City would be made in a Pullman passenger car.

Dustin made the transfer with Cindy, making sure her belongings were put on the correct train and she was made as comfortable as possible. She was not easy to make comfortable and was very vocal about it. Dustin was glad this part of the trip was short. At Kansas City, Dustin made arrangements to stay a few days at the Grand Hotel to let Cindy rest up before starting the wagon trip the rest of the way home.

While she rested, Dustin made the necessary arrangements for an old military ambulance like the one Colonel Gibson had used. This one had been retired and was in need of some repair. Dustin took the old thing to the blacksmith at the east end of town. This big, ornery, German fellow shared a shop with an Irish cabinet maker. This odd combination of nationalities often made for some robust conversations and even fisticuffs between these two craftsmen. They were very much the talk of the town when things were slow. Particularly when there were no scandals with one of the towns leading citizens and one of the late night girls, who were working the entertainment district.

Dustin knew and liked both these fellows and admired their workmanship. He had a plan as always and explained to both men his situation with Cindy. He told the men he was wanting to fix up this old army wagon for her so she could survive the trip. He'd like it to be as pleasant for her as humanly possible. He also stated he realized they couldn't do much of a job of fixing the wagon up with the primitive tools they had to work with. He would appreciate if they tried their best to make it nice for her. He'd be glad to pay whatever it cost for the extra time and effort. It was important that the wagon be in perfect repair. He could not take a chance on a breakdown on the way. Cindy could not make any part of the trip horseback. Each of the two craftsmen assured Dustin that their part of the work would be done satisfactorily. Dustin knew that the pride and competitive spirit between these two friends and rivals would guarantee a good job with the wagon.

He left the men with the ambulance and took the harness to the saddle shop to have it looked over. He next went to the mercantile to purchase supplies for the trip. He bought Cindy a parasol and a few other nice things he thought she might enjoy on the trip. She might be able to sit up part of the time and enjoy some of the travel home.

Dustin's funds were getting a little short so he went back to the fort to requisition some horses to pull the ambulance. While he was there, word came back from Montana about the 08 cattle. Things were a mess and not nearly all the cattle had made it but Bliss was in control and making everything work for now. There wasn't anything Dustin could do for him now but he'd get up there when he got Cindy settled in at home. Cindy had been walking around her room some and looking a little stronger the last few days.

The day before they were to leave Dustin gathered everything together for an early start in the morning. The horses were shod and Dustin couldn't even recognize the wagon. The two men had gone overboard in fixing it up. The wagons suspension had been completely gone over and buffed up. The seat had been upholstered with a deep, soft padding and covered with beautiful leather. The Irish cabinetmaker had cut large windows into both sides the length of the ambulance. These had shutters and could be opened and closed as desired. He'd built shelves under the bunk to accommodate the supplies and keep them out of the way so as to allow as much room in the interior as possible. The old German had even painted the whole contraption a bright, clean white with, on the insistence of his Irish partner, emerald green trim. He'd also contrived a set of shades for both side windows and also for the seat as well. If Cindy was able to set up front, she could also lean back in a reclining position due to the ingeniousness of this team of immigrants. They had designed the seat so that the passenger side could be laid back in several different positions from upright to nearly tipped back completely. The extended back was more like a barbers chair than a bench. The idea in fact came from an old dentist/barber friend of the twosome.

Dustin paid the men for the horseshoeing and wagon repairs and offered them a bonus for their creativity but they declined the extra money and wished Dustin well. He had already picked up the repaired harness and drove to the mercantile to load the previously purchased supplies and then on to the hotel livery to load all but what they would need tonight and in the morning to travel in. Dustin put the horses in stalls and parked the wagon where he could load their luggage easily and then went up to retrieve it from the room.

When he entered the room terror struck deep within him. There on the floor laid Cindy. She appeared dead. Dustin rushed to her and rolled her face up. She smelled strongly of whiskey. When he stood up with her, he saw an almost empty bottle on the stand by the bed. There was no controlling the rage running through Dustin's mind. This might set her recovery back months or even worse, it could kill her. He laid her on the bed and headed downstairs. Dustin grabbed the man at the front desk and asked how in the hell Cindy got a bottle of liquor.

This poor fellow had no idea but would get the bartender for Dustin if he would just let him go. No one in the establishment confessed to delivering the bottle but assured Dustin someone would be reprimanded for the mistake. This did not appease him much. Dustin calmed down some and very quietly explained that if Cindy suffered any ill effects from this breach of his explicit instructions he would come back and burn this shit hole to the ground and kill every son-of-a-bitch in it. He gathered up a doctor and had him examine Cindy. His diagnosis was the same as the doctor in New York.

"This didn't help her any, Mr. Thomas, but she's not any worse off than she was before this...accident. You must not allow this to keep occurring. It will shorten her life even more than the tuberculosis has already. She'll have a little headache tomorrow but will be all right to travel."

The night passed slowly. Cindy spent most of it either throwing up or cussing Dustin for a variety of transgressions, real or imaginary, she held him responsible for. Dustin spent it cleaning up after her and trying to make her comfortable, bathing her head in a manner similar to what Teresa had done for him in his moment of suffering in the little Mexican village one time that seemed so long ago.

Morning finally arrived to find Dustin loading the last of Cindy's belongings and hooking up the team of horses. When finished, he went upstairs to carry Cindy down and get this last leg of their trip underway. The start wasn't too unpleasant as Cindy slept for many hours while Dustin covered a good distance.

The first night's camp was quiet. Cindy was lounging on an Indian death chair Dustin had the Irish cabinet maker build in the style of Nacatan's. This simple recliner was covered with quilts and Cindy was continuing a silence that had lasted all day. He made a good supper and Cindy ate enough so that Dustin felt she must have been enjoying it. She chose to sleep in her bed in the wagon instead of on the ground by the fire. Dustin wasn't going to press her too much. He knew that it would take a solid month of travel to cover the distance from Kansas City to the Morton home on the frontier in the New Mexico territory. Cindy would soon enough forgive him for not being on time to save Louis and all the other horrible neglects he'd been unknowingly guilty of.

Days passed mostly uneventful, with little more than a change of scenery. They crossed the wild country known as the Indian nations. Very few white men would dare cross the nations unless in the company of a large group of armed men riding fast horses. Dustin was unafraid and was crossing where he pleased to afford the easiest and most comfortable passage for his precious cargo. He several times encountered Indians along their way. His fluent linguistic capabilities in many Indian dialects kept his trip nonviolent and his scalp intact. Many of the bands he came in contact with had heard of him from Yoshela's people and he was treated with great respect and rode along for much of the journey in the company of mounted warriors; these either out on hunting parties or just patrolling their land bringing back reports of the movements of the white settlers. The migration westward was starting to build again and most all the tribes left in the nations could see clearly the end of life as they knew it. This one white man, who acted more Indian than white, might be the link they needed to help them survive the transitions they were about to be forced to endure. Several times the hunting parties brought fresh meat to Dustin and Cindy as they passed by.

By the second week on the trail, Cindy started asking questions about the various tribes of Indians and differences in their cultures. Once when Dustin drove close to a rather large encampment of Chirracaua Apaches who were leaving the nations and going to old Mexico, they were asked to join the fireside and eat. Dustin started to decline but Cindy asked if they couldn't please go. He was very surprised by her reaction and accepted the invitation. She sat very close to Dustin the entire evening. At one point she even put her arm through his and held tightly. Cindy was enthralled by the stories being told, interpreted by Dustin. These people held Dustin in very high esteem and treated them like visiting dignitaries. She watched every move and every gesture of these now nomadic people and was very polite while eating the meal. Apache stew and maze flat bread is definitely an acquired taste but she ate a respectful amount and tried to make it look delicious.

When it came time to retire, Cindy leaned heavily on Dustin's arm. She was able to walk considerable distances now but Dustin didn't hesitate to carry her the last little way to her apartment on wheels when she said she'd had a wonderful time but was feeling a little faint. Dustin tucked her in bed and she thanked him for letting her go to the camp. He assured her it was he that was glad she'd gone. The sun was high when Cindy woke the next morning.

"How far have we come?" she asked in her little voice that Dustin had remembered.

"All together or just this morning?" Dustin asked wanting to give her the correct information.

"Both! I want to know exactly where we are," she stated.

Dustin started explaining to her just where they were located and told her when they stopped for dinner he would get out a map he'd gotten before they left and pinpoint their location for her. She rose and stepped up into her recliner next to Dustin and set it up straight.

"Their eyes were so sad. They reminded me of Momma's and Daddy's so long ago when we left home," Cindy said reflectively but definitely to Dustin.

"I'm surprised you can remember, Cindy. You were sure small," he responded.

"I don't remember much, just that look of emptiness in their faces. It scared me. I've never really felt safe since then. All the terrible things that happened to your family, they scared me even more. It seems that there is nothing you can really count on in this life. Everything can be taken away so easily, so quickly."

Dustin sat quietly and let her ramble on. She spoke of the disappointment of life in general more than of any special events in her own life.

At noon Dustin stopped and made a larger than normal dinner. Cindy hadn't eaten much since the trip started but she needed to eat a little several times a day. She was steadily consuming more and more and her strength was growing as well. Evenings around the fire Cindy would walk, just a little at first and gradually farther and farther. Dustin would walk along with her and listen to her talk or just stroll along in silence if she didn't happen to feel talkative. Her times of depression and resistance were growing more rare.

Cindy still had coughing spells from time to time and these worried Dustin to no end. She would be weak for hours after an episode of these convulsions. He would sit by her bedside and wipe her forehead with a moist cloth until she settled enough to fall to sleep. Between these seizures Cindy was becoming more and more pleasant toward Dustin. He was enjoying her metamorphosis more than he'd ever dreamed possible. She started asking him about his adventures and he would tell her of all the things he'd done. At first he was careful not to be too graphic in his depiction of the events of his life. As they became more familiar and comfortable with one another again, he told them as they happened. He even embellished a few if he could see he was shocking her or intriguing her with some tale or adventure. By late in the trip, Cindy was swapping tale for tale with Dustin and shocking him even more often than she was being shocked by him.

As they approached their destination, Dustin was almost sorry the trip was ending. He and Cindy had become more dependent on one another with each of the last eight hundred miles. Cindy had never apologized to Dustin for anything nor did he ask or expect her to. She had talked of her time in Europe freely and openly. She'd told Dustin of Louis' gambling but never did she mention his propensity of using her to help him perpetuate his bad habit. She told of the grand life she'd lived and the wonderful things she'd seen. She talked about the beautiful music she had heard in Europe and how much pleasure it brought her. Dustin never even once felt used, in spite of the fact it was he, who under false pretense, financed her whole fling abroad. He instead was thrilled by the fact she'd been able to see so much of the world and had enjoyed it so very completely. He never made her feel guilty in any way for abandoning their marriage plans or lying about needing more money to return home and then not coming back or even for marrying Louis and financing his exile to the states with what was left of Dustin's money. She was there with him now and that was all that mattered. Now that they were almost home he'd have to share her with Matt, Mom, Kathy and, of course, little Wesley. The latter of whom she'd not asked about at all. This itself concerned him greatly. Dustin was sure she would come around once she was with Wesley again, like she had done with him on their trip home.

Wesley wasn't so little anymore. He'd gotten old enough to go out with his Aunt Kate when she rode out to check the cattle that were in close to the ranchhouse. He had to wait home on the days she rode the far country. Wesley was the ideal child. He somehow seemed to know he was all but abandoned by his mother and that Grandma had her hands full with Grandpa since the stroke. He didn't understand about the strokes, of course, but he did know Grandpa was sick for a long time and now he was gone. Grandma had more time for him now that Grandpa was gone. He knew he liked that part. At five you don't think much past how things effect you. He was a little afraid of going with Aunt Kate the first time. Once he got away from the house and had the wind blowing in his little face and felt the rocking motion of the horse along with the security of Aunt Kate's body and arms holding him in front of her in the saddle, he was hooked. He wanted to go every time he saw her leave the house. He would not cry or mope around when he was unable to go but would sit quietly watching out the window for her return. He'd run out to help her unsaddle her horse and then he'd walk back to the house and listen to her talk about what she'd seen that day. Sometimes Aunt Kate would stay out at the ranch house. Often she would let Wesley come out and stay with her. He loved the ranch already and went every time he was allowed to go.

Dustin didn't know any of this as he'd been away also. He was counting on nature's bond between mother and child bringing Cindy close to Wesley once they were together again.

Dustin pulled up in front of the Confederate Cantina and helped Cindy down from her seat. They strolled into an empty saloon, being it was still relatively early in the day. There behind his bar was Matt staring off into space. He had a sinister snarl on his face and was mumbling inaudible words to some villainous figure no one else could see.

"Hey Matt, come back to earth, partner. Look who's come home!" Dustin said just a little embarrassed he'd caught his friend daydreaming again.

"Damn Cindy, you look terrible! Did Dustin here make you walk the whole way home?" Matt tried to joke as he walked hurriedly around the bar to embrace his sister, he too was embarrassed to, again, be caught daydreaming.

"Hello Matthew," Cindy replied rather formally.

"Little Juan, watch the place while I take my sister back to the house," Matt ordered the young Mexican who helped him in the saloon.

"Mom's going to be so happy to see you! Wesley, too. He's been asking questions non stop since he found out you were returning," Matt said as he led his sister out the side door and the few steps down the lane to the hacienda style home that had come with the cantina.

Mrs. Morton was standing in the door having heard Matt's commotion all the way down the lane. She looked twenty years older than the last time Cindy had seen her, but then, so did Cindy. Each tried hard to conceal their shock in the other's appearance. They embraced and walked to the settee in the sitting room.

"I'm so glad you are home, dear. We all missed you terribly. Your father especially. He asked for you until the end," Mrs. Morton almost wept to Cindy.

The latter letting the guilt being heaped on her lay for the moment.

Mrs. Morton continued, "I can hardly wait until you see Wesley. You've been gone so long you'll not recognize him, I'm sure," again with more guilt.

"How about Kathy? Hasn't my absence devastated her life also, doing untold psychological damage, rendering her totally useless as a human being forever?" Cindy said and walked toward the hall. "Which cell is mine, Warden?" she asked Matt.

Her brother pointed to a beautiful room on the right with a view from the window toward the old ranch.

"She's been through a lot recently and she's very ill. We'll have to all be easy with her for awhile," Dustin said then asked, "Where is Wesley?"

"He's with Kate as usual," Matt answered.

"Kate?" inquired Dustin.

"Yea, everyone's been calling her Cattle Kate lately. She loves it too. She's doing a hell of a job out at the ranch, Dustin. She sold a big bunch of steers to the new Major up at the fort. Some Yankee too young to have fought in the war but old enough to have gone through West Point. I think he's a little sweet on Kate too," answered Matt.

"Good, how's she feel about him?" Dustin asked excited for her prospects.

"She don't know there is another man alive in this whole damn world but you. She says you'll come around some day and if she has to wait till your ninety, she'll be there for you when you want her! Seems plumb silly to me after all you ain't never showed no interest in no one but Cindy. Kate don't care! She knows you'll wake up someday," Matt finished.

"Damn Matt, I had no idea she felt that way. I thought she was joking about sharing the ranch as my wife. I ain't never done nothing to lead her on," Dustin proclaimed.

"Nothing but be yourself. I guess you are pretty much all of our hero, Dustin. You've done things that men three times your age only dream of doing. Believe me, I know Dustin. You are an easy man to admire. There ain't nothing wrong with the way Kate feels about you. Cindy looks seriously ill. You might need Kate's help before this is all over."

At that moment, "By god he'll have it too, if he wants it! Hello darling!" Kate said as she rushed in and threw her arms around Dustin and kissed him full on the lips.

Right behind her was Wesley trotting to keep up.

"Hello, little fella," Dustin said.

"Where's my Mommy?" demanded the tough little guy.

"She's in the room we fixed up for her, Wesley," Matt answered.

"Can I see her?" the little boy asked.

"She's very tired. She'll be out soon. You can see her then," Matt answered.

"I'll wait!" Wesley stated then asked, "Is she sleepy tired or tired like Grandpa was?"

"She's tired from her trip, Wesley. Come on, we'll help Dustin put up his rig," Kate said extending her hand.

"I better wait. Mommy will want to see me when she wakes up," Wesley said and sat again in the same place reconfirming his conviction in staying.

"OK buddy, I'll see you after while," Kate said and turned to Dustin, "Are you tired too or would you like to ride out and get Chief?"

"I feel great! Let's take the wagon out and leave it at the ranch. I'll ride Chief back in tonight," Dustin said.

"Hell good looking, I may not let you come back in tonight," Kate said quite robustly and yet a little more sensually than Dustin remembered ever hearing a woman sound.

Indeed Kate was a woman now. There was no question about that. She might need a little smoothing out to be what most would consider a lady but no one on earth could imagine her as anything but all woman. She was beautiful, healthy and full of life. She bubbled over with excitement and enthusiasm at every detail of the ranch as she showed it to Dustin. She'd tied her saddle horse behind the wagon and lounged very enticingly on the reclining seat Cindy had ridden much of the last part of the trip on. Kate teased Dustin nonstop except when she was pointing out cattle or showing the wonderful range conditions.

Her proudest moment came as they pulled up to the house and Dustin sat a moment speechless then said, "Kathy, it looks beautiful. Did you do this all yourself?"

"Most of it. Some I let those goofs at the fort help with. There are a couple of them boys think they got a chance of moving into it with me. It's been real handy and it's developed into a great market for our beef," Kate teased.

"What are you saying, Kathy?" Dustin demanded acting very jealous.

"I'm a woman in a man's world. I have to show a little petticoat at the dances and giggle at their stupid jokes but that's as close as they'll ever get! When we're married you can dance with the drunk bastards to get them to buy our cattle!" Kate said matter of factly.

"Kathy, you know that Cindy...I mean that me and her...," Dustin struggled to find words and was glad when Kate jumped in.

"I know, you love Cindy! You are going to marry her, that is if she don't steal all your money and run off again first. I know all of that, Dustin. The fact is I love you all the more for your misplaced loyalty toward Cindy. You don't owe me nothing. You've never been nothing but honest about the way you feel. I won't be nothing but honest with you either. I love you, Dustin, and I always intend to. You go on and marry Cindy and take whatever abuse she dishes out, and I'll wait right here for you. Hell, I even fixed up the house for you two lovebirds. I've built me a room out where you used to stay at the barn. If she won't marry you I can stay here at the house and help take care of her and you can stay down at the barn. Either way will suit me fine," Kate explained.

"You are really something. You would be the easiest person in the world for me to love back. You know that don't you, Kathy?" Dustin said holding onto her shoulders and looking her passionately in the eyes. His own eyes searching her face as if he'd been blind his whole life and had been granted this one long look at real beauty. He wanted to drink in every drop of her, being very careful not to let any feature go unmemorized.

"You do know that don't you?" he repeated.

"I'm counting on it, darling. Absolutely counting on it. Come on let's go look at Chief. He'll be glad to see you too!" Kate said tossing her beautiful, long, brown hair back over her shoulders and heading off toward the barn.

Dustin followed her and was as surprised and pleased with the barn as he was the house. Kate had renovated the barn completely and had added a very complete saddle shop next to his old apartment. This too had undergone a makeover.

"Impressive! Just how much petticoat did you have to show to get that harness stitcher?" Dustin asked almost accusingly.

"Do I note a touch of jealousy in your inquiry, Mr. Thomas? I certainly hope so!" Kate teased then said, "That cost us a good mare and an attendance at an officers ball that I thought would never end. By eleven I considered letting the military keep their old equipment and just go home. I just kept thinking how handy that stitcher would be for us in the years to come. This country probably won't have a good saddle shop in it for a long time. We'll not be dependent on them Texas boys to repair our saddles!" Kate explained.

"I sincerely appreciate your sacrifices, Kathy. You are the best partner a man could have," Dustin exclaimed.

"That's what I've been telling you all this time!" Kate added.

The two walked around looking at the apartment and the barn and from one of the stalls came a nickering.

"Hello Chief! How ya been? Goodness sakes fella, you are as fat as a hog!" Dustin stated.

"The mean bastard won't let anyone ride him. I have to take my life into my own hands just to feed the sorry S.O.B.!" Kate told him.

"You must be fearless, Kathy! He looks like you been risking your life five times a day!" Dustin laughed then added, "He looks great, Honey. Thank you very much for taking such good care of him for me."

"For us! I've bred him to several mares already. He's a very aggressive breeder. He'll make us a great stud! Yes sir, Chief really loves his work," Kate elaborated.

"Damn girl, you talk like a sailor. If you are ever going to be my wife you are going to have to leave that corral talk to the men," Dustin scolded.

"Well I be! I've got you talking about it already. I'm way ahead of schedule. I can talk as clean as a bishops prayers if it will keep you thinking that way!" Kate declared.

"Let's get saddled and get back. You are frustrating me some and confusing me even more! I thought I had everything worked out in my mind, until now that is," Dustin said with a pleasant smile that made Kate say, "Fine darling, you just keep on figuring things out. I'm young still. I've got lots of time."

Chapter 20

Big Bill rode into Kansas City and was overwhelmed at the number of cattle on the plains surrounding the quickly developing town. Just a few months ago it was little more than another railroad tent city. There was some law now, mostly comprised of rejects from more developed communities. Most were of more objectionable character than the citizens they are holding sway over. It was the standard operational procedure by the general population to handle most problems themselves without involving the trash that was passed off as the law. This worked well for the most part. The occasional deviation from the rule caused ample problems to occupy the time of these despicable tramps with badges.

Bill happened along at a time when these boys of the law had nothing else to mess up. He had walked into a saloon accompanied by his 08 trail hand companions. The bartender caused a scene because Bill was black. He refused to serve him and Bill was going to leave. His friends refused to let him go and insisted he be served. Each pointed out Bill's superior character traits and his right to drink where he pleased. The bartender pulled a bunghammer and got his head cracked with a pistol butt for his effort. A couple of the bartender's friends took offense to his being knocked unconscious by a bunch of saddle tramps accompanied by a black man. The fight was on shortly, all in good fun, until some cowardly bastard pulled a gun and shot one of the citizens in the belly. The fight stopped at the report of the pistol shot.

While the crowd jointly cared for the injured patron, the shooter fled out a side door, but soon returned with the local delegates of the politically corrupt magistrate. They took things in hand immediately by arresting the black man on the spot. Bill did not resist but refused to be put in cuffs. Bill simply said he would go along quietly but he would never wear chains again. A blow from one of the deputized lowlife's rifle barrel sent Bill to the ground and a second from the butt of another knocked Bill out. One of Bill's companions, Jason, protested too adamantly and was shot dead. The others in Bill's company refrained from further objection and allowed the arrogant constables to drag Bill to the jailhouse. The boys got together and laid their dead partner out on a faro table next to the one the gut shot taxpayer was on.

In the morning two of the boys, Andy and Jake, went to check on Bill while the other two, Jeff and Slim, took care of the undertaking arrangements for their dead partner. The two men that chose to look in on Bill paid with their freedom. They were arrested upon their arrival at the jail. They also found Bill had been dragged from his cell in the middle of the night and beaten severely. A small boy who held no fondness for the local, official gentry got word to the remaining two cowpokes they'd better leave and come back with help or not come back at all.

Jeff and Slim took heed. They left post haste and didn't look back. They'd left enough money to bury Jason and would come up with a plan to get the other men out of this chickenshit jail and town, as soon as possible, from a safe distance, of course.

Once outside of town the boys checked up a little and tried to compose an escape plan. They decided to go to the quiet little community of Levenworth, not far to the north, to see if they could find some kind of justice. They came up empty in the sympathetic ear department. Jeff decided they'd better try to get word to Del Rio and maybe enlist the aid of one of the influential cattlemen at home. The only direct wire from Levenworth to Del Rio was the new one between the forts. The boys were able to get a wire off to Del Rio and more importantly found an ally at the telegraph office at Fort Levenworth.

The sergeant at the wire volunteered to help with the release of their three compadres. A series of messages were sent and a Federal Marshal named Wallace was contacted. The marshal was in St. Joseph, Missouri and responded to the sergeant's request for assistance. He would be in Kansas City in a few days and would be glad to look into the matter. He had received several complaints about the city officials in the wild and woolly cattle town and would also send a wire to them forewarning them of his coming. Marshal Wallace felt the wire might prevent any further injury or torture from being inflicted on the three cowboys. Slim and Jeff offered some money to the sergeant for his auxiliary efforts on behalf of their friends. He refused their offer and explained he'd been in that jail once and was held without being charged until the Army intervened on his part and forced his release. He was glad to help out. He also pointed out that Federal Marshal Wallace was an ex-military man and was known for his fairness and honesty. He would help their friends receive justice.

There was also a response from a United States Circuit Court Judge Maynard who would arrive in Kansas City about the same time as Marshal Wallace. The judge, also having received many complaints from the citizenry of the young cowtown, would be pleased to look into this situation as well. The boys were in disagreement as to how they should proceed until their help arrived. Jeff wanted to just lie low until the marshal and judge got to town. Slim thought they should go into town and get word to Bill and the others that help was on the way. They could not agree and decided to each follow their own plan. Jeff stayed at the fort and Slim rode into town.

The City Marshal had received word from U.S. Marshal Wallace that the prisoner's were not to be further harmed. This pressure from a higher authority was more than City Marshal Ambrose wanted to deal with. The testimonies of these cowboys would be enough to remove him from his very lucrative office if not land him in prison. He could not allow these men to talk to either the U.S. Marshal or the Judge. City Marshal Ambrose had Bill brought out of his cell and told him he'd decided to let them go on the condition they left immediately and not return.

Bill had already talked to Slim who had snuck around to the cell's outside window. Bill declined Ambrose's offer stating he was fairly sure they'd all be killed and the Federal Marshal would be told it was in an escape attempt. Bill knew their best chance was to remain in jail until they had opportunity to speak with the Circuit Court Justice.

Marshal Ambrose was livid! He told Bill he'd kill them all in their cells and tell Marshal Wallace it was an angry mob that had done it.

Bill explained that there were still several of his company around town and any such action on his part or his allowing any assassins to sneak into the jail for the purpose of their murders would not go unpunished. Bill advised Ambrose to arrest the Deputy that murdered Jason and the fellow that shot the citizen and make them the targets of the Federal Officers investigation. Bill was sure the Deputies had too much on Ambrose to let them testify to a federal judge but it at least got Ambrose to consider other options.

Near midnight all hell broke loose in the alley behind the jail. Bill told Andy and Jake good by. He was sure their murder had been planned. In a moment every lamp was lit and the jail was light as day. Just moments after the shooting and shouting in the ally, several Deputies, some Bill had not seen before, came carrying the bodies of two men into the jail office. One was the deputy that had murdered Jason and the other must have been the man who had gut shot the saloon patron who had died from the wound just this evening. Several of these men came back to the cells and dragged Bill, Andy and Jake out.

"This is it boys! It's been good riding with you," Bill said as they were led into the office.

The little room was full and more people were gathered outside, one of whom was Slim, afraid of the worse. City Marshal Ambrose called for silence.

"Gentlemen, I'm afraid there's been a terrible miscarriage of justice here. If not for the fine work of two of my special deputies, this might have become an irreversible situation. They caught these men you see laid before you here, sneaking around in the ally attempting to assassinate these three, poor prisoners to keep them from testifying as to what really happened to those unfortunate men at the saloon the other evening. They had to defend themselves against these corrupt agents of the law, unfortunately killing both of them in doing so. Let this be a lesson to all the fine people of this fair city that no corruption or abuse of authority in this office will be tolerated. We owe an apology to these three good men that have been held wrongly, but most of all we owe our thanks and appreciation to the noble and brave deputies who's fearless and steadfast efforts have brought this unpleasant matter to a just and quick end.

"The first rounds on me, boys! Let's go across the street and enjoy the benefits of living in a town free of the depravity and dangers all too familiar in most frontier cowtowns!"

The crowd roared its approval at their City Marshall's victory over crime. Bill was handed his belongings as were Andy and Jake by the deputy who had been brought in by Ambrose to correct the problem the best way he saw fit.

"This is twice I've spared your life, Bill. I can't keep doing it, even if you do make the best biscuits I've ever eaten. People will start to talk," laughed the special deputy. It was Bowdry, Bill had not recognized him in all the excitement. Bowdry continued, "You've had to ride away from a lot of injustice in your life, my friend. I suggest you ride on this time as well. Waiting for the Federal men now would be extremely unhealthy."

Bill understood completely and gathered the boys. They got their horses from the stable and rode out to the south. No one even considered waiting to talk to the Federal Marshall. They rode a crazy trail, leaving headed south a while then west then south some more and at one point turned and rode due north just to make sure they had been allowed to leave unmolested. Bill became a little paranoid and continued this evasive trail for several days until he was sure they'd not been followed. Once satisfied, the men started south toward home again. Bill insisted on posting a guard nightly for the next full week just in case. The other men felt Bill was being overly careful because of the beating he'd taken. They had no way of knowing Bill's concern was so well placed.

One day Bill suggested they back track a ways and watch their trail awhile. He felt certain they were being followed. The boys were all against loosing another day and all wanted to press on. Bill told them to go ahead if they wanted to and he would watch the back trail awhile then catch up. Everyone agreed that they would continue on and wished Bill would reconsider and just come on with them. Slim went so far as to tell Bill he was being plumb silly about this and he should just come on with them and get home. Bill wouldn't go against his gut feeling and headed back over their trail. The other four 08 trail cowboys rode out south for Texas. Bill actually liked traveling alone and was more comfortable in his own company than with a large group.

Bill camped off the trail a good distance and built no fire. He stayed two days and still couldn't shake the foreboding feeling of impending doom. Bill packed up and rode hard to catch up to the other men again not because he craved their company but because of this haunting feeling that was getting stronger by the moment. Bill stopped at the camp he'd shared with his former companions. He didn't stay overnight because of this pressing feeling eating at him. By noon the following day his worst fears were

brought to fruition.

There just off the trail were the four 08 men and their fire. The men had all been shot and robbed of all valuables. They were shot from a distance and lie where they fell, dead. Bill couldn't believe that his detouring and back trailing allowed whoever had been following them to get ahead of them and simply wait in ambush. Bill was sickened by the cold bloodedness of this killing. The perpetrators had laid in waiting allowing their four victims to unsaddle their horses and make camp then shoot them before they even ate their supper.

This was not the style of Bowdry and his murderous raiders. They would have rode down their prey and shot them face to face. Bill rode a big circle looking for some indication of who these assassins were or where they came from. The more evidence Bill gathered the more certain these ambushers were not Bowdry or any of his men. Bill's premonition had been correct but not in every detail. These murderers had not come from Kansas City. The unshod hoof prints he found had led in from the southwest. It appeared there had been six horses coming in. It troubled Bill that he could only find three sets of foot prints other than the 08 men near where the horses had been tied. The three new sets of prints all were of boots also. That didn't fit with the unshod horses. He expected to find moccasin prints or possibly even sandals, commonly worn by the Mexicans of the area. There was more to this story than Bill could read from the available sign. He knew two things for sure, one is someone killed his comrades and whoever did rode out on 08 horses headed northwest.

Bill crudely buried his four friends and instead of following the tracks of the murderers, he tracked them the direction they had come from, trying to answer some more questions about what actually happened here. There was a direct trail leading into camp. Nowhere was a sign of these shooters laying in wait as he first suspected. Bill found empty cartridges just off the trail with no human footprints near by. This indicated these men shot his friends from their horses. This was no small task. These cartridges were every bit of two hundred yards distant and the accuracy was incredible. Two of the men had received head shots and the other two were shot dead center. Few men could make these shots from this distance using a bench rest. Shots like this from a horses back was almost super human. Taking in the possibilities that one of these men might have made two of these shots made the prospects of overtaking them even more frightening.

The 08 men had died where they sat, none of them even having time to stand. This would imply all four shots were simultaneous or fired very rapidly by at least two expert marksmen. It would be impossible for anyone to get off three shots before a man had the time to stand up. Bill kept assuring himself there were four shooters. Maybe one was injured and never dismounted or held the horses while his companions saddled the 08 stock. He wasn't sure just what he was up against but it wasn't too comforting either way.

One scenario was that there were at least four cold blooded killers all with unbelievable skill as marksmen. The other is that there were only the three murderers and at least one of them was quite possibly the finest shot to have ever lived. No real consolation either way.

Bill intended to follow to where these killers had camped last in order to see just how many people were involved. He knew there were at least three, possibly as many as six but he did not think there were any more than four. From the sign by where the 08 saddle horses had been tied it looked as if at least two sets of pack boxes were set on the ground and then repacked on different horses.

It was early next morning before Bill found any solid evidence of what was going on. He rode over a ridge and below him in an open clearing was a terrible scene that told of another ambush and several killings. There before him was a wrecked wagon with four dead mules still in harness and lying around it were the bodies of eight Indians and two dead ponies. Bill remained secluded and watched for sign of anyone else anywhere near. After convincing himself he was the only living person for miles, he approached the site of this battle to try and read its signs.

There in the wagon, besides the usual plunder men need in traveling cross country, were the remains of several broken crates once containing new Winchester 73 lever action rifles. There was also much ammunition left behind as well. Bill rummaged through the wreckage and found three rifles which had been overlooked and left behind by the men testifying to the extreme hurry with which they fled the scene. Bill loaded these beautiful "seventy threes" wrapped in a wool blanket, also from the wreckage along with a large supply of ammunition, into his bed roll tied to his pack horse. He studied the scene as carefully as he had the camp of the 08 men and found this another confusing scene. He discovered a dead saddle horse not far from the wreck. This horse was shod and had been unsaddled where he lie. From the tracks, Bill could reasonably assume there were three men. They were gun runners. They had been attacked by an Indian ambush but it was the Indian ambushers who were surprised. These sharp shooters apparently ran a very short distance until their fatally wounded mules fell wreaking their wagon and spilling their load then just picked off their assailants at will. The bodies of the Indians were strewn about behind rocks, still kneeling, weapons in hand with the tops of their heads blown off. Several had been shot off their horses. Those ponies apparently ran away after loosing their riders. Bill found the hiding place not too far from the original ambush site where six ponies had stood tied and had been discovered and led off by the booted men. Bill reviewed the whole scene one last time and then headed after the three murderers who had escaped being murdered themselves.

It seems there were three men, one riding a saddled horse and two in the wagon hauling the Winchester rifles. They were attacked by a hunting party of very young Indian braves. Bill found nobody older than twenty years of age. This was extremely rare and added to the mystery of this encounter. Bill knew it was a hunting party and not a planned assault or act of war for two reasons. First, there were several field dressed deer carcasses near where the six ponies had been tied, and secondly, none of these young men were wearing any of their ornamental battle array. This looked like an impromptu attack made by these eager young hunters. They had no way of knowing the skill possessed by their intended victims. This lack of preparation and knowledge of their enemy were fatal oversights by these once noble, brave, young men now lying dead at the hands of their intended prey.

After the fight the three riflemen were momentarily afoot. The discovery of the six ponies allowed their hurried escape from the ambush site. The rider saddled one pony and unless the other two had saddles in the wagon, they rode bareback. The remaining three ponies must have been packed with the cases containing the bulk of the Winchester rifles.

Bill had no plan. He would simply follow these men until he came upon them and decide what course of action to take at that time. He knew he could just ride south and let what happened be, but Bill could no more do this than he could just ride off to San Francisco to tour the world instead of returning to the herds to make sure Dustin's cattle drive had its best chance of some small amount of success after the raw deal Mullen and Wilson had handed him. Bill was loyal and honorable to a fault. He knew his chances against these three deadly shots were very slim, yet he could not let his friends' murderers go unpunished. The big black man rode boldly, silently, and watchfully into the unknown.

Chapter 21

Dustin and Kate rode to the little carriage house that had stalls built in it for Kate's horses when she was in town. They unsaddled and put Chief and Peso up for the night and walked to the house giggling and talking about the ranch and Dustin's mess with the cattle drive. He'd received partial reports about the herd being scattered or stolen. More reports of the sell of two fifths of the cattle by Mullen and Wilson in Denver.

"Kathy, I'll tell you things went to hell for sure. I thought I was going to get rich," Dustin said reflectively.

"You never cared a bit about money, Dustin! Hell, you've given away more money than any fifty people out here will ever make!" Kate said supportingly.

As they came down the alley by the window of Cindy's room, there was a light on and someone moving around in there. Once they were nearer they could hear the dreaded coughing coming from inside. Dustin rushed around and into the house followed closely by Kate. Wesley was still awake way past his normal bed time and was standing outside his mother's door.

"Is my Mommy all right?" he asked his Aunt Kate. "I been waiting all day to see her, but she hasn't asked for me yet." The little fellow said so sadly that it killed a little piece deep inside Kate and she knew it was just one more thing she would never forgive her sister for.

"She'll be OK, honey. Come here with me," Kate said and reached down to pick the little fellow up. She held him so he could see Cindy better and then took him to his room, comforting him as much as possible. Dustin went into the room with Cindy and Mrs. Morton. Cindy's convulsions had subsided but she was racked with pain. Dustin hurried out and returned with the first of the laudanum bottles and gave Cindy a small spoonful. Almost instantly Cindy relaxed and fell to sleep peacefully.

"Damn it, that is strong stuff," Kate said just returning from Wesley's room.

"It's for pain, Kathy. The doctor in New York said Cindy would need it more and more as her condition worsened. I didn't think it would be necessary this soon," Dustin said very concerned.

"Let's let her sleep. I'll take these things out and wash them," Mrs. Morton said carrying out an arm load of bloody towels and linens.

"Mom, how sick is she?" Kate said near tears.

"She's very, very ill, Kathy. I'm afraid we're losing her," Mrs. Morton said without a tear.

She'd shed all the tears she had in her already, she told herself. She had dealt with much sorrow and would try to stand up under this loss also.

Dustin went back out and brought in the large case of bottles of the magic Laudanum and placed it under Cindy's bed.

"Mom, give her this sparingly. The doctor said it was very potent and addictive as well. Just use your judgment," Dustin said as he slid the case of bottles under the bed. "Damn!" Dustin said in frustration and walked outside and on down to the stable to see Chief.

Kate did not follow him, respecting his desire for solitude. Dustin found himself wishing she would come out to him. He'd enjoyed her company a great deal today and was having mixed emotions about his feelings. Dustin didn't like having to think about his feelings at all. He wanted to live life like the Indians did, simply and honestly without pretense or guilt. Everything was so confusing lately he often wanted to just run off to find Yoshela and his village and live the non hypocritical lifestyle of the Chiricahua Apache. Even in these trying times the Apaches were able to retain their closeness of family and their freedom to express their love of one another without the guilt of white European social standards applying.

Dustin returned to the house after everyone had gone to bed. He went into Cindy's room and sat next to her bed. He'd grown accustomed to sleeping close to her on their trip. She had one little coughing episode during the early morning hours but nothing like the one earlier. At sunrise, Dustin left to walk down and feed Chief. Upon his return Cindy was awake and in an unpleasant humor.

"Well, it's nice of you to finally come check on me! You drag me away from my home, bring me back to this hovel in the wilderness and then abandon me immediately. I saw you and Kathy drive off together. Did you two enjoy spending the night together while I lie here in my cell on my death bed?"

Dustin couldn't respond to Cindy's hurtful words and was relieved when he heard Kate's voice, "Calm down, dear. Dustin spent the night sitting on the floor right there by your bed. I do feel you should know, dear sister, that he is more than welcome to spend his nights or any part of them with me. He, however, has chosen not to. For some reason he'd rather sit on a hard floor next to you than lie in a soft bed next to me."

Mrs. Morton interrupted, "Girls! Stop this right now! Cindy I'll get you something to eat. Kathy come help me."

Kate walked out and into the kitchen with her mother. Standing in the doorway was Wesley.

"Are you my mommy?" the little fellow asked.

Dustin stood watching the anticipation on Wesley's face and waiting for Cindy's response. Finally Cindy set herself up and motioned for Wesley to come over by the bed.

"Don't I look like your mommy?" she asked.

"You look too old. My mommy's real young, like Aunt Kate," the innocent little guy said honestly.

Cindy turned cold instantly, "You are right young man. Your mother was very young and very foolish as well."

She was so unfeeling and harsh to Wesley it unnerved Dustin greatly. Wesley backed away slowly at first then ran out of the room and into the kitchen crying to the safety of Grandma. Dustin stared at Cindy in disbelief.

"Let's see how good he'd look if he'd been through all that I have," she said as some sort of perverted justification of her treatment of this poor child.

"Damn Cindy, he's just a baby. Your baby. He's not old enough to know better," Dustin exclaimed.

"This is all your fault! Don't you try and blame me. If you would have minded your own damn business I'd still be in New York City, not out here in this God forsaken wilderness being subjected to insults from that spoiled child. I hope you're happy!" Cindy snapped and had herself so upset she started coughing uncontrollably again.

Mrs. Morton rushed in with warm towels and held Cindy while she convulsed.

"Dustin, you are upsetting Cindy. Please wait outside!" Mrs. Morton said very accusingly.

"Good Lord, Mom. He's the only reason she's even alive!" Kate scolded.

"Stay out of this Kathy. Help me with your sister," Mrs. Morton demanded.

Dustin left and went to the barn. He saddled Chief and rolled his bed tying it behind his cantle. He mounted and rode Chief away. He glanced into Cindy's window and saw Kate holding Wesley, both crying looking out at him as he left.

Dustin knew he had upset Cindy and he also knew what to do to make it up to her. Cindy loved music. She talked a lot about the high toned culture of European life style and pleasant times she had playing music for the English heads of state. She must play beautifully. Dustin could almost hear her playing the classical songs of those famous, dead, foreign composers she'd told him so much about on their trip.

Dustin had been thinking about what he could do to make Cindy's life more pleasant. He knew this must be hard on her, being brought back here to face her family again. It was all his fault. She would see that it was the right thing for her. She would thank him as soon as she started feeling better. He'd give her a little time to get well then she would begin to feel differently about life here in the west, about living at home again and having little Wesley around her, maybe even about him. He'd always wanted her to feel about him the way he felt about her. She'd said and done many things Dustin just didn't understand. He never had stopped hoping she would care for him someday. He'd tried every way he knew to show her how much she meant to him. He'd make her happy now. This time he'd do the right thing.

Dustin rode to where he had left the ambulance he'd hauled Cindy home in and in it headed east. He knew what he was looking for but wasn't real sure how far he'd have to travel to find it. Distance made no difference to Dustin. He was doing something for his Cindy. Making her happy was all that was important to him. The look on her face when he got back with her surprise would make all the hurt go away. He'd make her happy this time, that's for sure.

The railroad town of Wichita, Kansas was where Dustin finally located his treasure. Appropriating it was an altogether different matter. It was a beauty, a real rare find this far west. The problem was it was the only one for hundreds of miles around and was one of the main attractions in a young town which held too few attractions at best. Acquiring this prize would be costly, to say the least. Dustin had been too far to be denied his trophy. This was going to be the one thing that no one else had been able to give Cindy. She'd see he was still the man to get her the things she needed and desired. He would have his reward no matter what the price.

Dustin was so intent on making his purchase he got careless, something he never did. He was talking with the saloon owner and was offering a very large sum of cash and was being overheard by some local ruffians that one, thinking clearly, would normally be wary of. Dustin was told that there was another person who, as part owner, would have to be consulted before a sale was finalized. This new stumbling block was just a minor inconvenience for the determined adventurer and was met head on.

Dustin and the saloon keeper left out the rear door of Wichita's finest liquor emporium and house of ill repute and proceeded on a well built wooden walkway directly to Wichita's only house of worship. They knocked on the door of the rectory, which was positioned just to the right of the larger door into the chapel itself, the latter being the one the walkway led to. A Reverend answered and the unlikely trio walked into the church proper to hold their conversation. The Reverend confirmed that the church was indeed part owner of the property in question but considering the small flock and financial problems a young growing ministry is faced with, he would certainly consider any reasonable offer for their share. He would not, however, go against his co-owners wishes concerning the sale. Neither were able to make the original purchase of this object of Dustin's desires by themselves. They had become the strangest of bed fellows to make the purchase of this beautiful, cherrywood, upright piano, delivered all the way from St. Louis. This wonderful example of the craftsman's skill was the life of the party nights throughout the week but on the Sabbath, as well as Christmas and Easter, it was rolled across the wooden passageway to another world, one where it traded its honky tonk melodies for a more reverent refrain, filling the little church and the hearts of its parishioners. It would then make the trip back across to the nether world. It was this versatile instrument that had brought so much pleasure and joy to the local townsfolk and the travelers passing through, that Dustin had set his sights on. A piano, he had started out for just that!

As the trip had dragged out, he'd thought about a simpler music maker, like a guitar, violin or even some sort of flute. Cindy had talked about the beautiful pianos she'd seen in Europe and a piano it would be. Not having any idea of what a piano was worth, on top of the fact that the saloon keeper didn't want to sell this one, Dustin was about to be robbed in the most nonviolent way he'd ever imagined. When the saloon keeper named his opening price, after listing the finer attributes of this exceptional instrument, the preacher, out of embarrassment, excused himself explaining that whatever price they agreed on would be fine with him. It's hard on a man of the cloth to stand by and witness such blatant thievery as was about to transpire on the sale of their piano.

Without debate, Dustin handed the saloon keeper the price asked and enlisted the assistance of three of the ruffians to help him load his purchase. Dustin was not a fool by any means but wanted this piano and wanted to get it back to Cindy as soon as possible. The price was not an issue now. He was going home to his Cindy with a gift that would bring her some happiness, a gift that just might bring them together, and that would be priceless.

As Dustin headed back across the long trail home with his prize, the ruffians drank in silence. They started remorsing the loss of their beloved eighty eight and cursing the obviously eccentric and rich outsider who was now traversing westward, growing more distant with each passing drink. There was only one thing to do, they would ride out and just take their piano back. To hell with this bold stranger. First, a few more drinks, there was no hurry. After all how fast could he travel with a wagon load of piano. The next round led to another, as is its custom and then still another. Before long it was unanimously decided to put off retrieval until tomorrow. The tomorrow never came for the would be piano rescuers. This, as many other noble efforts, ended with several rounds toasting the memory of their magical music machine. Their attention became focused on the new one that the saloon keeper was ordering from the east. This one was actually supposed to play itself. The concept was very old, music boxes had been around for a long time. It was the scale of a full size piano playing itself that had everyone's imagination captured.

Dustin drove the team steadily westward with just enough stops to feed and rest them. The trip was an uneventful one until he reached the nations. Dustin had enough experience to know this wild stretch was as perilous as any to be covered on this earth. He knew it going into this trip and weighed the dangers as light indeed when compared to the possible reward of Cindy's affection and gratitude. Most would not make a trip so potentially wrought with danger as this for any reason, to make it for something as seemingly frivolous as purchasing a present for someone, made it almost ludicrous. This opinion was meaningless to Dustin. He alone realized how truly important this trip was. He didn't consider his cargo merely a piano, it was a symbol of his affection for the woman he loved, a display of the continuing effort he was willing to expend to please her. Cindy's happiness was paramount in Dustin's life. To see her smile again, to hear her laugh and sing, would be worth any hardship he had to encounter. He knew this was the act, the show of love and loyalty he needed her to see, to understand somehow, that he was the one she needed. He more than Tim Burns, that degenerate, or this Louis fellow that had her living in squalor and allowed her to become and remain severely ill. He, Dustin Thomas, was the man who would love her and care for her forever and always, as she deserved to be. She would see this beautiful piano and love it and just maybe love him too, a little, for getting it for her. She would play it and he would listen to her as long as she played. The piano could bring them together. This was his cargo and a heavy cargo it was, both figuratively and literally.

The heavily loaded wagon was pulling slowly and with great difficulty in the sandy soil of the Indian nations. The early part of his return trip was on the main trail west, not an extremely heavily traveled roadway but more so than the pony track he would have to follow from the time he headed southwest off of it. He was pressing onward, fighting the good fight against the distance. He was making tracks.

That was just the problem. He was sure making tracks, deep tracks as only a very heavily loaded wagon could leave. Dustin knew any band of wondering Indians or marauding bandits seeing these deep wagon tracks would think at the end of them would be a large payday. Either supplies for some town or camp, maybe weapons, or it could even be loaded with gold. Whatever it was, this wagon would draw some unwanted interest out here in no man's land. Dustin had to remove the box top off the ambulance while in Wichita in order to fit the tall instrument in the wagon bed. He had covered it with a canvas tarp to protect it from the elements but now he left it uncovered during the day. If someone was trailing him or just happened upon him, they would see he was just a nut hauling a piano across hundreds of miles of wilderness, not a gun runner, a paymaster or even a merchant carrying dry goods. Maybe he could avoid trouble and possible ambush by bad men whose curiosity would otherwise be peaked by seeing the tracks alone.

This worked well for a while, then one moonless night while Dustin took a few moments of much needed rest, a shot rang out. Dustin heard it hit the wagon. The wind had picked up while he slept and his fire had blazed to life again making him an easy target. He kicked dirt over it and pistol in hand, peered in the direction he thought the shot had come from. He heard nothing more and daylight found him well removed from the area. He stopped after the sun had risen and discovered his worst fears were well founded. The bullet had indeed hit the wagon. Worse was it had passed through the planking of the wagon sideboards and had torn a hole into the end of the beautiful cherry upright, leaving a hole and an ugly scar. Dustin was heart sick but helpless to do anything about the attack or the damage. He pressed on. He did not sleep again the rest of the trip. The final four days he never closed his eyes. He still stopped to rest his horses, but not for as long as he had before.

173

Finally he arrived on the hill overlooking the little community where he could pick out the outline of the Confederate Cantina on the skyline. Even with the bullet hole in its end, Dustin was very proud of his present to his lovely Cindy. He drove the team harder than need be. He wanted Cindy to see the piano and to see he had gotten it for her. He wanted to see her smile and thank him for his love and thoughtfulness. He wanted to see her! Cindy had said harsh words to him when last he saw her. Even her mother had been stern and accusing. That would not matter now, for now he had his prize. The gift no one else had given. He was giving her music. She could play and get well, sing and be happy and he would listen.

He drove by the cantina without stopping but not without drawing attention. Matt ran out after him, admiring the beautiful piano and praising Dustin for successfully completing such an unbelievable feat.

"We didn't know where you'd gone or if you were coming back! Where did you get it?" Matt asked.

"Wichita," was Dustin's response.

"Why a piano?" Matt asked.

"It's for Cindy. She plays beautifully, I'll bet," Dustin stated.

"I didn't know she could even play," remarked Matt.

Dustin was thrilled to see Kate's horse was tied in front of the house. He didn't know why but he really wanted Kate to be proud of him too. It was important to him what she thought. That emotion confused Dustin some, but he gave it little heed now. He had to be ready to accept his just rewards from his lovely little Cindy.

"Hey, you girls in the house, come out and see what this crazy Dustin has done!" Matt yelled.

Kate, carrying Wesley, and Mrs. Morton with her arm around Cindy helping her walk, came out on the porch. Kate was big eyed and as pleased to see Dustin as she was surprised to actually see a piano.

Mrs. Morton said, "What a magnificent piano! It's beautiful. Look Cindy, Dustin's brought you a piano! Isn't it wonderful?"

"Wonderful? It's got one end shot off of it. Looks like he found it laying on the trail," Cindy said and shot an evil glare at Dustin that he felt cut into his heart.

He had been afraid the bullet hole would upset her. Maybe when he got it set inside it would look better. He was numb while he, Kate, Matthew and two neighbors slid the giant instrument from the wagon to the porch then from the porch to the house.

Kate said, "It's the most beautiful piano in the world and you are the most wonderful man!" and kissed him on the cheek, trying to comfort him some. She, being able to see the pain Cindy had inflicted on him, hurt for him, deep inside herself.

Dustin went into Cindy's room and hoped Mrs. Morton would leave so he could tell Cindy how much she meant to him and how he wanted her to have a piano to play and remind her of Europe. She seemed so happy when she talked about it. Mrs. Morton didn't leave. She seemed to be intentionally hovering over Cindy in some needless effort to protect her from him.

"Cindy, I bought it for you. You told me how much you love music. I want you to be happy, Cindy. That's all I've ever wanted! I'm sorry about the bullet hole, maybe I can get it fixed. Cindy, don't you like it?" he asked pitifully then added, "What's wrong Cindy?"

"WHAT'S WRONG!" she shrieked at him. "I'll tell you what's wrong, you bastard! I can't play. I never could play. I lied! There, are you happy now? You just brought it here to humiliate me. You knew I couldn't play it. You just had to show everyone, just had to make yourself look big and important! Well, you've done it. I hope you're satisfied, you sick son-of-a-bitch," she finished more growling than speaking.

"Cindy, I didn't know you didn't know how, I mean you said you…It doesn't matter, you can learn now. There are books in the bench. I thought you'd like it is all, that's the only reason I…" he didn't finish.

Cindy stood weakly clinging to her mother and with her free right hand slapped Dustin so hard, the sound of the blow brought both Matt and Kate into the room. Then Cindy threw the blow Dustin would feel forever.

"You jealous, meddling trash! You've wanted me your whole life. You have made a fool out of yourself over and over trying to make me love you. You are pitiful, Dustin Thomas. You drag me here to this hell hole to die and then you run off without saying a word to anyone, then come crawling back with that shot up, hunk of junk wanting everything to be hugs and kisses. Well, my simple minded friend, it ain't gonna happen! Not now, not ever! You make me sick to my stomach just looking at you standing there. You are not half the man Louis was on his worst day. I'm glad I'm dying and you caused it. I hope I do it before I ever have to see your face again. Thanks for ruining the only fantasy I had left to cling onto by bringing that pile of rubbish here to remind me it was all just a dream. Well, you've killed the dream and me along with it. I pray one of us is rotting in hell long before I have to see the "great Dustin Thomas" again."

Cindy swung out, more weakly this time, but still making contact with Dustin's reddened cheek. He turned and walked past Matt and Kate who were speechless and by little Wesley who was crying and pulling at Kate's leg to be picked up. Kate glared a look of pure hatred at her sister which fell on uncaring eyes, then turned toward Dustin, leaving Wesley to Matt's attention.

"Dustin, wait," she said. He did not. "She's sick, she doesn't know what she's saying," she added. He kept walking. "Dustin, it's a beautiful piano," Kate said at a loss for the right words to say to a man who's heart had just been ripped out and stepped on.

He looked back, he would not soon forget the look on Kate's face as he rode away. He hadn't realized it at that moment, but they were both crying. That long look burned itself into each of their souls and welded them together with a bond that even time couldn't weaken.

Dustin walked down to the stalls, saddled Peso, as his horse was still out at the ranch, and rode by the Cantina where Matt had taken Wesley after the blow up. He stopped and entered the saloon. There stood Matt, leaning on the bar staring off into space again.

"Hey Matt! I'm leaving. You want to ride along or are you just as happy dreaming about life as you would be living it?" Dustin asked seriously.

"That's not fair, Dustin. You know I'd go, if I could. I've got responsibilities. We all can't just pack up and ride away from our obligations," Matt returned having had his feelings hurt by Dustin's remark.

"Yea, I guess you're right Matt. I know you'd like to go. See you around sometime brother," Dustin said and walked out of the Confederate Cantina. "Tell Kathy I'll leave her horse out at the ranch. She can pick him up when she takes the wagon out.

That day he rode off east on Chief, bitter for the first time in his life. He'd been dealt some sorry hands before but he'd never felt so deserted as he did now. When his family was murdered, he was broken hearted and felt a terrible loss but he never felt lost before now. He rode two hard days east before stopping.

Chapter 22

He came into Ft. Sumner late the second night and entered the saloon outside the fort perimeter. Dustin had encountered many battles with Mescal since his first one at Teresa's but did not consider himself a real drinker. He was in such a state of turmoil at the moment he thought maybe a good long drunk might be just the thing he needed. He started cautiously at first and then became more reckless as to volume and time of consumption. He was soon spinning slowly out of control, unable to allow his mind the menacing luxury of pondering on one hurtful memory or another for more than a brief instant. This was useful in the heartache department but he was also unable to concentrate on just exactly where he was. Neither was he able to do anything about it during the flashes of coherency that came to him from time to time. He remembered making the decision not to drink anymore when he realized he'd tipped over backwards in his chair and was just lying there looking up at the ceiling. Two of the young ladies working the establishment helped him up and one led him to the stable where Chief was stalled. She made Dustin as comfortable as possible and promised she would come out and check on him later. He passed out immediately. She kept her promise and came out after the saloon closed and found Dustin sleeping soundly, so she returned to her quarters at the back of the saloon.

The next morning Dustin woke early because the stable man was feeding the horses and they were excited to be receiving his offerings. Dustin was a little hung over but nothing he couldn't live with. He did realize shortly that none of his problems had gone away. They were still very much with him and now he had this terrible headache and woozy stomach to deal with as well. He decided drinking might not be the means to the end he'd hoped for. From now on coffee or a single shot and a beer or two was going to be his self imposed limit.

"Hell, a six year old child could have rolled me and taken everything I owned last night. I'll not let that ever happen again," he said to Chief, who seemed to understand.

Dustin wanted to thank the girl who had helped him last night. She could have stolen him blind but didn't touch a thing belonging to him. Her honesty deserved reward. The saloon hadn't opened yet so Dustin strolled over to a cafe supporting a sign which boasted, 'fine dining, morning, noon and night', out in front over hanging the wooden sidewalk.

"That sounds like the spot for me," Dustin said to himself.

He ate a meal that would have amply fed five, large men and while finishing his second gallon of hot, black coffee asked the plump, old, German woman waiting on him if they had anything sweet for dessert.

"Goodness gracious, son. What you gonna do when you blow up from too much of my good food?" she asked very seriously.

"Did I over do it a little, Ma'am? I'm sorry. My manners are a little rusty. I ain't eaten nothing this good in a while. Now what about dessert?" Dustin repeated.

"Ya sure, we got dessert! We got strudel like you never had. I'll get you some and just keep coming with more 'til you explode!" she said disbelieving the capacity of this big, young man.

Dustin finished two kinds of strudel, apple and cherry, drank a little more coffee and thanked the old woman with a very generous tip.

"You come back soon! We start serving dinner in just three hours, at eleven. You need to get started so you can be done by suppertime. We start serving it at six. You'll want a fair start because we close the doors at nine and throw you out, done or not!" the big woman teased.

"I'll do my best," he retorted.

Dustin walked to the fort, checked in and wired around trying to gain information about his cattle drive. He got very little news anywhere except from Fort Macvett in Texas where this all began. He received official word of Gibson's death, the theft and sale of Mullen and Wilson's herds in Denver, the loss and only partial recovery of Miller's herd, his death by drowning, Epps disappearance and assumed murder of him and all his men. Supporting evidence that Epps herd was stolen and sold by a man named Bowdry, in Kansas City.

Of all the information Dustin received, the story of how Big Bill, the cook, rode from Denver to intercept Miller's herd, helped gather the scattered cattle, drove them to join Bliss in Montana, stayed through the winter helping build a ranch, then just left without a penny of payment for his invaluable service, absolutely amazed Dustin.

He was pleased to hear the ridiculous goat herd idea had been a grand success, thousands of abandoned calves had been saved and the Mexicans had even started sheering the angoras and had found a ready market for the fleece, possibly keeping the ranchers, who lost so great a percentage of their cattle on the ill fated drive, alive until finally the war department honored part of their agreement to purchase the cattle that were actually delivered.

The association had convened and estimated percentages of ownership of the delivered stock and by not honoring Dustin's agreement, all came out fairly well after all was said and done. All moneys had been distributed to the association membership and they were at present organizing another much smaller drive to the forts being built in the Colorado territory, to start soon. Bliss refused to cut Dustin out, knowing full well he was responsible for what success the drive had obtained and wired full payment for the one hundred head Don Diego Augustina had given Dustin, to his banker Mr. Rogers in Del Rio. He also had retained Dustin as partner on the cowherd he was staying in Montana with. Bliss also chose to keep many cows and bulls the Army had backed out on purchasing for the reservation Indians. He and the 08 men remaining with him had built a fine ranch and were raising ample beef for the governments needs, both military and Indian. Dustin's twenty-five percent interest would be honored on every head Bliss held in Montana.

With Mullen and Wilson working themselves to death for Horace Tabor in the tunnels of the Great Rocky Mountains, only Bowdry, the apparent murderer of Epps and his men, was left to settle with for the wrong they committed to the 08 herdsmen. Dustin would make this his cause. He would somehow find his friend Bill and pay him for his great and unusual loyalty and he would find this evil Kansasan Bowdry and kill him and every man who stole a single cow from a trail herd anywhere up or down the length of this wild country. He would personally see to it that future herds would have one less worry on their long arduous drive. He would see to it that these bands of thieves and murderers were too afraid to leave their homes to wreak any further havoc for these hard working drovers.

Dustin left Ft. Sumner immediately after leaving word with the military to notify Big Bill he was being sought by Dustin Thomas, who owed him a great deal of appreciation and gratitude. Dustin would base his operations out of the fort at Levenworth, staying in the field between there and Kansas City and would greatly enjoy entertaining and compensating Bill for a job well done. This message, along with a description of Bill, was to go out over all lines and everyone was to be on the lookout for this noble gentleman.

Dustin rode hard and covered many miles in short order. He was in the Indian nation for several days when he sighted a rather large encampment of Indians. Dustin, sure he'd already been seen, rode on in. There was some uneasiness as he entered the camp but knowing their customs, Dustin ignored the stares and mock threats and rode directly to the chief's council fire located in the center of the encampment. He introduced himself and asked permission to dismount. His ever more fluent Apache, again opening doors otherwise shut, made him welcome. Dustin was invited to stay as he might be of some service to the Chief as an interpreter. They were expecting white guests any day and his ease with both languages might prove very helpful. The Chief, Mantibo, had not dealt with these men before and did not know just what to expect from them. Dustin assured Mantibo he would be proud to talk for the great Chief. Mantibo was not really a great chief, rather a very minor one who normally led a small pack of beggars and thieves. This assembly was very impressive in size and number of fighting age men, so Dustin would allow his graciousness some freedom while addressing this suddenly powerful war chief.

When asked where he learned of their language and customs, Dustin told the stories of Nacatan and Yoshela and of being at Nacatan's side at his death. A great commotion arose among these Chiricahua renegades. They had heard of the brave white man returning the body of the mighty warrior and chief Nacatan. He was asked directly, "Are you this man?"

Dustin responded, "I am no brave man. I was with a brave man at his end. The great Nacatan spoke his last word to my ear only. I was honored to see how fearless a Chiricahua Apache warrior chief faces his death. Yes, I am that white man. I am Dustin Thomas."

The counsel ordered a feast be prepared for their honored guest. He would share their best tonight. These Indians were in no way dissimilar from any others Dustin had known when it came to celebrating. These boys could and would party. Dustin had invoked his drinking limit just in time, unfortunately the Indians had no such rule. The Indian equivalent of Mescal was a noxious concoction called many things, mostly it was known as tiswin. It tasted like an inconsistent mixture of turpentine, kerosene, horse urine and wood alcohol. It was, however, very effective in its purpose. Indians did not drink because they particularly enjoyed it, they drank to get drunk. This tiswin served this end well. The blindness often occurring from drinking it, was seldom permanent and that was comforting to Dustin who had to at least appear to consume some of the celebration liquid, it was after all being served in his honor.

After about ten o'clock, Dustin slipped off to the outskirts of the encampment where Chief was tied to spend the remainder of the night. He'd not now be missed. All he would have to be careful of is not being hit by the ricochet from a shot fired by a celebrating drunk and all would be well.

Dustin survived the feast which was still weakly going when he arose the next morning. He prepared breakfast and then strolled over to camp, arraying the still half full gourd cup of tiswin he'd left with last evening.

Mantibo looked up at Dustin standing, drink in hand, looking fresh as anyone just waking from a full nights sleep and said just barely coherently, "It's no wonder we're having so much trouble with you white men. You are the toughest man I have ever seen."

This said, the Chief slid into the slumber over indulgence in its final mercy brings. Dustin laughed to himself and walked through this camp comprised of several different bands of Apache sects. He wandered around looking for anyone he might know. He saw several of the middle aged men he'd seen before but did not know any of them well.

It was well after noon when Mantibo woke from his tiswin induced sleep. He sent for Dustin and had a meal prepared from leftovers of last night's feast. The two men talked of many things but primarily of the probable fate of the Apache nation. It was a gloomy prospect at best. Dustin had overheard a high ranking officer discussing the likelihood of allowing the Apaches to retain some of their White Mountain homeland instead of sending them all to Florida or the Oklahoma territory or even further north. Mantibo felt this would be satisfactory. He asked Dustin to take a message to the White Chief that he, Mantibo, would bring his people in quietly and stay in the White Mountain range, with no further trouble. They would never go elsewhere to live. This was their home, they had lived on all the land from here to the Great Mountains. They would go there and live or would die fighting to be allowed to remain free.

Dustin said he would be happy to bring this news to the soldiers at the fort in Levenworth. They could get word to the white chief. During their meal the conversation turned to Dustin and the reason for his being this far east of his home. Dustin explained the two main reasons, first he was looking for a man who had done him much good service and he wished to find and honor him. He went on and described Bill to Mantibo and asked if he had seen such a man.

"No, I have not seen this particular black white man. I do understand the bravery and fearlessness of these black, white men. Many times in battle since before the great war the whites had with themselves, when there were any of those black white soldiers facing us, they were always the first sent in to do battle. The greater the odds, the more black, white soldiers went forward. Only after the battle field was covered with the bodies of these black white men did the white soldiers advance. We Indians have always suspected these black white men were your best and bravest soldiers. I am glad you want to show honor to this Bill. We have never thought the white men treated the black white men with the respect they had earned, even though they do allow them the privilege of being first into battle every time. That may be honor enough for these brave black white men," Mantibo resolved.

Dustin told the Chief the second reason he was there was to kill a man or men who had done much wrong to him and had killed a friend of his and thirty men who had worked for him.

"How many men are there that they could kill thirty armed men?" Mantibo asked.

Dustin wasn't sure but they were border raiders and the Chief must have seen them along

this part of the Indian nation. They followed and stole from the cowherds traveling to the railroad. The leader's name is Bowdry.

"I may know this man. I have seen him and a very large company of men riding fast and at night. He has not caused me any aggravation," the Chief declared.

"When did you see him last?" Dusitn asked.

Before he was answered a commotion was raised on the other side of the encampment. Three riders were approaching. They were leading pack horses and these were the cause of the excitement. The pack horses were loaded with cases marked Winchester. The Indians could not read but could recognize the picture this word made. It was not the cargo causing the uproar, the leader of these men, all three of whom had their own rifles cocked and in hand, shouted for Mantibo by name, like one would call a dog. This alone brought great disfavor by the Indians. Even this disrespectful manner was the least of these three men's problems. Several warriors brought the men to Mantibo's fire.

"I sure as hell hope you're Mantibo! I'm Jackson," the leader said.

Mantibo spoke softly to Dustin, "We were to buy rifles from a man called Jackson. This must be him. I am concerned deeply by the fact these men lead the horses of a hunting party of young men I sent out several days ago led by my own grandson. Ask these men where these ponies came from."

"Chief, I too am concerned. They also ride horses belonging to me and my trail herd. Do you see the 08 brand on them? I recognize two of the saddles as well. Let me get these men off of their horses and see if we can't get their weapons away from them. See how ready to shoot us they are? You tell your braves our plan. I'll act like I am interpreting for you and invite the men to eat. As soon as they are off guard, your men can jump them and we'll get the story of your grandson and my friends from them."

"What the hell are you two blabbering about, half-breed? Is that Mantibo or not?" demanded Jackson.

Mantibo shouted loudly Dustin's plan and his men moved in closer.

"The Chief says you are most welcome to his camp," Dustin said loudly in English, then continued, "He is delighted you have come and brought his rifles."

"By god, they ain't his yet! Not by a damn sight. We had hell getting here. There going to cost him more than we'd told him!" Jackson stated.

"Come and join us please. We have a meal prepared and wish you to share it with us. Get down, rest your tired horses and yourselves. The Chief is a wealthy Chief, he has much gold but few rifles. He will gladly give you the heavy gold. It is of no use to him. The rifles are what he needs. Come join us," Dustin said very theatrically, motioning grandly with his arms.

"Come on, Jackson. Let's eat and get paid," one of Jackson's partners said.

"I'll be glad to help the old bastard with his heavy gold," said the other of the trio as he slid off his horse.

"Not till I have the money!" demanded Jackson.

Dustin turned and asked Mantibo if he had the money for the rifles and was assured by the Chief tossing two rather large sacks of gold coins to Jackson and telling Dustin, "This is a great deal more than our agreed on price."

Jackson surveyed the coins and readily able to tell the amount was more than satisfactory placed the sacks into his saddle bags and said, "Well, all right. Now we'll eat," and stepped off his horse as well.

His left foot was still in the stirrup when they grabbed him. All three were dragged to the ground and disarmed. Dustin and Mantibo walked to where they were being held.

"Now, Mr. Jackson, could you explain how you came to be riding my horses and leading his?"

"These are our horses, by God! We bought them!" Jackson shouted.

"Did you buy them saddles too?" Dustin asked.

"They're ours. We've had them for years. Turn us loose, are you crazy?" demanded Jackson.

"Why yes, I am crazy! I'm crazy enough to believe that old A fork saddle on the 08 bay over there belongs to a friend of mine named Slim. I'm crazy enough to give you one more chance to tell me the truth before I take the saddle off and look underneath at the tree for Slim's name. If it's there, I'll know where you got my horses. Then I'm going to let Mantibo's boys get you to tell them where you got his ponies. You won't enjoy his questioning nearly as much as mine," Dustin said evilly.

"We didn't want to kill nobody! Jackson, he made us kill them fellas. We needed the horses," the second man confessed in terror.

"Shut up you silly bastard," Jackson ordered to no avail.

"We shot the two Indians that was chasing us horseback then Jackson wrecked the wagon killing our mules. It was him went back and killed them other Injuns!" the third man cried out.

"I'll kill both you fools! Don't you know what these savages are going to do to us?" Jackson snarled.

Dustin turned to the Chief, "I am sorry to tell you, your grandson is dead and all of his party. So are my friends. This man Jackson is the blame but his two companions helped him."

The Chief gave a quick signal and the order to execute these cold blooded killers was official. The ponies were unpacked and the 08 horses were unsaddled and all were turned out with the tribes other horses. The Chief was sickened by the loss of his grandson and sent a small band of men along with the tribes holy man out to hold their service over the bodies of their fallen young.

Mantibo let his warriors pass out the weapons and ammunition according to position in the tribe. He kept Jackson's Spencer rifle for himself. Mantibo offered Dustin a rifle but he was happy with his own and gave his to a brave not too near the head of the list who might not otherwise have received one. The tortures of these three men reminded Dustin too much of scenes from the past and he refrained from watching, much to Mantibo's displeasure.

"Killing a man is no great task, Dustin. Killing him slowly takes much skill. You should learn this. It might serve you well someday," the Chief said.

"I have seen this all before my friend. You forget I knew Nacatan well. He could keep a man dying longer than I ever knew was possible," Dustin stated.

"Yes, he was a great man!" Mantibo said proving he had not picked up on Dustin's sarcasm.

"Each man must live life as he sees fit. There are places on earth for all beings, for the eagle and the snail," Mantibo continued after a moment of reflection. "The eagle is free, possessing the greatest freedom of all things. He must pay for this freedom by the need to kill all he must have to eat. If he does not work hard at his hunting, he will starve. This dangerous life of the hunter is the price of his freedom," again the reflective pause then once more the Chief continued, "The snail has no freedom. He travels nowhere, he sees nothing or at best very little. He has the security of the lake waters feeding him. Always washing food into the snail's mouth. He too pays a price for this security. He pays with his lack of freedom.

"My people were once eagles. We hunted to feed ourselves and were free. We took the risk of starving and accepted it gladly. We are now being asked to become snails. To live in our shells and be fed by your government like the lake feeds the snails living in its boundaries. We no longer have the choice to be what we please. The white chief has chosen for us to be snails. This will be difficult for my people. We have flown as eagles since the Great Father created the earth and put our people here. I have had many dreams recently. I know that we must become snails in the lake of the white man or die fighting to remain eagles. If the decision was for myself alone, I would not hesitate to die like the eagle I was created to be. The deaths and capture of my people's great chiefs have left this choice mine to make on behalf of all the children and women, young and old of my tribe. I have spoken at the counsel. My people want to live. The fathers want their sons to have the chance to become men. The mothers want to hold their daughters' babies in their arms.

"I had these men bring me rifles so we could die fighting in spite of what my people wanted. Now my heart is full of sorrow at the loss of my grandson. I want no more death to come to my people at the hands of the white man. I will go with you to this place called Levenworth and tell its chief we will stay in the mountains you call White. We will be half eagle and half snail. We will live on the white man's reservation like his snails but we will hunt and be free like eagles within its boundaries. You can make this happen for us, Dustin. We will go tomorrow and see this chief," Mantibo said feeling as if the decision was made and final.

"Chief, I've got a suggestion you might want to think about. I believe like you, the only future your people have is to go to the reservation. I do worry about some of the men that the great chief in Washington has representing him out here. I would have some men take your new rifles and hide them on the reservation. I believe the men at the fort will want to take your weapons away from you. You will need your good rifles to hunt with in your new home. The white soldiers don't need to know everything. Mantibo, you are a good chief and a wise man as well. I will help all I can. I am not a chief of my people and have no place of importance at our council tables but I will speak loudly and strongly for Mantibo and his people!"

This talk served several purposes. First it occupied Dustin and Mantibo while the warriors had their way with the three gun runners. The end had been prolonged an incredible period of time and finally the Apache women who had lost sons at the hands of these men were allowed their turn. Dustin stepped out with Mantibo just as these women were set free on the captives. The savagery of the war hardened braves paled by comparison to that of these heart sick mothers. They inflicted so grievous and brutally inhuman torture that the end came soon. The bodies were left tied and the camp dogs were given last turn, finishing the job completely.

There was then preparations made for another celebration. Dustin was beginning to think the festivities held in his honor the night before were going to be held anyway and his name was attached to it spur of the moment. This bunch of Apaches would do well on a reservation. They enjoyed partying too much to be allowed to roam free.

Mantibo and two elders of the tribe accompanied Dustin the next morning on his way to Levenworth. Not an hour out of camp Dustin saw a solo rider sitting in the middle of the trail holding a pack horse.

"Dustin Thomas! I couldn't believe it was you down there. Your friends saved me a pretty chancy encounter with those three ex-gunrunners," Bill said as he shook Dustin's hand.

"Bill, I've been looking for you to say thanks. If not for you, not one of Miller's cows would have made Montana. What the hell you doing here?" Dustin asked.

After Dustin introduced Bill to Mantibo and the boys, Bill told his whole story from Denver till now. Dustin told Bill he might not want to ride along with him on this trip. After he talked to the presiding officer at Fort Levenworth on behalf of the Apaches, he intended to kill Bowdry. Dustin explained that he understood the notorious border raider had spared Bill's life twice and he did not expect Bill to assist in his assassination. Bill made no response but continued along with Dustin and the Indians.

It was several days ride to Levenworth and the men arrived in good time, ready for the official surrender of one of the last large bands of Chiricahua Apaches. Fort Levenworth was a major center of military intelligence and there was always an abundance of high ranking military personal on hand. Dustin led the three Indians into the fort unceremoniously and requested a meeting with Brigadier General Stone, the highest ranking officer currently present at the fort. The General granted Dustin a hearing immediately and he and his three guests were shown into a large office. All four men waited anxiously, there were just four because Bill had chosen to wait with the horses. In a matter of moments the General and an entourage of fellow lesser officers entered the room. The General congratulated Dustin on bringing the Apaches in. Just as Dustin started his dissertation, he was abruptly stopped by soldiers rushing into the office. They grabbed the Indians and put them in chains.

"What the hell are you doing?" Dustin shouted and tried to release Mantibo.

185

He was struck from behind and knocked to the floor by the blow. He heard Stone order the Indians taken away and he tried to rise but was held down by two soldiers.

As they were being led out Mantibo said to Dustin, "Tell my people to flee into Mexico and join the other Apaches taking refuge there. They will have need of the new rifles soon."

Dustin raised his head and spoke his agreement to comply to Mantibo's request.

Dustin rose and turned to Stone and said, "They came in voluntarily. What did you do that for?"

"Yours is not to question why. You did a fine job, son. Don't spoil it now!" General Stone said and walked out.

Dustin was escorted out and Bill came running over to him, seeing he'd been injured.

"Come on, Bill. We've got to warn the camp! I've been tricked," Dustin said ashamed of being involved in this mess.

The two men rode hard, pushing their horses near their limits but arrived at the encampment, confident of not having been followed. The Indians were not fit to travel when Dustin and Bill reached them. It seems they had been celebrating the big pow wow being held in Levenworth on their behalf. Dustin roused them into a state of action. He told Bill to catch the 08 horses and saddle them. They would lead their tired horses and ride the fresh ones to a safe place Dustin knew of, not far from Kansas City.

While Bill caught the horses, Dustin explained what all had happened, gave Mantibo's instructions to the remaining elders and helped the Apaches pack up their camp. In a matter of hours, the Indians were on the move south. It had always amazed Dustin, how quickly an entire village could be taken down, rolled up and hauled off, leaving very little sign of its ever being there.

When Dustin got to Bill, he was all ready. Every horse was saddled and both Bill's and the 08 boys pack horses had extra saddles thrown on top of their packs.

"What the hell are you doin, Bill?" Dustin asked finding humor in the scene.

"I wanted to take the boys rigs back to their families in Del Rio. It ain't much but they're all their families will have left of them," Bill justified.

"Good idea, my friend! Let's get gone before anyone sees us aiding and abetting our national enemy."

The Apaches headed south picking up the burial party on their way. Bill and Dustin headed southeast with even more urgency than the fleeing Apaches. Dustin took Bill to a different location than he had originally planned.

"I almost forgot you was headed to Del Rio, Bill. This is more on your way," Dustin explained his change of plans.

"I wish you'd forget this getting even business and come home with me," Bill offered.

"No, Texas ain't my home. Mine's west of here," Then after a short sigh "or it was anyway. I got no place to be now," Dustin said so sadly Bill couldn't even respond.

Once at the beautiful little spring and oasis of cottonwood trees nestled around it that Dustin had changed course for, the boys stopped and started making camp.

"If I remember correctly, you used to be a pretty fair cook. I'll take care of all the horses if you'll unload your pack horse and fix supper," Dustin bargained.

"Sounds good to me. Is it safe to build a fire here?" Bill asked.

"Yep, I camped here with Cindy on our way back from New York. You can't see this place 'til you are right on it. It's hard to tell from here but this spring sits in a little hole hidden by swells in the landscape."

"New York City?" Bill said, maybe remembering something, maybe just amazed a little.

"Yep!" Dustin answered, then completely unsolicited began to tell his story.

He even flashed back to his early childhood and covered most every detail, down playing any heroics or bravery on his part. Bill could read the boldness of Dustin's actions into the results of each tale anyway.

When Dustin finished the part about him being at Mantibo's when the gun runners rode in and ended his story, Bill said, "Back there years ago when you found that loot in the fella's saddlebag, got me to thinking. These gun runners didn't have no place to spend the money they took off the 08 boys. I'll bet it's still in their saddle bags," Bill said setting his coffee cup down.

"Hell, let's go look, Bill! I'll bet them Indians cleaned them out though," Dustin added not yet rising.

"I'm sure you're right. I'd forgot the Apaches had them saddles for several days," Bill said setting back down.

Dustin jumped up child like giggling and made a run over to where he had stacked all the tack saying, "I'm gonna look anyway. Them Chirichaua's was sure celebrating hard and I ain't been right about nothing for a long time!"

Bill jumped up also and laughing the silliest laugh Dustin ever heard a grown man laugh, ran past Dustin with amazing ease. Dustin thought to himself, this big, black fella could out run some horses he'd owned and probably carry more weight too! They started through their spoils of war and found all the personal belongings of the four 08 cowmen along with the money they'd have been taking home to their families, if they had not gotten themselves killed.

"This is wonderful!" Bill said.

"No, this is wonderful!" shouted Dustin as he threw a large bag of gold coins at Bill.

"Lordy, Lordy! Them boys was sure too busy drinking!" Bill said in amazement then asked, "What you gonna do with all that gold?

"Well hell, Bill, I'm gonna give it to you, for all you done for me," Dustin declared.

"You ain't gonna take it back to the Apaches?" Bill asked.

"They got their guns and there ain't no place for them to spend it where they're going. Besides I seriously don't believe they would accept it back anyway. Their Chief gave it as payment for the rifles and to them that was the end of it. If they would have wanted it, all they would of had to do was reach down and get it. They had it nearly a week. No, I'm giving it to you. You can buy a ranch or a cowherd or both. There's a lot here," Dustin stated.

"There's too much here! Too much for just me, I'll split it with you," Bill demanded.

"All right, half and half. But you have to do me one more favor. I borrowed a lot of money from a banker in Del Rio, a Mr. Rogers. He never hesitated a second lending me that money for Cindy and I ain't paid him back yet. You take my part and give it to him. If it don't cover what I owe him, you tell him I'll be sending what I can along to him," Dustin explained.

"Consider it done, my friend," vowed Bill.

"Let them 08 horses wear the boys saddles home too. I got no use for this many horses. I will keep the pack horse, I'll be living off of him now," Dustin said thoughtfully.

"You know I would sorta like to, now that you mention it," Bill said.

"Like to what, Bill?" asked Dustin not understanding.

"I'd like to buy a cow herd, not a ranch so much, just a trail herd and make another drive. I've talked to a lot of drovers since we made our drive. Very few run theirs as well as you did. I'd like to make another drive with all my own cattle so no one else could make no decisions. I'd run it like you run ours and sure make it work too!" Bill said determinedly.

"Well, you damn sure got enough money for a start. Just remember how my drive turned out," Dustin reminded him.

"Your drive got three fifths stolen, two thirds of that by the cattle association representatives themselves, another herd scattered and a third lost, again by an association leader and with a herd and a half arriving at your destination, still made the cattle owners money and saved their Texas asses! You are the only one that lost on that drive," Bill said.

"I didn't have nothing invested but my time and them cows Don Diego Augustina gave me. I did use what was going to be part of my profit to borrow against to get the money for Cindy," Dustin said reflectively.

"You still got most of them cows, Dustin! Bliss has them for you in Montana. Them and a share of the ranch," Bill reminded him.

"Why didn't you stay and take a part, Bill?"

"It's too damn cold for me up there! I spent one winter shivering, that's plenty for me," Bill said adamantly.

"You'd like my place in the territory. Kate has done a real fine job with it, Cattle Kate! That's

what she's called now. It used to be just plain old Kathy when she was just a kid," Dustin said dreamily.

"Why don't you go back, Dustin?" Bill asked tenderly.

"I will someday, Bill. Maybe someday. You'd sure like it, Bill. Yes sir, it's a fine place," again Dustin said with real emotion.

"Hell, we'll just go together, Dustin! You and I. How's that sound?" Bill said encouragingly.

"You bet my friend, someday we'll do that," Dustin said sadly and walked into the darkness.

Chapter 23

Morning came and the men took their leisure breaking camp. Bill made biscuits enough to feed several dozen men and insisted Dustin take all the uneaten ones with him for the road. The men finally parted with the assurance Bill would take care of Dustin's banking and Dustin would make the trails a safe place to travel in case Bill decided to make the drive again. Each man kept his word!

Bill had an uneventful trip but had to show the bill of sale for the horses, Dustin had insisted he take with him, twice to sheriffs along the way. A black man leading several, saddled, riderless horses did cause a little curiosity from a sworn official in Texas.

Bill was pleased by his reception at the bank in Del Rio. Mr. Rogers was exceptionally friendly and would not give any accounting of Mr. Thomas' financial situation to anyone other than Mr. Thomas himself. He did assure Bill all was well with his accounts and he would tend to this deposit as well. This wise and frugal banker tried to encourage Bill to invest some of his new found fortune, but Bill told him of his plans to put together a drive next year and wanted the money close at hand. Seeing the futility of any further explanation, he simply placed Bill's money in a safety deposit box and gave him a key for it.

Dustin, on the other hand, had quite an eventful time ahead of him. Not far from Levenworth, while he was camped and sleeping, shots woke him suddenly. One struck the coffee pot sitting on a rock at the edge of his little fire ring, just a few feet from his head. The other hit his bedroll close to his left side. He rolled out trying to determine just what the hell was going on and with pistol in hand searched the area surrounding his little camp. On the other side of the clearing, he found tracks of someone kneeling by a large tree with an unobstructed view of his bedroll. Whoever this was had run to a horse tied a short distance away. Dustin had determined this was either a professional trying to scare him off for some reason, or a rank amateur, the more dangerous of the two apparent options. He had been an easy target to hit but to miss took either great skill or terrible marksmanship.

Studying the tracks, Dustin knew this was no professional. There were boot prints all around behind the tree, there were holes in the soles of both boots and the heel caps looked to be worn plumb off. Going up to where the horse had been concealed, Dustin saw that it to was in poor repair, missing the right front shoe.

Dustin made breakfast leisurely and found that a large twig sharpened to a point and jammed into the hole in his coffee pot, would slow the leak to a still useable volume. He'd begun talking to Chief again, which had been his usual custom shortly after Bill departed and now, there was certainly something to talk about.

"I'll not be run out of my camp by some damn fool wearing wore out boots! What in hell do you suppose that was all about, Chief? You should have woke me up. I know you smelled the horse. I'm going to get me a dog! Yes sir, a big mean bastard. Some damn fool with wore out boots slips right into my camp and shoots my coffee pot all to hell, then escapes on a near barefoot horse! Aint that a hell of a note!"

Dustin ate his breakfast and then, as always, had a plan. He'd felt badly about the mess at the fort and knew that it was probably inevitable that Mantibo serve some time eventually but not by his doing.

Dustin located a new camp, well secluded and not too far from the fort or from Kansas City either. He left his camp set up and his pack horse picketed out. Late at night Dustin slipped around the guards and into the main fort complex. He started a fire in the Quartermasters stockroom and then waited quietly for it to take hold. He had no idea how rapidly it would burn. This thing went up like kindling. Soldiers were running everywhere. Finally, they started a bucket brigade and Dustin walked into the stable and led out three horses in the shadow of this huge fire. Then he went over to the guard house and simply let Mantibo and his companions out. He escorted them out of the fort and into the little town adjacent to it, where he'd tied Chief. He bid his friends farewell and as they headed for Mexico, as quickly as possible, Dustin ran Chief toward his own camp.

He changed to the 08 horse and hurried on into Kansas City being very careful no one saw him enter town or the saloon. After just a brief moment, he rose from his concealed corner table in the crowded saloon and tipped it over demanding, "give me another bottle you son of a bitch! Make sure this one ain't half full of water either or I'll kick your big dumb..."

That was all Dustin had to say before the gentleman bartender struck him a blow with his bung hammer that Dustin wished had really knocked him out. He pretended it had but this was another part of one of his plans he hadn't thought out very well. Someone ran and told the city Marshall. He sent a deputy back saying the jail was full, just put the drunk in the store room of the saloon for the night.

The deputy went through his pockets and took all the money he found and gave the barman two dollars for the broken table leg. Dustin had intentionally left his horse loose with the others in the stable yard and placed his saddle on the rack with all the others. He hid all but twelve dollars in his saddle bags and also left his guns and other valuables at the stable with his saddle. He knew the local law would take all the money he had on him while drunk. If he had none or too little they'd not be satisfied and maybe hold him until he produced more. The twelve dollars, consisting of change and one ten dollar gold piece, worked just right. He spent the night resting comfortably on some flour sacks in the store room. Comfortably, that is, except for his head. It felt as if he'd butted heads with a buffalo. He was going to have to work on some aspects of his planning skills. They had nearly always served him well overall, but many times there were parts of them that damn near killed him too. This was one of those times.

After they went through his pockets and drug him into the storeroom, he heard at least ten different people including the bartender himself, swear he'd been there all evening drinking heavily but hadn't caused no trouble till just now. That was a good enough alibi for him. It was a necessary one as well.

"Dustin Thomas? Is that you, mister? Hey wake up you! Is your name Dustin Thomas?" the city marshal asked kicking Dustin in the ribs.

He lie there taking the abuse trying to act like a waking drunk and found he didn't have to fake it much, his head was killing him.

"Yes! Yes, I'm Dustin Thomas. Please stop kicking me," Dustin said.

"I figured as much. I'll go send a confirming telegraph," the marshal said to someone outside the room.

"I don't understand, sir," Dustin said as the marshal helped him up.

"Someone damn near burned down Fort Levenworth and let some prisoners escape last night. They put it out over the wire you were wanted for questioning in the matter cause you had brought the Indians in and was upset at the treatment they got. I wired them back and told them I had you and maybe you was upset but you was drunk and unconscious as well. You couldn't have done it, you'd been here all night. Sent the names of a dozen witnesses along just for good measure. Between you and me, I don't care if you did burn the place down. Aint no love lost between me and them federal boys. No sir!" the marshal said as he led Dustin over to the bar and had the barman pour them both a cup of coffee.

"You got any money?" the marshal asked.

"Yea, I think I got ten dollars," Dustin slurred as he searched his pockets.

"We got that as your fine. Do you have any for a place to stay?" explained the marshal.

"Yea, why is that?" Dustin asked making sure not to be the least bit abusive with his tone.

"Just didn't want to leave you hurt and broke too, is all," the marshal explained very friendly like.

"Oh, thank you," Dustin said rubbing his head then, "I meant why no love loss for the federal men?" Dustin asked.

"A while back, we had a little unpleasantness here and I've had a damn federal judge and marshal hanging around ever since. You might have heard about it. They were 08 cowboys," the marshal said and watched real close for Dustin's reactions.

"Don't know nothing about it but I'm riding one of their horses," Dustin admitted knowing full well the marshal had already seen his horse before coming over to the saloon. Them Indians must have got 'em or something. I speak a little Apache and ran across this big camp. I don't know this country and got myself lost looking for a fort or town or anyplace I could get me some food and trade for a horse, mine had gone lame. He was sure a good horse too. Anyway this sorry old Indian traded me an old bay with an 08 brand on him for my good horse and my granddaddies gold watch. It didn't work but hell, the old bandit couldn't tell time anyway. You aren't going to tell me he's stolen or nothing are you?" Dustin finished his lie very proud of himself for its believability.

"No, you can keep your horse. Did the Indians talk you into interpreting for them or how did you come to bring them in?" the marshal asked just interested, not interrogating.

"Yea, like I said, I talk a little Indian and had contracted to do a little scouting out west so I knew the army had a reward offered on most of those old farts and so I brought them in. I was mad because I got cheated out of my reward not because they locked up them old guys," Dustin finished making even more points with the disgruntled marshal.

"Well, I gotta go now. I hope you'll hang around awhile. You seem like a pretty good fella. Just stay away from the liquor! You don't do too well on it," the marshal laughed and walked away.

Dustin finished his coffee and as he walked to the stable, he saw the marshal coming out of the telegraph office.

"They've called the dogs off you, Dustin. There blaming the Indians now. Good luck!" the marshal shouted from across the street.

Dustin collected his horse and saddle and rode indirectly back to his new hideout campsite. He found everything just as he left it and no sign of anyone having traveled near.

Two days later, Dustin rode his 08 bay into Kansas City to get some information on Bowdry and his gang. First he rode out to talk to some trail herders who by now were coming with more frequency. The gangs had indeed been active. Dustin received reports of at least eleven deaths directly attributed to the border gangs. Bowdry and his bunch were still by far the worst of them but now there were several others vying for position as the most productive or destructive band of cattle thieves and murderers in the territory. Now, also it seemed, there had been several attacks by parties of renegade Indians. Apparently tired of begging for the few steers as before, they were now running off entire herds at night, imitating their white counter parts, making driving cattle more and more life threatening and less and less profitable for the owners of the cattle. Dustin would do what could be done and try to make these snakes hunt a hole. As always he had a plan. He'd hang out in town, maybe take a job at the stock pens. He'd soon see just who was bringing in what cattle.

Dustin moved in from his camp and boarded Chief and the 08 bay at the livery. He walked straight to the marshals office but saw Marshal Ambrose before he got to it.

"Hello, Marshal. I come to hang around town awhile. I thought I'd check in and see if there were any special rules I should know about," Dustin said quite friendly.

"Good, Mr. Thomas. Glad to have you if you stay sober, at least part of the time," the marshal fainned sternness and then chuckled.

"Don't worry about that! My head's still hurting," Dustin declared rather truthfully.

"I'll bet that's honest enough! The only rule is I like my deputies to be the only ones wearing guns while in town. I have a little trouble enforcing it when the herds hit town but we do our best," the marshal stated.

"Have any trouble with the border gangs?" Dustin inquired casually.

"What border gangs? Who have you been talking to Dustin? I'm not aware of any raiders working out of Kansas City," the marshal said nervously.

"I bought another horse from a cowman who said he'd been troubled by some bad cattle thieves. Thought he'd seen some of the rustlers in town before. He's a big good looking sorrel with lots of white," Dustin added.

"What? Oh, the horse you bought. Fine, fine. If you see any of those badmen you are worrying about, come tell me and I'll handle it. I don't want to send a wire to your family telling them you've been killed from not minding your own business! By the way, where are you from?" asked the marshal pleasantly, considering how threateningly he'd made the statement before.

"Out west on the Rio Grande, New Mexico territory. They know me at the fort," Dustin said remembering the marshals lack of communication with the army.

"Good enough, just be careful," the Marshal said as a commotion broke out just ahead of where he and Dustin had been walking.

A young man came backing out of a store pointing an old navy colt pistol nearly as big as he was. The store keeper was raising hell and wielding a meat cleaver wildly. As the young fellow backed to the street and reached for the reins of a poorly kept and very old horse, Dustin stepped in behind him and picked him up from around his waist with one arm and removed the big colt with his free hand.

The Marshal said, "What's going on here! Damn it, Belcherman, put that damn thing down! You are going to hurt yourself with it," he said to the store keeper.

The young fellow was struggling so Dustin squeezed a little tighter and whispered, "Settle down and I'll get you out of this and not tell the marshal you tried to shoot me the other day." The young fellow calmed instantly.

Belcherman still quite excited stated, "That damn kid stole food from my store and when I caught him, he pulled that cannon on me!"

"Is that what happened, son!" the Marshal asked.

"I ain't your son! No, that ain't what happened at all. I took an apple and bit into it and this crazy bastard took a swing at me with his hatchet. If it hadn't stuck in the counter he'd of got another swing at me. I just used Dad's old pistol to keep him off so I could get away, is all," the young fellow said.

"A man has a right to protect his property, Marshal!" declared Belcherman.

"Cutting a boys head off for stealing an apple don't seem quite right, Belcherman. Here's a nickel. That'll pay for the boy's apple and the one I stole an hour ago. I don't want you coming at me with that damn cleaver. I might not have the self control our young friend here has and shoot you. Then who'd run your store? You go back inside. I'll talk to the kid," the marshal ordered.

Belcherman went back in, grumbling all the while.

"What's you name, son?" he asked.

"Michael! It's Michael!" the young fellow said pulling loose from Dustin's relaxed hold.

"Got any family, son?"

"I told you before, I ain't your son and no. No family except for Lightning here!" the youngster said and fed the old horse the rest of the stolen apple.

The two were a sight that touched the heart strings, sure enough. This young waif in ragged, worn out clothes so big they just hung on him and a hat that came down so far on his head as to almost cover his eyes and that noble steed Lightning had seen his better days years ago. Probably not much better from the looks of the old work bridle he wore as his only piece of tack. Its blinders had been cut or torn off to make it appear more like a riding outfit instead of a plow bridle. The bare back was swayed a little and the back bone stood out some. Just from age though, Lightning was in good flesh. Michael made sure his horse ate well even if he didn't.

"How old are you son, I mean Michael?" the Marshal asked.

"Sixteen last March," the boy said without hesitation even though his smooth face and slight frame shouted nearer thirteen.

"Well, well, Mr. Thomas, what do you think we should do with young Michael here?" the Marshal asked very officially.

"Well sir, if you could find a way to keep Belcherman from pressing formal charges on him, you could release him into my custody. I was looking for someone to help me out at my camp. I'd like the company. That's sorta why I come into town. I'd be much happier out there with a little company. I was thinking about buying me a dog too, Marshal," Dustin said.

The Marshal started to reply when the youngster burst out, "Oh yes, a dog. Could we please get a dog. I've never had one. Please mister, can we get us a dog?"

195

The Marshal grinned big and said, "Looks to me like I just took care of two potential problems. You'll keep the kid from stealing and he'll keep you too busy to be sticking your nose where it don't belong. I know a man outside of town who raises good dogs. Big leggy buggers that can run with a horse all day. They get kinda protective, sure enough good watch dogs and will hunt and work cattle too." The Marshal finished by giving Dustin the directions to where the dogs were located. Then he left on his other business and Dustin and his new charge stood looking at Lightning.

"He ain't as old as he looks, Mister. He's just had to work real hard," Michael said.

"Let's take him over to the livery and get him shod. I don't want his feet to break up on us," Dustin suggested.

They walked over to the livery leading Lightning. About half way there, Michael swung up and rode saying, "These old boots hurt my feet some, Mister. I'd better ride."

"Call me Dustin, please. You are going to work for me, but we'll be friends too, OK?" Dustin requested.

"OK, by me!" was the answer, then softly "I ain't never had one."

Dustin just caught the last part but tried to pretend he hadn't. It was one of the saddest and most lonesome statements he'd ever heard.

At the livery, Dustin asked the man to have Lightning shod and to feed him well, being careful with the grain because he'd not had much hot feed in some time. Dustin also asked the stable man if he had any good used saddles for sale. Michael's eyes lit up but he stood silently just watching Dustin. The stableman's eyes lit up as well and he in fact had several very good saddles that happened to be for sale. Dustin looked through all the man's saddles and picked three as good enough for his new protégé.

He turned to Michael and said, "Pick them up and see if you can handle one better than
the others. I think this one is the best but it's a little bit heavier than the other two."

"I'm real strong, Dustin," he said and lifted the larger saddle with some effort but easily enough to satisfy Dustin.

"All right, I'm convinced. Pick one out and we'll get the rest of your outfit put together."

Michael took the one Dustin liked best and the stableman threw in a good matching bridle and a serviceable wool blanket.

"We'll let Lightning get shod and rest up and you can ride the 08 bay for a while," Dustin said and caught up Chief and the bay.

They saddled up and Dustin was pleased that even though Michael had been riding bareback, he knew the workings of a saddle well. He needed no help at all and checked and adjusted it for fit very carefully.

196

"Where to boss?" Michael said as he swung up on the big bay.

"Let's get you some new clothes from hat to boots. I'm a pretty important scout for the army and can't have my aide looking too shabby," Dustin said as if there were just no choice in the matter.

"I can't let you do that! I'll be two years working off the price of the saddle," Michael insisted.

"Look, you have to be presentable to hang out with a person of my standing in the community. If you don't want to owe me for them, I'll make them a gift or I'll buy them and just lend them to you like the bay! No harm in that, is there?" Dustin said cleverly.

"I guess not," Michael said, a little reluctantly.

He was using the bay and loving it already, some clothes would be nice, especially the boots. These were about to cripple him. They went into a mercantile that specialized in clothing for the frontier families as well as for town folk. They had a grand selection and Michael's eyes got even larger, if that was possible.

Dustin walked up to the lady at the counter and said, "My friend here needs some new clothes, from the skin out and the top down. Fit him up good. None of this city stuff. We're going out to the nations, he'll need good cowboy gear. Get him a couple pairs of heavy pants and several shirts and a good brush coat. He'll need the best boots you got that'll fit him and a good hat too. Anything else you think of also and let him pick out anything there is a choice in. He'll need a good heavy canvas warbag to put the extra stuff in too. You two take care of this, I'm going down the street and see a fella. I'll be back in an hour and we'll go eat," Dustin said and walked out after Michael's affirmation that all would be fine.

In about an hour Dustin came in carrying a large sack and stood speechless at the door for a second.

"Well?" Michael asked. "How do I look, boss?"

"Like a sure enough rooten tooten cowhand, I'd say! Look at those boots! Black with red tops, just like mine. Do those tiny, little boots really fit your feet or are you just buying the color?" he inquired looking at the clerk first.

"They fit like gloves. I've got small feet. Those old ones were my dad's," Michael said.

"OK, if you are sure. Here put these on them then," Dustin said handing Michael the most beautiful silver spurs and stamped leather straps available in Kansas City.

"They're beautiful, Dustin. Just beautiful!" Michael exclaimed and Dustin thought he saw tears welling up in Michael's eyes.

"Come on, let's go get something to eat, you look weak!" Dustin proclaimed.

Then to the clerk he whispered while he paid for all the goods, "Why in the hell did you let him pick out a shirt that big. You must have some smaller."

The lady clerk answered shortly saying only, "Michael likes them large for room to grow," and winked at Michael after defending their selections.

Dustin paid and thanked the lady for all her help, then said to Michael, "Grab your warbag and we'll just tie it on behind your saddle for now. We still have to put you a bed together. We'd better eat first. You're looking a little puny."

They rode to just outside the edge of town to a road house that advertised hot meals, pulled in and dismounted.

"Here put this on, you are going to hurt yourself or me with your dad's old gun. This is the newest thing. It fires cartridges. No more reloading black powder. It's a thirty-two caliber and the holster fits up high on your waist and cross draws. A little jacket totally conceals it. I got you a couple of cases of ammunition also. I'll teach you to shoot it good enough that you'll be able to save my life someday," Dustin said while Michael strapped on the beautiful holster carved to match it's belt as well as the spur straps.

It fit perfectly. Again Dustin saw signs of tears.

"Good Lord, boy pull yourself together. Ain't nobody ever done nothing nice for you before?" Dustin asked teasingly.

"No," was all the answer that came back.

"Damn!" Dustin said more to himself than anyone and had to fight back what he was afraid might be tears of his own.

They ate like starving dogs, Dustin because he liked to eat when he had the chance and Michael because he was starving, or nearly.

Watching him eat Dustin said, "Damn boy, I wished I'd thought of this sooner. Is that why you shot at me back in camp, hoping I'd hurry off and leave something to eat behind in my rush?"

"Yea, it usually works," Michael said finally starting to slow down some.

"How long you been on your own?" Dustin asked not wanting to pry but wondered anyway.

"Daddy died six months ago. He'd been real drunk for a long time again and died puking in his sleep. I been sort of drifting around ever since."

"Damn!" Dustin sighed again. "Let's ride over to get us a dog and then we'll go back through town, pick up the makins for a bed roll and get Lightning. Then we'll head out to camp and make us some big plans," Dustin finished.

"Can I pick out our dog and can I name him too?" Michael fired the questions.

"Yes, yes! Let's make sure we like what he's got first," Dustin reasoned.

They rode out to the ranch where the man with the dogs lived and were greeted by a pack of large, mostly gray colored hounds that reminded Dustin of some he'd seen one of the Cavalry General's traveling with, some kind of European sight hounds. Closer to the house there were some smaller working stockdogs. Dustin had seen this type before. They were excellent cowdogs. They couldn't keep up with or whip the wolf hounds but could easily stay up with a horse under normal conditions and were as smart as people. Dustin told the man of his interest in buying a watchdog for a companion and was pointed out several that were excellent hunters and were already trained for several commands. The two most important of these were come and attack. Dustin turned to ask Michael which one he liked best of these almost indistinguishable dogs and saw Michael up at the house with a puppy about three months old in his arms. This was a black ball of fur with white and brown markings on his face and chest and four white feet.

"Damn!" Dustin said again. "Michael, I wanted a grown dog who could watch camp now."

"Go ahead and pick one for you then, this is the one I want!" Michael said and stepped up on the bay, holding his treasure and then added, "I named him Sugarfoot!"

That was the end of the discussion. Dustin looked helplessly at the rancher who now had twice the dollar signs in his eyes as before. Dustin didn't really care, he was spending the money the gunrunners had on them, over the money they'd stolen from the 08 boys. He'd tried to split it with Bill too but Bill said he had more than he ever needed and if not, he had Dustin's share he could use too. Dustin laughed out loud thinking of the silly look Bill would get on his face when he tried to tease Dustin about spending his money.

"Pick me out a good one, Mister, at least a year old. One that kinda needs a friend," Dustin instructed the rancher.

"I've got just the dog for you. He might be the best dog I've got," the rancher said.

"Yea, I bet and the highest priced too!" Dustin said sarcastically.

"Oh hell no, he ain't worth a damn to me. I hunt them in packs and this is the killingest son of a bitch I've ever seen. Problem is he kills other dogs too. Here, I have to keep him tied up in there. He don't bother horses or cows unless you sic him on them but he can take down a full grown bull by himself if you'll encourage him a little."

The rancher opened a large stall door. "There he is!" the rancher said proudly.

Dustin looked into the dark stall but didn't see anything at all. Then suddenly, he saw a long pink tongue at about chest level.

"Damn!" he gasped. "He is as black as midnight. I couldn't even see him till he stuck that tongue out. All the others are light gray, what's the deal?" Dustin asked.

"The most of them are his litter mates. He's a throw back to their ancestors, I guess. He's heavier than the others too. Weighs over one hundred sixty pounds and is just fifteen months old," the rancher explained as Dustin walked foolishly into the stall.

He felt somehow strongly drawn to this huge beast.

199

"What does he eat?" he asked.

"Pretty much anything he wants to," was the serious answer.

"I'll bet. I mean what do you feed him?" Dustin asked.

"Truth is I haven't fed him a bite in a year. I pen the other dogs up at night and let him loose. In the morning he usually has a carcass of some kind or the other. He's never killed a domestic animal to eat. He seems to know the difference. It's funny, he could travel for days with you and never look at your horse then you could sic him on to it and he'd kill it for you in a second."

"Damn!" one more time. "What's his name?" asked Dustin.

"Satan's his name but he comes better to boy or fella," the rancher said.

"I'll have to change that name. Too many people have already accused me of traveling around with the devil to give them that much more ammunition to work with as well," Dustin said and then asked, "Can I have the chain also? I'll want to keep him close for awhile until he gets used to me some. I'll take him and the pup too, but only if he don't hate the kid," Dustin said.

He called Michael to ride over and see what a dog should look like.

As Michael rounded the corner, his mouth dropped and "Damn!" gasped out.

"That's my boy!" Dustin said to the rancher, who had not heard the word used so many times in one day.

The big dog walked over to little Michael, still holding his tiny puppy and wagged all over. He sniffed the puppy and then Michael, who's face was just tongue high and licked both with a saddle blanket sized tongue.

"That settles it! We'll take them both. How much for the pair?" Dustin asked reaching for his folding money knowing this was going to cost plenty.

"I'm going to give you the big black bastard just to keep me from worrying about him killing my other dogs. You can pay me for the chain if you want to. You'll have to pay my wife for the pup. The shepherds are her's," the rancher said.

"Sugarfoot is already mine, sir. Your wife gave him to me."

"Damn!" gasped the rancher and all three laughed loudly.

"Well, you might as well keep the chain too then. Unless there's anything else we can do for you that I can charge you for," still laughing said the rancher.

"Well sir, there just might be. Is that a quilting rack on the porch?" Dustin inquired.

"Why yes, it is. My wife makes the finest, most durable quilts in the country," bragged the rancher.

"Do you think she might have a few she would be willing to part with, for a fair price of course. I insist!" Dustin said.

"So do I!" the rancher said and all laughed again. "I'm sure she does. I never pictured you as a fancier of beautiful quilts," the rancher stated.

"There's no better soogans in the world than a couple of good heavy quilts. We're building a bedroll for my friend here and I left most of my stuff behind me. I could use a couple of good blankets myself them being plum pretty don't hurt a thing. Michael run in and pick yourself out three good heavy ones and if she has them, get me a couple as well. I'll be right in. I need to talk to our new friend for a moment," Dustin explained.

Soon Michael came out with the rancher's wife and the large stack of beautiful quilts and many heavy wool blankets the woman had hand woven in a style very similar to the Indian fashion. Dustin and her husband were standing in front of the house holding Chief, the 08 bay and another darker bay with Michael's tack on it. The 08 bay had a pack saddle with panniers hanging on each side and a halter on in place of Michael's stock saddle and bridle. Dustin had a good piece of tarp folded over his shoulder and handed his dog, he'd decided to name Midnight, to the rancher to hold while he showed Michael how to make up a cowboy bed. He explained that you roll it for travel in a wagon and then showed him how to fold it for a pack horse.

This done, he tied it on top of the new pack saddle on the 08 bay and said, "Have you two agreed on a price? If not I've hurt our bargaining leverage considerably, having already packed it on our horse. If you have Michael, how much and if not, start haggling. I've already let her husband here out trade me on this sorry old horse and this pack outfit. See how you make out with the Misses," Dustin said grinning like a possum.

He looked at the rancher, who Dustin had indeed over compensated on his own insistence and against the wishes of the rancher. The old gentleman looked at his wife and smiled widely and winked. She, very business like, gave the details of her fine craftsmanship and superior materials used in their creation. Then stood straight and named a price of not nearly what the quilts alone were worth, let alone those fine heavy wool blankets.

Michael listened to the offer and replied, "For each one?"

"No, for the lot," answered the Misses.

"Just a moment please," Michael said and whispered to Dustin.

"I believe they're worth more than that, don't you?" Michael said out loud.

"This is your deal to make, take it or make her an offer," instructed Dustin.

Michael thought for a moment then said, "They are so very beautiful and you worked so hard on them. We insist you take double that amount. That's my offer!"

There were three simultaneous gasps, "Damn!"

The Misses covered her mouth as an apology for the slip and looked at Dustin. He handed her double the amount she'd requested and laughed so loudly Michael scolded him.

"It's not polite to gloat when you've bested someone in a trade." Shaking his small index finger at Dustin.

"I'll try to remember that in the future," Dustin said and when mounted he reached for Midnight's chain.

The rancher handed Michael his puppy, and leading the 08 bay loaded with the most valuable bed west of anywhere, Michael rode off following Dustin and his huge beast of a dog. They did not stop again until they were at the livery. They picked up Lightning and Michael insisted putting his pack on him and Dustin's on the 08 bay. They were ready to head for camp and make their plans as to how to go about the eradication of the border vermin.

While he was settling up with the livery man, he purchased a rifle scabbard and slid the new Winchester seventy-three, Bill had insisted he take, into it and tied it on Michael's saddle.

"Now, there ain't no man alive's got a better outfit than you. Hell, most of it's better than mine!" Dustin said approvingly.

They rode out to the secluded campsite, unsaddled and unpacked.

"This will be our home for awhile. Make it as comfortable as possible. There is plenty of grass and water in this little box canyon for the horses. We can tie Midnight on the clearing side to watch nights for us and you can put your dog... well put him anywhere you want to," he teased.

"You just wait, someday Sugarfoot's going to be the best cowdog on the frontier!" Michael claimed proudly.

"I've no doubt about it, if me and old Midnight don't get hungry first and eat the fat little rascal," Dustin continued to tease.

"That kind of talk could get a man shot in his sleep, Mr. Thomas!" Michael snapped back.

They put together a good camp and made a feast of stew and biscuits with hot coffee for a late supper. They talked and shared stories 'til they fell asleep in the early morning hours. Shortly after the sun was up good, Dustin came walking back into camp from taking Midnight out to walk and hunt a little and was surprised to smell breakfast cooking.

"I thought you'd still be asleep," Dustin joked.

"I wouldn't be much good to you if I couldn't hear you and that horse size dog of yours leave camp, now would I? How did he do?" Michael asked while finishing breakfast.

"He did great! We probably won't have to chain him for long. We will for a while, just in case. He ran down rabbits so easily, you wouldn't believe it," he answered.

"Dustin, we need to talk. I mean, I need to tell you something. I should have told you yesterday before you spent all that money but it was such a wonderful day, I didn't want to ruin it. I didn't ever want it to end," Michael said then paused looking at Dustin.

"Let me guess. You didn't think I'd like you if you were a girl? Is that it? Hell, I've always liked girls better than boys and you are a very beautiful girl at that," Dustin said like he'd always known.

"You son of a bitch! Damn, you Dustin! How could you let me feel so guilty all night long. I hardly slept a wink worrying about how to tell you," she said.

"Well take your hat off and take your hair out of that bun and let's see what you were hiding," he told her.

"I was so afraid you'd be mad," she said.

"Mad! Hell, I'm relieved. I was worried about how good you looked to me in your new clothes and how pretty I thought your eyes were. I'm happy you're a girl. Michele, is it?" he asked.

"Yes, it's Michele. You think I have pretty eyes?" she said as she let her hair loose.

"Yes, very pretty eyes and absolutely beautiful hair! Damn! You're a lot better looking girl than you were a boy. I was real stupid not to notice at first. The big baggy clothes made you look like you could have been a sissy boy. Soon as I saw those tiny feet and the shape of your bu... backside, I knew something was wrong or I mean right. Then those little tears from those pretty, pretty eyes. That's when I knew for sure. I'm really glad you are a girl, Michele. I'd of had to leave you off somewhere if you was a guy and looked this good to me. Is that it or is there anything else you need to tell me?" Dustin said casually.

"No, that's it for now but if I think of something I'll let you know," she said, so relieved she started to tear up again.

"That will probably need to stop. You should put your hair back up when we go places. You can leave it down when it's just us, if you want to," he suggested.

They had their breakfast and talked about yesterday's day of fun.

"You're really going to let me stay, Dustin?" she asked matter of factly.

"Let you stay? I insist you do. We've got your outfit put together, now the work begins. As for my being worried about you being a woman, you survived with nothing for six months before we met. I believe you'll do fine with me, now you've got an outfit. Let's clean this breakfast mess up and make our plan."

Dustin and Michele spent most of the next two days getting Michele familiar with her new weapons. Dustin found her to be a remarkable shot and it was apparent she had missed him intentionally back at the old camp.

The plan of attack was for Dustin to keep an eye out for anyone watching the trails and then when they were ready to make their move, he would eliminate the threat however he could. Michele would move the camp and take care of Dustin's outfit while he was out. This would allow him to travel up and down the trails and when quick action was called for, he'd not be encumbered with all of his worldly possessions in tow. This alone would give Dustin the mobility necessary to be effective in his attempt to make the trails a safer place to travel. He explained to Michele that this would be a dangerous assignment. Even though his seemed a noble mission, he was executing it with evil intent. His motive was revenge, his method would be savage.

If Michele did not feel comfortable with participating in this attempt at a total genocide of these murderous border gangs, she was free to find safer refuge elsewhere. Dustin would locate her a safe house to stay in until he had the time necessary to take her to his place in the territory. He'd told her all about Kate and Matt, Mrs. Morton and little Wesley. He even told her a little about Cindy. He didn't tell her much because he found it difficult to explain to Michele why he cared so much for Cindy. Everytime he told a story of their limited times together, Michele would point out how confused she was about Cindy's seemingly cruel manner in her treatment of Dustin. Michele was able to read the selfish and thoughtless way he'd been treated by this girl he was so adamant about being devoted to. He finally told Michele that he'd always loved Cindy and just having her to look out for and love, even if it was unrequited, had given him a purpose. He was surprised that he'd admitted that this love he'd held onto so dearly was, in fact, one sided. He'd never before considered the possibility she didn't love him as he loved her. Dustin told her all about Kate and the ranch. He told what a wonderful job she'd done with the place in his absence.

"Sounds to me like you may have fallen in love with the wrong sister," Michele said.

Dustin looked across the fire at this pretty young girl who'd had such a hard and sad time, yet still she was so excited about life and living it. He questioned everything he thought he knew about his feelings toward Cindy and Kate. He tried to understand his feelings for Teresa, the beautiful Mexican girl of the evening, who had doctored him back to health. He pondered the differences between the fond feeling he held for Waynola, the old Chiricahua Apache woman who had also cared for him and nursed him in his time of need. There had been some wonderful females in Dustin's life. He'd not thought much about his ever really loving anyone other than Cindy and he was beginning to suspect she may never love him back. This all was discomforting and confusing to Dustin and he'd just as soon not deal with it all right now.

He asked Michele if she wanted to accompany him on this hazardous and questionably legal venture or wait until his thirst for vengeance was adequately quenched, then travel with him to the ranch in the territory.

Her answer was swift and simple, "I'll go where you go!"

"Fine," he said, "let's move out about a weeks drive down the main trail and we'll find a good camp to strike from. So, you're sure you want in?" he asked with some reserve.

"To the end! You are stuck with me. Who knows, you may even learn to like the idea," Michele said a little coyly.

"Hell girl, I already like the idea. Now let's move our camp."

They headed out and luck was on their side. From a ridge Dustin saw a dust cloud that, since the near extermination of the buffalo, could only be caused by a trail herd. There was a small spring not far off the trail but Dustin felt it had been too recently camped by. They moved southwest for several more miles and came to a perfect spot for them to use as a base of operations. Dustin helped set up camp and located Midnight where he could warn Michele of intruders in Dustin's absence. Dustin had everything prepared to go on his first scouting circle, but kept finding little things he could do to make camp more comfortable for Michele.

Finally she said, "Look, Mother, why don't you stay here and make some curtains and I'll

go shoot me some border raiders while there's still a few left!"

"All right, smart ass, I'm going. You sure you are going to be OK while I'm gone? It could be overnight," he asked.

"I'll try to survive out here all by myself with only three fine horses and two dogs, one the size of an elk. This arsenal of weapons, that would be the envy of a rather large army, will have to suffice for me to use to defend myself in case a rabid squirrel should challenge me for possession of this old oak tree. Now get out there and kill a bunch of those bastards so we can go to the ranch and live a life of relative peace raising cows."

"Damn!" said Dustin, "Did all that just come to you or have you been planning it for a while?"

"Get, so you can get back sooner!" Michele said and gave Dustin a big hug and kissed him on his cheek. "I'll be fine, go on," she said and handed him Chief's reins.

Dustin rode out and made sure his tracks were not visible, leading any pursuers back to the camp and Michele. He was originally planning to ride to the herd and check with the foreman as to any signs of raiders. This became unnecessary because a few miles ahead of the herd, Dustin saw a single column of smoke blocked from the herds view by a little bluff between the fire and trail.

"These bastards are getting so bold their building camp fires, Chief," Dustin said to his faithful horse.

Dustin rode as close to the smoke as he felt wise to get some idea of how many raiders there were. Shortly, he realized this wariness was unnecessary. There wasn't even a guard posted. Against his better judgment, Dustin rode down and untied the picket rope that all the would be raider's horses were tied to and just led them off. It was many miles to anywhere and theirs would be a hard trip out on foot. Dustin took his string of twelve saddled horses and rode to the trail herd. After introducing himself, he asked the foreman if he'd had any problems with raiders yet.

"Dustin Thomas? Yea, I've heard of you sure enough! You are the fellow that out drew and killed that mean S.O.B. Sanderson down in Texas some time back, ain't ya?" When no answer was given he continued, "No we ain't had no trouble, but our other herd ahead of us sure did. They got run at three different times. Lost over six hundred head. We ain't seen anyone but a few Indian beggars so far," John Black the foreman said.

"I believe you were about to have a little trouble. A day's drive up the trail waiting for your herd, are a dozen heavily armed men. They are now afoot, partially due to their own careless boldness. If you have no objections, I'll ride with you past where they were hiding and then I'll go back down the trail to see if I can't discourage some more of these boys," Dustin said.

"Welcome! Step down and eat with us," Black offered.

"If you don't mind a suggestion, I'd double the night guard in case these boys were waiting for reinforcements. They sure didn't act like they were, but who knows? I'd volunteer to ride night hawk but it might seem suspicious me just riding in here like this. If something happened with me out there, you'd always wonder about me. So, as much as I hate just sitting around a coffee pot and getting a full nights sleep, I guess I'd better," Dustin said with a big grin.

"You are sure a thoughtful fellow, Mr. Dustin Thomas. But if that were true, how else could you explain your leading in twelve saddled horses? You can pull the late shift with me. I'll enjoy your company," the foreman answered back.

"Well, you can't blame a fella for trying," Dustin laughed.

The night passed and Dustin enjoyed the cattle and the drovers company more than he'd remembered. There were no intrusions by raiders or Indians. The following day the herd drove to within a few hundred yards of the mouth of the draw the raiders had been in. The herd was bedded down and camp set up as usual. Black was nervous about the plan Dustin had suggested and then implemented. Shortly after dark, it started to seem like a better idea.

"Easy in the camp! We're coming in. Don't do nothing stupid," came a voice from the dark.

Black stood and put his hand on his pistol. He was wearing it, as were all the men on the drive, especially for this expected encounter with these raiders. Pistols were never regularly worn by cowboys. They are heavy and awkward at best. They're very dangerous to wear while riding a horse and working cattle. They were always stored in the wagon or rolled in their beds. Dustin's warning prompted their extraction from storage.

"Get your hand away from that pistol, mister! We've got men all around you. Just stand easy!" the voice demanded.

A group of four men walked into the edge of the light and the man spoke again," We're taking your cattle and horses too. You don't have to die for these damn cows if you do as I say. Now drop your guns."

At that moment, Dustin stepped out from the other side of the wagon behind the intruders, pistol leveled on the speaker of the bunch.

"No, I don't believe we will drop our guns. I'd propose you boys drop yours instead," Black said calmly.

"By god, I've killed dozens of dumb ass cowpushers like you already. What would keep me from killing you too?" the man snarled.

"Me, I guess," said Dustin, startling the men terribly, causing them to whirl around.

Dustin extended his arm and stuck his pistol into the speaker's open mouth. The intruder dropped his pistol and so did his companions.

"I see you think so, too. That's a shame. I was really looking forward to killing all of you. Mr. Black, would you have some men tie up these confessed killers. I'll have the others brought in," Dustin said feeling genuinely sorry he'd not just shot the raiders dead.

Dustin called to one of Black's other trail hands and in a moment led in the remaining eight rustlers. All were tied and several looked as if they'd put up a fight.

"Now Mr. Black, I suggest you tie our guests head to foot and then tie them to the wagon," Dustin said.

"Sounds like a lot of unnecessary trouble to me, my friend. I'm just going to hang all of them anyway," Black said coldly.

Dustin stood silently, knowing he could talk Black out of hanging these men and take them to Kansas City. If he could keep them in jail until the federal justice came around, they might get a conviction against the mouth piece for confessing to some non specific killings. Most likely they'd all walk. Some would quit from the scare of being caught and tied, but most would be stealing and killing again within a month.

After a little soul searching, Dustin spoke up, "All right, hang the bastards! You can do whatever you want with their horses and saddles. All I want is a list of their names. I will put in for any rewards if any have wanted dead bounties on them. Do you want to wait 'til morning to hang them?" thinking the wait might change Black's mind.

"No, I'll get you a list of names while the boys look for a tree. We'll hang them now. It

will be a message to the rest of their kind," Black said.

"There is a large cottonwood up that draw aways with a big, low limb. I don't think it will accommodate a dozen men all at once," Dustin said.

"We'll hang them in groups of three or four if we have to. I've had two brothers killed on this trail and their entire herds lost. These men here may not have been the ones who did it but they sure as hell would have killed all of us if not for you. When you get to Kansas City charge anything you need to the Black and Greenaugh Cattle Co. We sure owe you more than you can spend in a couple of days," Black said and shook Dustin's hand. "You are, of course, welcome to stay or if you would rather leave this to us, here is a list of their names. I hope to see you in Kansas City in a few days," he finished.

"You'll be seeing me up and down the trails until they're a safe place to travel. You see, Mr. Black, I've had men killed on these trails too!" Dustin said and walked over to Chief and rode out in the darkness toward camp and Michele.

The next several months passed quickly and the legend of Dustin Thomas spread widely. This avenger of the cattlemen became famous and feared. On one visit to Kansas City, a small gang of rustlers saw and recognized Chief who was also becoming quite famous, tied outside the Marshal's office. They fled town, turning themselves in and confessing to the sheriff in the nearby town of Independence, Missouri. They begged to be placed in custody and under protection of the sheriff's office fearing they might be the reason for Thomas' visit to the neighboring town. As ridiculous as this tale sounds, it was not the only such incident of criminals doing everything in their power to avoid the sure and not always swift fate of becoming the target of this avenger of the trails.

Another example of the extent the fear Dustin had instilled in the hearts and souls of the raiders, bandits, and murdering rustlers spread all over this wild raw land, is the time that he and Michele rode toward a small fire they'd seen from a distance. When quite near to where they expected to find this not very well concealed little camp, a gun shot rang out from its direction. As always, in the face of danger, Dustin, pistol in hand raced directly toward the sound of the weapons report with Michele close behind him. They found a single man lying still on the ground, a self inflicted death wound in his temple. The Grim Reaper had not fully collected his prize when Dustin knelt down beside the dying man.

"I knew it was you! I didn't kill no one, just stole the horses. It was..." he died before he was able to pass blame for a murder Dustin hadn't even been aware of.

"We're starting to make a difference, Michele. The word's getting out that murder and rustling aren't going to be tolerated out here no more!" Dustin said with no emotion of any kind in his voice. "Let's get these horses to town and see who it was this fella and his companion killed to get them," he added.

"I'll get the horses saddled while you see if he's got any identification on him that might help us," Michele suggested.

Dustin liked the sound of the "us" in her words. He felt warm inside when she was near him. Michele kept him from feeling alone and abandoned but for a reason even he himself could not fully explain, Cindy still had some kind of hold on him. She'd made it painfully clear she wanted nothing more to do with him the last time he saw her. She even strongly suggested that she had never wanted any part of him at all. That their whole relationship had existed entirely in his own mind! She had been very ill and he held out hope someday he would ride into a town somewhere and there would be a letter waiting, asking him to come back to her. In his heart he knew this was never really going to happen, still he would continue to be faithful until he heard from her again, just in case time softened Cindy's heart and she wanted him to come home. Until that time came, he and his always loyal Michele would continue to rid the trails of the murderous element that had thus far plagued and terrorized the trail herds and had taken the lives of so many young cowboys.

During their wild and exciting time together, Dustin and Michele became very close but not physically involved. They were companions and had a bond to each other that words have yet to describe. The fact that they had never been intimate with one another was partly due to Dustin's unexplainable commitment to Cindy.

The main factor determining the status of their relationship was one night when Dustin had returned from a particularly bloody episode and was obviously shaken from the carnage he had just been part of, Michele delivered another revelation. It came out unexpectedly to both of them. The man she had told Dustin was her father, in actuality was just the last of live-in male companions of her mother's. This one happened to be around when her mother died of a combination overdose of opium and rye whiskey. He too was an addict and drunk and abused Michele regularly. This had been occurring long before her mother died and only increased afterward. After a particularly rough and disgusting occurrence, Michele ferreted out his pistol and while he lie in the slumber copious amounts of self indulgence brings, she shot him dead. She'd fled the little community they'd stayed in and not looked back since. That was the main reason for the disguise she'd been wearing when they'd met. She was sure the law was after her and she'd be hung for murder. After several months, the paranoia wore off some and the needs of survival took over.

Dustin was close to six years her senior but she was pretty and at times beautiful. Dustin had seen the hurt and disgust in her eyes as she stared into the fire and revealed her heart breaking story. Other than there being no sexual contact between them, they were as close as any man and wife could be. They had an added dimension to their relationship that allowed them a closeness not able to be shared by most friends. He felt this was more than any man could ask for. They never argued about things the way most married couples do from time to time. He grew more and more fond of her with each passing day. Michele had never even met a decent man, let alone spent any time with one. Dustin's honorable manner and good kind heart drew her to him unquestioningly and unconditionally. She truly would walk into fire for him if asked. He never asked. His protectiveness of her privacy and feelings was so complete as to almost seem excessive. This was the way of things, at first anyway.

Once when Dustin was helping her move to a new camp over on the Dodge City Trail, as it was recently named, they were ambushed by well hidden snipers. These assailants had planned this well and Dustin had gotten careless. He sent Midnight up and around the general area where one of the rifle men was located. Shortly there was a scream, a shot and another scream, then silence. Pinned down, Dustin was worried about Michele and the horses. He thought maybe they should surrender then try to shoot their way out once the ambushers came out to take them. He knew this would probably not work because these boys would just shoot them where they stood from long range.

Dustin turned to tell Michele to jump on Chief and make a run for it while he fired cover shots. She was gone. Sugarfoot, now seven months old, was gone also. He looked for her but was so badly trapped he could do little but fire a shot once in a while and hope to get lucky. He could have rode Chief out of the trap if he'd been alone. He wasn't alone, Michele was out there somewhere now and he wouldn't leave her.

Midnight soon returned to Dustin's side and had been slightly wounded along his side and much of his hair was burned away from the gun powder. He'd been shot point blank but the bullet grazed off his shoulderblade.

"Where is she fella? What in the hell does she think she's doing?"

The firing had subsided from all but one position now and he could move some and improve his position. Several more shots were fired from this last strong hold of these ambushers. None of them struck around Dustin. He tried to see what was going on when suddenly Michele stepped up on a rock and Sugarfoot jumped up beside her.

"Hey Dustin, bring the horses and come up here, would you? I've got one that's only gut shot. These cowardly bastards didn't mastermind this ambush. They were hired or ordered here by someone else. I had Sugerfoot try to make him tell me who it was but I can't get him to talk and want you to help him with his confession. Come on, you got to hurry. He ain't doing too good."

"Damn!" Dustin said and jumped on Chief and rode up and around to where Michele was standing. Acting as mad as he could, while barely able to conceal his surprise and pride, "Are you trying to get yourself killed?"

"No, I was trying not to! Look! Calm down. I know you could have gotten yourself out of that mess if I hadn't been there. I just don't ever want you to think I'm a burden. Hey, that damn dog of yours tore that poor bastard to pieces. What a mess. You gotta see it," she rambled, not nearly as shook up as Dustin would have thought she'd be in a situation like this.

They walked to the downed man and Dustin knelt by him.

"Keep that dog off of me!" he gasped.

Michele told Sugarfoot to sit in response to his request.

"Who hired you to do this?" Dustin inquired but received no answer, just moans of pain.

"Look, you are dead anyway. You might as well tell me," Dustin said honestly.

"Why the hell would I?" the wounded man asked in reply.

"Look asshole, you'll be two days dying from your wounds if I leave you be. Your choice is to tell me now and I'll put an end to your suffering quickly. I can have the dog work on you some more or even let that big one over there have a few minutes with you. You'll beg to tell me then. Let's do this the easy way," Dustin said.

The dying man had not seen Midnight before and looked in the direction Dustin had indicated the other dog was standing.

"Good Lord! What the hell is that? Please mister, hold onto that beast. Ohhhh, I'm hurting bad. Help me, please," he begged.

"Just the name and it's over," Dustin repeated.

"It was Bowdry! I swear it! He gave us each two twenty dollar gold pieces before and was going to give us two more after," the man swore.

"All right." Dustin rose and said to Michele, "Would you like to hold the horses over there a little ways?"

She answered by pulling her thirty-two and placing two quick bullets in the head of the down man, then said, "They'll be fine, Dustin. They've seen lots of gun play, so have I."

"Damn!" muttered Dustin.

After this episode, Michele asked and was allowed to accompany Dustin on many of his assaults on these now diminishing border gangs. She always carried her weight and though he worried she'd be hurt, Dustin never once worried about her ability to perform her assignments in the engagements. These two spread terror within the rustlers to a point that many more herds passed to the rail head unmolested than there were that had been disturbed.

"When are we going back to Kansas City to kill Bowdry?" Michele asked out of the blue one night.

"Soon, I guess," he answered reflectively. "Maybe we'll go kill the sorry son-of-a-bitch and just go on home to the ranch. I sent a letter awhile back telling Kate all about you and how excited you were about meeting her and seeing the place. I'll bet we got some mail back at Fort Levenworth waiting for us. If she seems happy about us coming home, that's what we'll do. Would you like that?" he asked the excited young beauty.

Michele could not control herself. She jumped up and ran over to Dustin, knocking him over backwards, hugging, laughing and shouting her approval of the plan! They had a big time going over all the stories he'd told her about Kate and the ranch and she made him describe the house, barn and corrals over and over again.

They packed up their camp and with the dogs running ahead of them, the two rode happily along on their way to kill a man. The contrast was almost ridiculous. To see them giggling and wrestling around the camp fire last night, it would be impossible to identify them as the vigilante assassins they'd become. Nowhere in history have there been so many people as afraid of any two executioners as there were of these two.

Back at Levenworth, "It says it was a nice funeral," Dustin said as he read one of his several letters the fort postmaster had been holding for Dustin's return.

"She died four months ago. Mom Morton had some kind of breakdown and Kate is raising Wesley. Matt married a widow who had five children and is now pregnant with his child. The ranch is doing great and all it needs is us to make it just right, Kate says. Well, that settles it! We'll finish up here and head for home!"

"Home! I love the sound of that word. I'm very sorry about Cindy," Michele said.

"Yea, so am I," he answered, not really knowing how he felt about any of the news except about going home, and he felt great about that!

As they started to leave, the postmaster said, "Dustin, there's a fellow says he knows you been asking around about your whereabouts. He said if I saw you, he'd be staying in the Palace Saloon."

"Damn!" Dustin said then added, "Thanks Sergeant. Don't wire ahead, I want to try and surprise him, a little at least."

Michele said, "How in the world do you suppose he found out?"

"The Indian territory ain't as big as it seems, I guess," Dustin said a little worried about losing the element of surprise.

They rode to the very first camp sight they'd had together those so many very violent months before. They didn't make camp or unsaddle the pack horses. Dustin tied both Midnight and Sugarfoot close by and asked Michele to please consider staying there until this was finished.

"To the end, remember?" she said and repeated, "To the end means all the way to the end! Besides you may need me to cover your back. Bowdry is waiting for you. He knows you are coming and is ready for you. I'll wait by the door if you want to make this dramatic," she teased.

"Let's go get it over!" he said.

They rode into town right down the main street.

"A little exposed, don't you think?" she asked.

"He's in the Palace! There's a lot of people in town. That herd we saw must have come into town also. I don't think he'll just shoot us down in the street. He'll have to make it a fair looking fight anyway."

As they rode past the Marshal's office, two deputies were so startled by their presence, one dropped his coffee cup. The other hurriedly disappeared down the ally.

"I am a little surprised they are surprised. We must have not been expected so soon, or maybe they thought we'd come in the other way," Dustin said.

They rode up in front of the Palace and a cowboy hollered in, "He's here! Dustin Thomas is here!"

Dustin slid off of Chief and handed Michele his famous horse's rein.

"Stay horseback and be ready to ride. This may go down quickly," he said and she nodded in compliance.

Dustin walked into the crowd of people that was parting like the Red Sea did for Moses. From the other end of the bar came a voice, "Dustin Thomas, I've been looking all over the nations for you."

Dustin recognized the voice and stood confused for a moment. As the pathway toward the voice opened up, Dustin readied himself for whatever may come up. When the last man stepped away from the bar, there stood the speaker.

"Damn!!" said Dustin.

"Damn? Is that all you can say to your old partner?" said Big Bill.

He was standing there his arms open wide and grinning like an opossum.

"Bill, are you who's been looking for me?" Dustin asked.

"Who the hell else would be looking for you?" Bill asked.

"Damn!" Dustin said and turned to run out to Michele.

The blast of the guns was deafening. There must have been ten different shots fired. As Dustin burst out the door, he looked into Michele's eyes. She fell from her horse returning his gaze. She hit the ground dead. Chief had been mortally shot as well. He staggered backwards dragging Michele's limp body several feet before he too fell dead in the dirt in front of the Palace Saloon on Main Street, Kansas City.

Dustin had his pistol drawn but never fired a shot. He walked to the street and knelt down by Michele and wept the bitter tears of loss and anger and rage. Bill ran out after Dustin and shot in the direction one of the fatal shots had come from as did several of his cowboys. They'd not turned in their guns when they'd come into town. Much to the Marshal's chagrin, Bill had refused because of the ill treatment he'd received on his last visit here.

"What the hell's going on, Dustin? Who were they?" Bill asked. Then seeing Michele, "Good Lord, who's the kid?"

Dustin stood holding the lifeless body of this fearless young girl and simply said, "Her name is Michele, Michele Thomas." He realized he didn't even know her last name and wasn't sure if she even had one. He gave her his name and it felt as comfortable saying it, as it did saying his own.

Bill looked confused but remained silent. Dustin walked toward the livery with Michele's body and Bill sent six men to watch him from a respectful distance. Then he had several men drag off Chief, after Bill took Dustin's rig off of him. He then sent several more men to try and find out if anyone saw who had fired the shots. All of this transpired before the Marshal and two deputies showed up.

"What went on here!" he demanded officially.

"By God, that's what we're going to find out, Marshal. A young girl was murdered sitting in the middle of the street," Bill said with a very threatening tone to his voice.

"I'll handle any investigation here. This is still my town," the Marshal said trying to gain some control.

Then Bill changed his mind for him with, "This was your town, Marshal. Not any more! If I were you I'd find the men responsible for this by morning or you better light out of town yourself. That young man has a lot of friends in town and we'll back his play, whatever it is."

"I'm the law! You can't talk to me like this!" the Marshal said weakly.

"I am talking to you this way and I mean every word I'm saying. I don't know exactly what's going on here but when we find out who murdered that little girl, they'll pay with their lives. You can count on that," Bill announced and his men roared in agreement.

The Marshal and his deputies backed up slowly and then turned and hurried away. In a few hours a list of names of possible participants was assembled. Every name on the list was a Bowdry man.

"Where can I find these cowardly Bowdry men?" Bill asked one of the locals.

Bill was told where the headquarters ranch house of the leader of the gang was located. Bill went to the livery and saw Dustin sitting in the shed row holding the young girls bullet riddled body. Covered in blood, the lifeless form glistening in the lamp light made an eerie red glow.

"Dustin, we know who did this and where he lives," Bill said.

"So do I!" came the voice of the very devil himself.

So horrible was the sound emitted that Bill jumped back a step and his blood turned cold. Dustin stood and laid Michele carefully down and covered her body with his coat as to shield her from the cold.

As he walked by Big Bill, Dustin said softly, "Her name is Michele Thomas. Take care of the arrangements for me."

Bill started to speak then, "Please Bill, please."

"You'll need help. He could have two dozen men out there," Bill warned.

"I can't take a chance someone else kills him, Bill! I've got to go alone," Dustin explained to his old friend.

"That don't make no sense, Dustin. It's suicide, son! They'll kill you too," Bill pleaded.

"You take care of Michele for me. She is very special to me. I want her treated with care. I need you to handle this yourself, Bill, I need your word you will take care of her personally." Dustin said adamantly.

"Of course I will. At least let me send some men with you," Bill added.

"No," was the only answer.

Dustin walked back to the saloon and stepped on Michele's horse and rode out of town. Just minutes after Dustin rode off, several shots rang out. As the crowd ran to the sounds of the shots, they saw the Marshal's office was in flames. Out front were two dead deputies and in front in the street was the Marshal holding his right arm which was bleeding badly.

"What happened, Marshal?" a citizen asked.

"We tried to arrest Dustin Thomas and one of my deputies got jumpy and shot at him. He killed them both and could have killed me too. He could have killed me easily, but he didn't."

The Marshal just knelt there bleeding, staring at the burning jail that had caught fire when one of the deputies knocked the kerosene lamp off the desk jumping for cover. The locals started a bucket brigade as fast as possible to keep the flames from spreading but just let the jail burn.

When he reached the bandits home ranch, Dustin rode directly into the Bowdry headquarters and shot his way right into the house, leaving Bowdry men dead or dying everywhere from the main gate to the front porch. He then jumped Michele's horse through the huge window in the front of Bowdry's home. The next few moments were just a flash and a roar to Dustin. He was being shot at from every direction and was returning fire equitably. He slid off his horse and started kicking doors open until finally he stood face to face with Bowdry himself, who's fear wouldn't let his legs hold him up. Dustin reached out and slapped the begging man as hard as he could, causing him to drop his unfired pistol. His surprise at Dustin's solo and direct assault fueled the fear that hadn't allowed him to even fire a shot.

He'd been as bad a man as had ever rode the plains and had dealt out more terror and murder than most dozen outlaws could, and yet when confronted by what appeared to be the very Devil himself he'd frozen, as afraid as any of his victims had ever been. He now wept, weakly staring in the face of certain death, knowing he was about to pay the price for the wickedness of his ways.

"If I had more time, I'd peel you inch by inch, you sorry bastard. If they kill me, they might be able to save you and that ain't going to happen. I give you my word." Dustin said as a mater of fact.

Dustin shot Bowdry five times in the stomach with the man's own weapon he had picked up off the floor. Any one of the shots would be, in itself, eventually fatal. The five shots insured there could be no surviving.

"There's one shot left Bowdry. It will take you hours to die or you could put yourself out of misery... but I don't think so!" Dustin said and fired the sixth shot into the floor.

"Don't leave me like this. Don't leave me, please!" the writhing, dying man begged as Dustin walked to the living room where Michele's horse was still standing.

He threw a lamp in the doorway of the office Bowdry was lying in and another one in the hole he'd just made with the horse. This second one spread wildly. The men outside started firing into the flames. They were waiting for Dustin to come riding boldly out through them but instead he rode out the back door and away into the safety of the darkness.

215

Dustin traveled directly to his camp and unloaded the packs. He turned Midnight loose. The big dog ran off a little distance then looked back teasingly, hoping for a response from his despondent master.

"Go or stay as you please, it's all the same to me," Dustin said coldly.

Midnight ran out a little further, then seeing he was drawing no response, he simply came back and lay down close to where Dustin was building a fire. Sugarfoot was not as easily ignored. When Dustin turned him loose, the shepherd ran circles around camp and back tracked Dustin's trail several hundred yards into the dark, looking for Michele. He eventually came running over to Dustin and whimpered sorrowfully. He'd spent many nights with Dustin gone but not one without Michele.

"She's not coming, boy! She'll never come back to us again," Dustin said while petting the confused dog's head. "I got the bastard that ordered it. Now I'll find the rest of the men that did the shooting. I figure I got a few of them at the ranch. I give my word on it, Sugarfoot. I'll get all of them if it takes the rest of my life," Dustin said and stood.

The shepherd seemed to understand and walked over to lie down with his head on Michele's saddle.

Dustin lay down and tried to rest for a few hours. He wanted to slip into Kansas City and say good by to Michele one last time but he thought better of it after the shooting of the deputies. He rode out to Bill's herd instead. He had developed extraordinary skills avoiding detection and could seem to just appear out of thin air. He had used his utmost ability in his approach of the cow herd. He was actually drinking a cup of coffee by the fire before Bill even saw him. Bill had ridden out to check his herd as Dustin knew he'd have to. Bill's cattle were to load out today and Dustin knew that the murders of a girl and a horse would not slow commerce.

"Hello, Dustin. How long you been here?" Bill asked his friend.

"A while Bill, not long. I see you got you a fine herd put together," Dustin said squatting cowboy style, sipping at his scalding coffee.

"Yea Dustin, got most of them from some old friends of yours. Mr.Rogers at the bank helped me swing the deal and said if I ever saw you to have you contact him," Bill said trying to just make conversation until Dustin actually brought up what he really needed to talk about.

Dustin still not quite ready said, "Yea, I bet he does. I must still owe him a bunch." He paused briefly, "Cindy died a few months ago," he added for no apparent reason.

"I'm sorry Dustin, that's pretty rough. What happened?" Bill asked not really sure which direction to go with this conversation.

"She had the consumption when I picked her up in New York. She was pretty bad off and didn't have long, I guess," Dustin said staring into his cup.

Bill just stood silently waiting for whatever came next.

"Bill, do you remember that little spring just off the trail back about three days drive?" Dustin asked.

"West of the trail by the mouth of that little draw with all the big trees?" Bill asked.

"That's it. Bury her there!" Dustin said and stood to leave adding, "Thank you my friend. I wouldn't trust anyone else to do this. She is very important to me."

"It will be taken care of, Dustin. You take care too! I pray I'll see you again. You know you always have a place when you need one, friend!" Bill said reaching to shake his friend's hand, for what he thought was quite possibly the last time.

"I'll see you along the trail someday, Bill. You know me! I got a plan. I'll be making these trails safer for you tired old cow punchers to travel on," Dustin said and smiled.

"You already have. There hasn't been a handful of cattle stolen on these trails since you went to kill... I mean exterminating these border gang vermin," Bill said to Dustin as he walked to his horse.

"I ain't quite done yet, Bill. There's still some more of them vermin, as you call them, needs exterminating," Dustin said with an evil smile Bill had never seen on him before.

"Hey, wait," Bill said, "I got your saddle for you."

Dustin stepped on the 08 bay and said, "Keep it friend. I'll ride this one, it was ... hers." then rode away disappearing into the nearby brush as quietly as when he had appeared from out of it.

Chapter 24

Dustin Thomas was a man of his word! He hunted down and killed every man suspected of being involved in Michele's murder. By the time the last one fell, Dustin had become obsessed with the annihilation of murderers and thieves from the Indian nations. He tracked men the conventional law had been unable to capture and had offered large rewards to the general populace for their assistance.

The next year passed seeing great changes on the frontier. The tracks extended further and the drives grew shorter and more frequent. They'd become more profitable also with fewer losses due to fewer border raiders. Dustin specialized in men wanted dead or alive and always felt dead was less trouble. The rewards paid to him, he sent to Mr.Rogers at the bank in Del Rio. He wasn't sure how much he owed still but was going to make good on the money Mr.Rogers had sent him for Cindy.

He still wrote Kate once in a while and would ride into a fort now and again to pick up letters she sent him. Her's were always positive and full of hope of his return. She had sent her sympathy after Michele's death and never tried to question his relationship with this young beauty. Kate always seemed to understand what Dustin was feeling and thinking. Never was she judgmental or critical of him or his savage life. She wrote often, in fact always, about his return to the ranch and her. She told stories about Wesley's growth and accomplishments as any proud mother would of a healthy young son. She had even understood Dustin's grief over the loss of Midnight when the brave and noble animal was shot to death defending Dustin after he'd been knocked unconscious by a head grazing shot from one of a pair of would be assassins. The ferocious beast killed both assailants before he crawled, himself shot nearly to pieces, to Dustin's insensible body and died quietly, while Sugarfoot licked at the big canine's many bloody wounds. After Midnight' death Dustin went on a mad killing spree that necessitated his fleeing deep into the nations until the legitimate law gave up the pursuit, deciding the men Dustin killed, on this run of terror, deserved to be shot anyway.

After his return to the edge of civilization, Dustin started losing the drive he'd felt for these last several years. He found himself looking more forward to Kate's letters than hunting down the remaining really bad men in the territory. One day he wrote Kate a letter telling her that he'd be in Kansas City in a month. If she would consider allowing him to, he believed it was time he and old Sugarfoot came home. That is if she'd still like to share the ranch with him as more than partners. He'd be at the Palace Hotel by the tenth of next month. If he heard from her, he'd head home immediately. If not, he'd more than understand.

Dustin found the long ride to Kansas City even longer than ever before. He'd gone north to Montana to talk with Bliss. He'd been received with open arms and shown a ranch as beautiful as any you could imagine. Beautiful for four months a year, that is. Dustin explained how much he appreciated Bliss' loyalty and honesty in his dealings on Dustin's behalf. If he had anything coming from the cattle operation, Bliss should give it to Big Bill.

"I offered Bill a percentage of my part, Dustin and he declined also," Bliss declared.

"Just send him whatever piece of the profit you think is mine each year. He banks in Del Rio where I do," Dustin said.

"It's a good thing I'm not sensitive. I can't even give part of my dream ranch away!" Bliss said not entirely in jest.

"It's not that I don't think it's a great ranch, Bliss. It's that I don't deserve any part of it. I know you think I do, but I don't. You send the part you think I have coming to Bill. He's trailing his own herds now and could use the money," Dustin told him.

He rode hard and arrived in Kansas City four days early. Before he checked into the Palace, he rode out to see if there were any herds close. Maybe he could find some old drovers to talk to. The towns folk had been so afraid of Dustin, that most men fled when he entered a room. The old cowboys treated him like the avenging Angel he'd been to the cattlemen through his unselfish purging of the border gangs from the trails. Dustin Thomas had made possible the continued marketing of the Texas cattle to the railroads and on to the rest of the country. These men who had faced the ravages of the trails before Dustin's efforts, knew what a tremendous accomplishment this one brave man had achieved. They indeed treated the name of Dustin Thomas and the man himself with due respect.

Stopping at the first herd just outside of town, Dustin had dinner with a trail boss he'd met several times before and liked well. Always he enjoyed the cattle and camaraderie of the trail men. When Dustin inquired about Big Bill, he was thrilled to find Bill had a herd out on the trail about two days back. He was holding his herd well off the trail grazing them until his shipping date which wasn't until the first of the week, still five days off. Dustin tried not to be too rude to his host who was obviously honored to have him in his camp. After a polite period of time, Dustin thanked his host and promised to see him in Kansas City later in the week.

Dustin hurried to find his old friend. He was excited to tell Bill about his letter to Kate. He rode directly into the camp in no way concealing his approach. It had been close to two years since he'd seen Big Bill. His friend saw Dustin coming and jumped on his horse, and rode out to meet him. They shook hands as vigorously as two patent medicine salesmen. The two talked, drank coffee and pet Sugarfoot all night. They didn't even stop when Bill had to ride the last watch, which was his custom. Dustin just rode with him, Sugarfoot following silently.

Bill was as excited about the possibility of Dustin's returning home as Dustin was. He had actually believed he'd never see his friend again. This was enforced by Dustin's absence last year from the Kansas City Trail. Bill brought a herd through hoping to see or hear from Dustin but went back to Texas disappointed.

Dustin explained he'd followed some fleeing members of a murderous border gang all the way to Oregon.

When the morning came and the two men rode in to eat breakfast, Dustin was shocked that Bill had hired a cook.

"Damn, Bill, you having a cook is like me hiring an interpreter," Dustin laughed.

"Don't you worry about my cook. I taught him to make bread and biscuits. Hey, the day after tomorrow is the tenth. Let's ride into town and see if you got any mail since you checked it when you rode through," Bill suggested.

"Hell, Bill, I didn't even check. I'm kind of nervous. I wouldn't blame her if she never wanted to see me again, let alone write and invite me to come back home," Dustin said obviously worried.

"We better get in there an pick up your mail! I bet you've got a trip to make!" Bill said encouragingly.

The two men headed toward town after breakfast. Bill told Dustin there was nothing to worry about. Kate sounded like as loyal and true a woman as there ever was.

"She's stuck by you all these years. I don't believe she'll quit you now. Yes sir, we'll have to buy you a new suit of clothes to go home in. We don't want the future Mrs. Dustin Thomas' first look at her prospective husband to be too great a shock. We got to rake some of the trail out of your hair and get it cropped a little, too," Bill rambled on making Dustin more at ease.

Then at a particular turn in the trail, "Have you been to see her grave yet?" Bill asked Dustin, noticing his companion looking back down the trail toward Michele's burial sight.

"Not yet this trip, Bill. I'll go see her before I leave," Dustin said making the conscious decision to go see if Kate had written him first.

They rode on into Kansas City the next afternoon late. Before they entered the town limits, Bill asked more seriously than jokingly, "Are you wanted for anything here in the civilized world?"

"Not at the moment. At least I don't think I am. I was for a while," Dustin answered intriguingly.

"What for?" Bill took the bait.

"For shooting a smart ass that used to be cook! And it looks like it might happen again," he laughed at the big man's reaction, then they both laughed together relaxing Dustin to his normal, carefree self.

The men pulled up in front of the newly renovated Palace. The new sign read "Welcome to the Palace, an emporium dedicated to providing the finest libations and entertainment available anywhere in the world".

"Damn!" Dustin said. "Things have sure matured some since I was here last. Seems kind of sophisticated and high toned for a cattle drover and... and whatever the hell you'd call me! What's it like on the inside, Bill?"

"The insides the same. Full of cheap whiskey and pretty girls! Outside is all they changed," Bill answered.

He paused a moment and looked up and down the wide main street of town and realized they were sitting on the spot where Michele fell.

"This place used to be plumb wild, Dustin, that's for sure. These sissy, pretty boy Marshals they got here now spend more time brushing each others fancy clothes off than they do protecting anyone. Those of us that remember what it was like before know what made it a safe place to live in, or who, I guess I should say," Bill said profoundly.

"What are you talking about, Bill?" Dustin asked not really listening too closely to his friend. He also was remembering this spot all too well.

"I'm talking about you, Mr. Dustin Thomas. All people have larceny in them. Some much more than others. Fear of retribution is the only thing that keeps them from being worse than they are. When you made it your life's work to stop all this wild and murderous activity, you became the motivation that stopped many a would be villain from taking the wrong road leading him to a life of crime. The mere multitude of bodies you've led down this very street, tied across their horses, is the reason this is the growing city it has become. They should build you a monument in the town square. The manner in which you avenged the deaths of those you knew and those you loved, was the sole deterrent strong enough to end the reign of terror the border raiders were inflicting on those innocent citizens of this once wild and woolly west. That's what I call you, Dustin, an Avenger!" Bill said with the pride of a father and love of a brother.

"Damn!" Dustin replied. "Did you say all of that without even taking a breath? That was something, Bill. You suppose I could get you to write all that down so I could read it to myself whenever I find I've got an hour or so to kill?" Dustin said trying to make light of the heavy load of credit and gratitude that Bill had just unloaded on him.

"And you called me a smart ass! Let's go see if you got any mail," Bill said shaking his head.

The two walked into the big door located near the corner of the Palace. The main entrance now was directly into the saloon and this side door had a sign saying hotel and restaurant with the outline of a big hand pointing toward the door.

As they walked in, a man dressed as if attending a funeral or wedding spoke to them saying, "Yes, may I help you?" looking at them like the tramps they appeared to be.

"Bill, I guess we are looking a little coarse for a place like this. I used to feel over dressed in this shit hole, if both my boots were on!" Dustin said a strong trace of wrath building in his voice.

"Easy friend, just check your mail and we'll go across the tracks and stay at the Drover's Cottage. They won't let me...That is I can't stay here because I'm bl."

Dustin interrupted his friend quickly and adamantly, "Because you're better than they are? That had best be what my friend was going to say, you sawed off little son-of-a-bitch!" Dustin finished, turning with the last words directly into the fancy dresser's face.

"Dustin just get your mail and we'll go," Bill repeated.

"Dustin? Dustin Thomas! Good lord, I had no idea. Please come in, you are welcome," and after a short pause, "Both of you gentlemen are very welcome. I should have known. We've been expecting you for several days now," the trembling little man said.

"Several days? Ain't today the tenth?" Dustin asked.

"Oh yes sir, the tenth, that's right. Yes, quite so, Mr. Thomas. But we've been receiving these since the first. I thought something was wrong with the telegraph machine at first so I requested the message be sent again. It came back the same each time," then he reached under the counter and handed Dustin a stack of telegrams.

"Damn!" both Dustin and Bill gasped simultaneously.

"Read em boy! What'd she say?" Bill urged his friend.

Dustin did not speak. He looked at each of the many telegrams dated at least one a day from the first of the month and several a day from the fifth. He finished his perusal of the papers and smiling with both eyes full of tears, handed them to his friend Bill, who took them and saw, "My darling Dustin," heading each identical telegram and each was signed, "Your loving Kate".

It was the body of the note that brought the tears. There was no message other than one hundred times the single word, YES! Bill smiled up at his friend and they embraced.

"This is good news I pray?" the still nervous clerk asked.

"Hell yes, it's good news. For you and me both, little man. You get to live another day and I'm going home!" Dustin said and grabbed the fancy little fellow by the shoulders, dragged him halfway over the counter and kissed the top of his bald little head

"Damn!" the little man gasped.

"Come on Bill, we got us some suits to buy!" Dustin said dancing around Bill, hanging onto the big black man's hands like a nut.

"Settle down, Dustin. You are going to pop a vein! What do you mean we have suits to buy?" Bill asked.

"You are going with me! You are going to be my best man. We'll sell your cows day after tomorrow and head west. I think I'll even have the saddle shop make Sugarfoot a collar with his name on it. Let's go, I got to send some wires!" Dustin said, to a now just as excited, Bill.

"We have a wire service here now, Mr. Thomas. I'll be happy to send your messages for you," the little man informed the still dancing pair.

"Good deal. I'll write them out and we'll get them sent," he responded.

Dustin sent the first one to Kate, saying he'd received her's and was the happiest man alive and that he, Bill and Sugarfoot would be there post haste! The second, Dustin sent was to the banker telling him he had a new beneficiary, Miss Kate Morton, soon to be Mrs. Dustin Thomas and to please send as much money as possible to cover wedding expenses. He didn't know if he had any cash money at the bank but if there was still some of that stock left in that Chicago Livestock deal, maybe he could lend him some on that.

Bill sent a telegram to Mr. Rogers also. His simply said to send Dustin ample funds necessary for a good start. He would back any shortage in Dustin's account.

As the two men started out, the clerk asked, "Would you like me to have your things taken to your rooms, Sir?"

"Our rooms? Hell, little fella, me and Bill wouldn't be caught dead staying in a dump like this! We may come back later and shoot up the saloon a little but that's it. Have a nice day!" Dustin said so menacingly that Bill thought the little clerk might swoon.

They walked out to the street and rode their horses to the livery which had also been renovated and increased in size. They left their horses, and then, with Sugarfoot at their heels, went to get proper outfits for their up coming festivities.

"Let's get cleaned up first, Bill, so we don't mess up our go to meeting suits trying them on. We'll want them to look brand new when we actually wear them back home."

"Sounds good to me. I ain't had a tub bath since we left home with these damn steers."

The two trail dusty men stopped by the barber shop first, then to the mercantile. This was the one where Dustin had purchased the clothes for Michele. The name was the only thing that was the same. It too had gone through a tremendous growing period. This was the largest store Dustin had ever been into. The men each picked out a complete outfit of trail clothes, from the skin out, to wear back from the bath house. They asked the salesman to put together some nice suits that would be proper attire for a wedding in their sizes and they'd be back later. He told them he'd be closing soon and for them not to tarry, he would only be open another hour. Bill saw Dustin's temper start to flare and spoke out before Dustin explained, in his usual manner, that he was not used to being rushed by a damn store clerk.

Bill tactfully offered, "Sir, this is Mr. Dustin Thomas! He is about to travel that glorious road of matrimony. He's going back to his home in the beautiful New Mexico territory to help his, soon to be, new bride run their ranch and build a grand life for them both. I know deep in my heart that you wouldn't want to have him start this new life tainted by your rudeness and thoughtless hurrying, causing him to leave this fair city, that he in fact more than anyone else is responsible for its being the peaceful burg it is, with your blood still fresh on his hands! Please, I ask you to reconsider your position, and if necessary, extend your closing time the few necessary moments to accommodate Mr. Thomas' very special circumstances. It will be very profitable for you as the nature of the occasion mandates our purchasing a large quantity of your very finest garments and your being brutally slain for the lack of common courtesy seems to me quite excessive, indeed. I do, however, assure you that is your only other option!"

Scared nearly to death at the mention of the name Dustin Thomas along with the threatening dissertation he'd just been subjected to, the clerk found it within his power to indeed remain open until such time as was convenient for them to return.

"Thank you for your kindness," Bill said graciously.

The men picked up the packages containing their new trail clothing and walked out onto the street.

"Damn!" Dustin exclaimed. "I don't remember you being so windy, Bill. Besides, we could have just come back tomorrow," Dustin said as they walked to the bathhouse.

"I know that and you know that, now. But I could see you wasn't thinking that then!" Bill said to Dustin who knew his friend had been right, as usual.

This bathhouse was quite a deal. They had a dozen tubs and offered fresh hot water for every customer. That was real classy for the times. Most only changed water when the patrons were getting out filthier than when they got in. There were several other men utilizing the tubs. This surprised both Bill and Dustin. This was relatively early in the evening and on a week day to boot! When they saw the frilly sissy suits hanging behind the occupied tubs, they understood. The Chinese, who run the laundry and bathhouse, would brush your suit while you bathed, if you wished. Bill and Dustin had their old clothes laundered to be picked up tomorrow as they were still good trail clothes, they were just dirty from wear.

Dustin never liked these pretty boy Marshals that came into these cow towns after the real rough had been taken off of them. They pranced around dressed like peacocks or pimps and took credit for cleaning up the city! Of course the attire was appropriate. Most of these fancy dudes were in fact just pimps and gamblers pretending to be lawmen. Any one of the Federal Marshals working out of Judge Parker's court in Fort Smith could chew up and crap out a dozen of these frail, wannabe famous badge toters.

He and Bill bathed and relaxed, while soaking off the road dust. The conversation at the other end was of no interest to either Bill or Dustin but was impossible to ignore. Most of it was just self gratifying bullshit spread for the benefit of their own pitifully weakened manhood from the mere presence of the two huge, tough new bathers. After awhile the local officials settled back into their previous conversation.

One story in particular caught Dustin's ear and Bill's as well. There was apparently a large fellow who owned a little business on the far edge of town. His failing fortune while everything around him thrived, caused him no little aggravation. He'd started drinking and beating his wife, whom he'd married to acquire the now failing business. Her first husband had owned and successfully operated the little store for several years until his untimely death in an accident. This large drifter had been working for the man at the time of the accident and was quick to move in on the widow. She had four children, the oldest a boy who could see through the drifters motives. The widow accepted the man's advances eventually and married him. Once in control of the purse strings Bill Abernathy, the drifter, became Mr. Abernathy, the entrepreneur. He started out seemingly well enough intentioned, then when his too frequent trips to the pleasure district down by the river started eating up too much of the profits for the little store to survive, the wife beatings and blatant abusive behavior began. He'd been jailed several times for his unacceptable actions. This usually came after much damage was done due to his size and strength. Abernathy was as big as Dustin and from the description resembled him greatly as well. So much so that one of the Marshals even remarked to his friends how he'd almost mistaken the freshly groomed new arrival for Abernathy. They had let Abernathy out of jail just moments before for his most recent and most violent beating of his wife and oldest step son. The boy was trying to defend his mother from this giant assailant and was nearly killed by the drunk. Since there were no laws governing the treatment of wives and children on the books, the Marshals could only arrest Abernathy for drunken disturbance. Once sober he'd pay his fine and the whole thing would repeat itself.

At the comment of the resemblance to this abusive drunk, Dustin flared instantly with, "The physical appearance may be close, you overdressed asshole, but I assure you, I am not an abuser of women and children. I prefer to vent my hatred and anger on even weaker, more pitiful creatures, like spineless fools who try to act like men to impress themselves by lying to each other about their trivial, meaningless lives as lawmen; not unlike the four of you lily white bastards."

The new Marshal and his deputies, who were not used to this kind of verbal abuse, were speechless. Especially ever since some idiot dime novelist, who had ridden the train out to this wild cowtown and was impressed by the clothing these foolish derelicts wore, had written books glorifying them to the eastern world. All of the Marshals were dressing, primping and brushing on one another, as pretty boys are wont to do, when Dustin, still bathing, made his comment. Bill reached outside his tub and held his pistol just out of sight, while Dustin continued bathing, both hands clearly in view. One of the officials took such offense to Dustin's remarks he pulled his own pistol and took a step in Dustin's direction.

"Come on over, asshole! Let's see if you are actually starting to believe the crap they're writing about you. Your friends there can tell everyone how bravely you died at the hands of the low life scoundrel, Dustin Thomas."

The man froze and gasped deeply and was so shaken by the name, he dropped his pistol. All he could utter was, "Dustin Thomas?"

"Yep, I reckon we ain't officially been introduced yet. You pretty boys came in too late to see any of the real fun this town had to offer. That's all right and probably for the best anyway. You would have gotten your frilly new clothes all dirty," Dustin said as intentionally aggravating as he knew how.

"We don't want no trouble with you. My deputy was just commenting on your physical resemblance to Abernathy. I assure you, sir, there was no slander intended," the Marshal said apologetically.

"Good, then there was none taken. I was just making conversation," Dustin said calming down some.

There was silence for a moment, it being necessary for the officers to pass behind Dustin's and Bill's tubs on the way out. The silence was broken when Bill uncocked his pistol and laid it back on the floor with a thud.

"If you get a chance while you're in town, Mr. Thomas, I've got a few new flyers come in on some train robbers wanted with big rewards on em, dead or alive," the Marshal said trying to ease the tension to where he felt safe walking past this notorious gunman.

"Sorry Marshal, not interested. I retired about two hours ago. Thanks anyway."

"There will be a lot of people glad to hear that news, Mr. Thomas. Unfortunately, most of them will be outlaws," the Marshal added meaning it as a compliment.

Dustin remained silent and the men started to pass out of the room. As they did, Dustin said, "Bill, better cover up. We got us a real live western hero behind us and one of his deputies is famous for noticing men's physical resemblance."

The men passed on by, not even hesitating at the remark.

"Dustin, how in the hell have you stayed alive so long?" Bill asked.

"Well Bill, I don't come to town much. That helps a little, I guess," Dustin said with a wide grin, looking slightly devilish.

"By god, you are something! Let's go get our new clothes bought and buy you a drink," Bill offered. "That poor salesman's probably getting a little tired of waiting for us."

Dustin laughed at his friend and said, "It's your fault! We could have just come back tomorrow."

The clerk was waiting patiently and had a nice selection ready for the two tardy customers.

As they looked at and tried on the jackets and pants, Bill said, "Dustin, this best man deal, don't you have a step brother or something? Won't he be mad or hurt a little?"

Dustin thought momentarily then answered, "Matt is Kate's brother, Cindy's too. We were kids together but we are different minded. The Apache's would say we have different spirits guiding our ways. Brother's are of the same blood. They have a common spirit leading them. In that respect, Bill, you are my real brother. Matt has always dodged his chances to really live life then apologized and justified his nonparticipation. Even when we were just kids, some challenge or adventure would arise and call me

into it and Matt would stand idly by. He'd then daydream about his bold involvement in the episode and become for a moment, in his mind, a hero to all people. He enjoyed all the glory of an adventurous, danger filled life without ever taking a chance. It is sad that he never will know the real thrill a true adventure brings a man, the freedom of spirit it gives him. A very wise old man told me once a story about the eagle and the snail. They can share the earth, in fact they must, but they can never be brothers."

"Damn!" Bill gasped imitating Dustin. "You were complaining about me being windy. If that is true, we must be brothers for sure. That was quite a little speech, especially the part about the buzzard and the tumble turd! Suppose you could write that down for me so I can read it to my crew late at night on the drive?" Bill said plumb smart alecky.

"Kiss my ass. Just pick out a suit and be glad that for once in your life you'll be the best man in the room!" Dustin shot back not to be out smart assed.

"Whoa, big fella, that was a little rough. Be kind, remember, I'm getting old," Bill responded.

They fooled around and purchased some extra things as luxuries. Bill purchased a pocket watch and when he realized they offered jewelry, Dustin picked out a beautiful, yet simple wedding ring for his future bride. While they were settling with the salesman, Dustin placed the ring box in his shirt pocket. Bill attached the fob to his new watch and they said they would pick up the suits tomorrow afternoon if the alterations would be complete. They were assured the suits would be ready and then they walked into the lamplight street. The lights were new too since Dustin had been in town and he liked the way the town looked dimly lit by these many, well placed little beacons of civilization.

"Bill, I ain't never been happier or felt better than right now. The miracle of it all is I know it's even going to get better when I get home to Kate!" Dustin announced.

The two walked down the semi lit street and turned toward a saloon where Bill recognized a fellow drover's horse standing tied out front.

"Follow me, big fellow and I'll introduce you to a man windier than both of…" Bill was interrupted by the blast of what sounded to be a cannon.

Bill turned to look at the door and saw Dustin staggering forward, drawing his pistol. From outside, through the crowd of people diving for cover from the gun shot, came a voice, a young crying voice, "God damn you, Bill Abernathy! I killed you like I said I would, you woman beating son of a bitch!"

Dustin, mortally wounded by both barrels of a shot gun blast to his back, managed to turn to face his assailant, pistol ready, hammer cocked. Dustin looked at the young boy's terror stricken face, realizing he'd just murdered the wrong man and was about to be shot dead for it.

Dustin did not fire, instead lowered his pistol to his side and gasped for the very last time, "Damn!"

He fell to the ground and into unconsciousness. Bill rushed to his side pistol ready. He stared at the youngster standing there with an insane look of sadness and fear in his eyes that prevented Bill from pulling his own trigger in anger.

Dustin was carried inside and two hours later, his strong heart lost its last valiant battle and ceased to beat. Bill wept uncontrollably over his dead companion. Sugarfoot jumped onto Dustin's lifeless body and would not allow anyone to remove him until Bill forcefully pulled himself together and held the lovingly protective dog in his arms while Dustin's body was carried to the undertaker, the same man that they had carried Michele to. The same man Dustin had made wealthy at the expense of the government by bringing in the bodies of wanted men too numerous to count.

Bill made all the necessary arrangements and had a large stone slab engraved with the words, 'Dustin Thomas.' Bill didn't know when Dustin had been born and didn't feel anything too flashy or sentimental would be appropriate, so he left it with just the name. He took Dustin's body to where he'd buried Michele's and placed him beside her. He knew as long as there were cattle being moved up the trail to Kansas City, drovers would pass by this spot and remember the man who made it safe for them to do so. He had considered trying to have the body shipped home to Kate but when he realized Dustin had been killed just feet from where Michele had fallen it seemed that it would be more appropriate to place him beside her again. If Kate wanted to, later they could move both bodies to New Mexico. Bill felt sure Kate would agree that the rightful place for his grave was beside this, one of the many cattle trails he had dedicated his life to protecting. Now he could continue his vigilance with his young partner Michele, for all eternity.

Bill had wired Kate to tell her there had been an accident and he would be bringing Dustin's things to her. He also wrote her a letter telling her in detail of his and Dustin's experiences of the last day of his life. He told her of the ring he was bringing her and the love Dustin had for her. He would see her soon to bring her the 08 bay, who had been with Dustin so long now, and Sugarfoot always at Dustin's side, indoors or out, loyal to the end. Bill would not press charges against the boy who killed Dustin. Since the town had no adequate accommodations for children prisoners, he was released into his mother's custody. Abernathy fled town when he heard about the shooting and was never heard from again.

Bill did not ship his cattle on time and might have never done so, but one of his foremen rode in and handled the affair in Bill's absence, who was busy with his friends final arrangements.

Bill rode to Kate's ranch on the western frontier leading the horses with Dustin's personal effects, all that was left of the "Avenging Angel" of the cattle trails worldly possessions, on just two pack horses.

Chapter 25

Sugarfoot trotted alongside Bill the whole long way to a home he'd never known. Bill tried to think what all he could say to this woman he'd never met about the life of this man they both cared so much about. Bill rode up to the Confederate Cantina and walked inside. There, staring off into space, was a man daydreaming about a life never experienced. Bill knew he'd found Matt Morton.

"I'm Bill, I suppose you'd be Matt?" Bill said in way of an introduction.

"What? Oh yes, I'm Matt," was the startled response.

"Where's Kate?" Bill inquired.

"She's out at the ranch with Wesley. They've lived there since I got married. I'll draw up a map for you. I'd show you the way myself...but I..."

Bill interrupted, "I know, Matt. You want to but you just can't, right?"

"Yea, Yea, that's it. I just can't. I got a business to run here. You know there's more to building a nation out of the wilderness than just chasing bad guys around and talking some tired old Indians into giving themselves up," Matt said defensively.

"Did Kate get my telegram and letter?" Bill asked, to keep from telling Matt what he really wanted to tell him about his last statement.

"I guess she must have. I didn't get to see them. They used to deliver them here to me first, but she moved to the ranch and kind of shut me out of her life. She had to of gotten them because she told me Dustin had been killed. I told him years ago he'd end up getting hurt if he didn't quit chasing around. I told him to grow up and take on the responsibilities of a real man. Not Dustin, he had to go off like a damn fool..." Bill cut him off by reaching out and grabbing his collar.

"Don't say another word mister, be real quiet and tonight while you are sitting staring out the window pretending to be part of the man Dustin Thomas was, maybe dreaming you had actually had the nerve to ride with him even once, you remind yourself that I wanted to kill you right now, but just didn't and see how much difference there is in doing a thing and just wanting to."

Bill turned him loose and walked to the door and turned back when he heard a little girl's voice saying, "Hi, Daddy!" and Matt's shaky voice answering, "Hello, Cindy."

Bill spoke very calmly and seriously, "Remember Matt," Bill paused and looked around at the Cantina Dustin had given his friend the money for, "Remember, you owe your life to Dustin Thomas. I'd have killed you just for fun if I didn't know Dustin wouldn't want me to. Good day, sir."

Bill and Sugarfoot walked out and as Bill mounted his horse he heard the little girl ask, "Daddy, who's Dustin Thomas?"

Bill did not wait to hear Matt's answer but choose to ride on out to the ranch. Matt did answer Cindy with, "He was just a man I used to ride with before I met

230

your Mama. We were kinda famous, Dustin and me," he said, still shaken by his very real near death encounter.

Bill arrived at the 08 ranch headquarters to a greeting more warm and genuine than anyone could imagine. Wesley shook his hand like the fine young man he was quickly becoming.

"Hello Sir, I'm Wesley Thomas. Aunt Kate say's you were with my dad when he was killed. Thank you for taking care of him for us."

Bill never flinched or faltered, nor did he look for a sign from Kate. Bill knew well the story of Cindy and the schoolmaster, Tim Burns. All that was not important now.

"Yes, I was Wesley." Then to Kate, "He bought you something in Kansas City. I have it here."

Bill reached into his pocket and handed the ring box to Kate and she held it to her heart without opening it. Seeing a pang of hurt in Wesley's eyes Bill continued with out hesitation,

"This is for you, Wesley. Your father picked it out for you just before he... just before the... the last day we were in town," Bill said and handed the boy the beautiful gold pocket watch and chain he'd purchased for himself at the same time Dustin had bought Kate's ring. The lad didn't seem to notice or care that this beautiful watch had not come in a box.

Wesley looked at the watch and smiled widely with tears running freely down his face.

"Aunt Kate, you were right! He did think about me too!" the boy said so proudly Kate looked Bill in the eyes with a deep gratitude and thanks so heartfelt, Bill's eyes filled with tears as well.

"You were the most important two people in the world to him, Son. He would rather have been here with the two of you than anywhere else in the world, but he had an important job to do. A job no one else was brave enough or tough enough to do. He was able to make safe, a country so wild and violent that all the soldiers and all the marshals in the country could not bring peace to it. He gave up being with you in order to make this a better place for all of us to live in. Your father, Dustin Thomas, was the finest, most fearless man that I have ever had the honor to know. You have a noble and proud lineage, Wesley, and I can see you're becoming the man your father would have wanted you to be," Bill said, thinking to himself Dustin was right, he was getting pretty windy in his old age.

Wesley looked up into the eyes of this giant of a man and said, "Thank you for being my father's friend. I feel better knowing he had someone who loved him by his side when he died." Wesley looked down at the dog sitting quietly at Bill's feet. "Is this Sugarfoot?" Wesley asked.

Bill couldn't answer because his tears were running so from the boy's statement. Luckily an answer was not required and Wesley knelt down and pet

Sugarfoot, who normally wasn't overly social, but the two were drawn to one another instantly.

Finally Bill recovered his emotions and said, "He's your dog now. He's a cow working rascal too."

"Oh boy! Come on Sugarfoot, I'll show you around," Wesley said as excitedly as only a young man with a new dog can be.

"Wesley, take the horses to the barn. We'll be down to unload them in a few minutes," Kate said.

"I'm sorry, Sir. I got excited," Wesley apologized and took the reins from Bill and headed to the barn.

"Ride him if you want. He's wearing your dad's saddle," Bill said as he handed Wesley the 08 bay instead of the horse he'd been riding.

"This one's wearing Dustin's old saddle. I'd kind of like to keep it while I'm still able to ride. It's pretty big for Wesley right now anyway. He'll of grown into it by the time I'm done," Bill said to Kate as Wesley rode ahead on the 08 bay leading the pack horses.

After unpacking and having dinner, Wesley went off to show Sugarfoot more of the ranch while Bill and Kate sat on the front porch.

"You've got a beautiful place here, Kate. Dustin was right, you've done a wonderful job here and with Wesley too. He's a fine young man," Bill said.

"Thank you for helping me with Wesley, Bill. I didn't know what to tell him about who his father was," Kate said.

"Don't you worry, Kate. Dustin would be proud for Wesley to have his name. Kate, I don't mean to seem pushy or anything but I want you to know, Dustin was the only family I've got and now you two are it. I've got a little money, if you two need anything I'd like to help," Bill said sort of awkwardly.

"Excuse me, Bill. You mean you don't know?" Kate said raising her hand to her mouth to cover a smile.

Bill noticed she had slipped on her wedding ring when she'd first gone into the house. It looked natural there but Bill had no idea what she meant.

"Don't know what, Ma'am?" he asked.

"Well Bill, it seems there was part of Dustin's life you or I, either one weren't aware of. Money won't be a problem for either of us ever again," Kate said.

"That's wonderful, Kate. I knew he'd wired his banker for some money but he wasn't sure he had any so I backed his loan," Bill explained.

Kate laughed openly this time. "Please, Bill, don't think I'm rude. I just didn't understand that even Dustin didn't know. Everything the banker sent me makes sense now. Bill, you are wealthy, comfortably so anyway. Dustin left you his quarter interest in the Montana ranch and Mr. Bliss has made a fortune up there. He sent a very large deposit to the Del Rio bank in your name, apparently just after you left with your last drive, and another just as large more recently. You will be receiving two deposits a year from now on."

"Damn!" he gasped and both laughed.

"You sound just like Dustin!" Kate said. "That's just what I said when I first got the letter from the banker, Mr. Rogers. Dustin invested some money many years ago in the then newly formed Chicago Stockyards. Even though he borrowed a lot of money from the bank to help Cindy twice, he had more than enough already in there to cover the amount both times and more. Mr. Rogers just kept investing the money Dustin sent him from the rewards he collected, and it's pretty unbelievable how much he made. Dustin died a very wealthy man, yet I would trade this ring, the watch you gave Wesley, and every dime of the money in an instant, all of it, and this ranch as well for one minute with him to say good by," Kate said suddenly weeping uncontrollably.

"Me too, Lady. Me too. I was right there and didn't get to say fair well or tell him how I felt about him. Where he could hear me anyway. What are you going to do now that you're rich, Kate?" Bill asked.

"I've been thinking a lot about that recently. Maybe you could help me. What I really want to do is build this into the largest ranch in the southwest. Have cattle and horses with the 08 brand on them as far as the eye can see. Thousands of mother cows running on tens of thousands of acres of land and hundreds of horses, the off spring of old Chief. We had twelve foals by him and have been breeding one of his sons to all my other mares and his daughters to our old stud. The problem is, I'll need an advisor. Someone that really knows the cattle industry and can lead men, but most importantly, I need someone who can make really good biscuits!" Kate said smiling ear to ear.

"By God, I believe I know a man that fits your bill to a tee. I knew there was a reason I bought cattle with my money and not a place. Hell Kate, if you think I'll do, I can start today. I don't even have to move. My home's been in that saddle hanging up out there in the barn. I'll write my foreman and have him and a few of the others drive my wagons out here. I've got four dandies too! They'll be handy around the place," Bill said and gave Kate a hug to seal the deal.

"Yes sir, Bill! You and me will make sure this old world don't ever forget the name Dustin Thomas or the 08 brand."

Chapter 26

Ten short years later, Bill, Wesley and the know famous Cattle Kate made their dream come true. The 08 ranch covered more of the territory than any two of the biggest ranches in the neighboring state of Texas. More cattle wore the 08 brand and more sure enough cowboy's rode 08 horses than any brand in the country.

Bill and Kate had bought controlling interest in the Montana place as well, retaining Bliss to continue managing it for them. The 08 brand would not soon be forgotten.

At this same moment in time, an overweight, prematurely gray, tired looking middle-aged man sat behind the bar of a newly renovated and renamed saloon. The New Mexico Restaurant and Tavern had previously been called the Confederate Cantina. The fat old man was telling stories to the new comers and children seated in the family dining section. These stories of daring adventure he'd added himself to and told just to people who didn't know better and anyone else who would listen.

His favorite was some variation of the following one and went; "The two men rode along in silence. The only sounds were of creaking saddle leather. This was not an ordinary ride. These life long friends were as different as beings from separate planets, yet in many ways were very similar. After last night, they now had more in common than they ever thought possible. They were wanted and were on the run. Their thoughts roamed back over the events of the past few days. Disbelief, apprehension, and trepidation filled their minds. Even a little fear and nervousness maybe, but absolutely no remorse or regret."

The crowd gathered closer to Matt Morton as he spun his yarn masterfully. This was history told to them by a man, who they were led to believe, was a participant in its making. They listened intently as he went on. Matt told his version of a history, that he had no real first hand knowledge of, often and to every group of newcomers that would listen. They would in turn repeat every word of it, as if it were gospel, to the next several generations of unsuspecting listeners, that is the problem with history. When a story gets repeated often enough people start to believe it as told.

These days few herds were driven to the railroad stockyards in the now booming metropolis of Kansas City. Since the tracks had been laid to Wichita, it was much closer for the Texas cattle. Now new lines were extending even further west and south almost to the gulf. Cattlemen were still kings of the west and would be for a while yet, but the days of the long trail drives were all but over, coming and going in less than two decades but not to be forgotten, ever. Maybe never remembered the way they really were, but at least remembered, by some.

Several hundred miles to the east of where Matt was misrepresenting history, some land speculators accompanied by two large buggies full of government officials and a wealthy railroad man drove along on a fine wide road that had once been the well used Kansas City trail. As this group of well dressed fat men rode comfortably along, they approached a little spring just off the old trail which was itself just a few yards from the new roadway. This well traveled by all sorts of frontier folk now, in complete safety without even the thought of how treacherous is was that short decade ago.

One of the men on horseback spotted a marble slab with a man's name on it and stopped to investigate.

"What is it?" another of the group asked.

"Looks like a grave stone," another replied.

"Who in the world would get themselves buried way out here?" still another questioned.

"Probably just some dumb sod buster who got lost and starved to death," another remarked.

The man on horseback rode closer to the stone. "I don't think so. No sod buster ever had an expensive stone like this," he said.

Finally the railroad man asked, "Well, then, who's name is on it?"

"Dustin Thomas," was the answer.

"Who was Dustin Thomas?"

No reply came. Sadly this is the way of history. A short decade after the fact, one man who played no part in it at all was telling the stories of how he dreamed the west had been and people were accepting it as truth, while other's sat in a luxurious buggy, staring history in the eye and didn't recognize it. Little did they know that here lies Dustin Thomas, the man that had a more active part in allowing the era of the cattle drives to exist successfully than any other single person or group of people, for that matter, in all of the west. Yet these same men setting in their fancy buggies staring blankly at this lonesome headstone can each name at least three of the four pretty boy, badge wearers, who were merely observers of the west's development. These fancy dressed, self promoting sissies that the dime novels glorified into a mock form of western hero, who at no time were ever as close to two real frontier fighting men as they had been once in a Kansas City bath house. This encounter with the real thing almost frightened these paperback princes to death. So much for the veracity of the printed word.

There is still one place, on a ranch the size of some large counties, where this man's deeds and sacrifices are not forgotten and never will be. On this ranch in the New Mexico territory, sitting on a hill over looking a valley filled with cattle all wearing the same brand, the 08 brand, are three riders: a huge, old black man, a young, tall cowboy, and a woman known to all around as Cattle Kate. These three will remember him, always! Never in this place once so wild, yet now so peaceful, no, never here will the question, "who was Dustin Thomas" go unanswered. These three will answer and answer proudly. These three who have lived the settling of the west, will help lead it into the future, but that is yet another story!

CPSIA information can be obtained
at www.ICGtesting.com
Printed in the USA
FFOW03n1408190418
46309311-47855FF